D0279584

FLOW OF FUNDS

Flow of Funds

A Conceptual Framework and Some Applications

R. F. G. ALFORD
London School of Economics and Political Science

Published in association with the London School of Economics and Political Science by Gower

Published by
Gower Publishing Company Limited,
Gower House,
Croft Road,
Aldershot,
Hants GU11 3HR
England.

Gower Publishing Company,
Old Post Road,
Brookfield,
Vermont 05036,
U.S.A.

Reprinted 1986

British Library Cataloguing in Publication Data

Alford, R.F.G.
Flow of funds.
1. Flow of funds —— Great Britain —— Econometric models
I. Title
339.2'6'0724 HC260.F55

ISBN 0 566 00517 4

Printed in Great Britain by
Richard Clay (The Chaucer Press) Ltd,
Bungay, Suffolk

Contents

Introduction vii

1 Introduction to the flow of funds accounting structure 1

1 A simple balance of payments account 1
2 The flow of funds framework 3
3 Quadruple entry 6
4 The purchasing power view 7
5 The presentation of the UK flow of funds matrix table 12

2 The UK flow of funds accounts – I 16

1 Considerations in the choice of columns and rows 16
2 UK flow of funds accounts: sector columns and presentations 18
3 UK flow of funds accounts: the capital account 22
4 The national income accounting background 24
5 CSO identity schemas 30

3 The UK flow of funds accounts – II 37

1 UK flow of funds accounts: the financing account 37
2 Sign rules in the flow of funds matrix table 40
3 Treatment of errors 42
4 Row terminology and hierarchy 51
5 UK flow of funds accounts: sources 56

4 Introduction to the use of the flow of funds accounts 61

1 Flow of funds and complementary data 61
2 An approach to using the flow of funds matrix table 67
3 Further aspects of the flow of funds accounts 77

5 Some applications of the quadruple entry approach 83

1 Manipulation of zero-sum matrix tables 83
2 Conjectural variation using quadruple entries 90
3 Syndrome entries 93
4 Macro-economic models and the flow of funds matrix table 97

6 Error entries in the UK flow of funds accounts 106

1 Error entries: the quadruple entry approach 106
2 Magnitudes in the UK matrix table 1971–82 112
3 Some implications of error entries 115
4 Error entries: the attribution method 123

7 Successive revisions in the UK flow of funds accounts 132

1 The scale of the problem 132
2 Revisions in the identified matrix table entries 135
3 Revisions in the error entries 143
4 The reliability of the UK flow of funds accounts 147

Appendices

1 UK flow of funds matrix table: current presentations 150
2 UK flow of funds matrix table: row headings of earlier presentations 154
3 The United States flow of funds matrix table 156
4 The relationship between e′ in Treatment 1 and e in Treatment 2 163
5 Construction of a specified zero-sum matrix table using compact quadruple entries 165
6 Some exploration of obstruction matrices 167
7 Two types of quadruple entry system 177
8 The overseas sector and the UK balance of payments account 181
9 Revisions and error ratios 185

Glossary of abbreviations 186

Introduction

Flow of funds accounts have been available for the UK for about twenty years, but they are still less widely used than might be expected. Several reasons can be found for this: many would-be users seem to have difficulty in perceiving any promising entry point at which to begin using the accounts; even practiced users can have problems with such an apparently straightforward matter as the signs of entries in the matrix table; and manipulation of the entries is difficult because of the constraints on the row and column sums.

These and other similar problems have arisen from the lack of a clear conceptual framework for the flow of funds matrix table. In Chapter 1 this is provided by the related concepts of the zero-sum format of the matrix table, quadruple entry and the purchasing power view. The application of this conceptual framework is the recurrent theme throughout the rest of this book. Chapters 2 and 3 look in some detail at the row and column structure of the UK flow of funds matrix table (and for comparison Appendix 3 gives some account of the United States flow of funds matrix table) while Chapter 4 looks at data which is complementary to the flow of funds figures and makes some suggestions on how the matrix table can be approached by would-be users. Chapter 5 considers some more theoretical aspects of the manipulation of the matrix table entries, and Chapter 6 looks at the error entries and some ways of handling them. Finally, Chapter 7 looks at the revisions over time in the flow of funds matrix table entries. In a work of this kind it is convenient to use a considerable number of abbreviations, and to help the reader a Glossary of Abbreviations is provided at the end of the book.

At an early stage I had useful discussion with the Central Statistical Office, and at a later stage the Bank of England was kind enough to look at Chapters 1 to 3, saving me from a number of factual errors. Any mistakes remaining in these chapters or elsewhere are my responsibility. In general, this book is written from the standpoint of the early months of 1984.

A number of tables have been reproduced from official publications. Tables 2.4, 2.5, 2.6, 3.6a, A1.2 and A2.2 have been reproduced from various issues of the Central Statistical Office publications *Financial Statistics Explanatory Handbook* and *National Income and Expenditure*, with the permission of the Controller of Her Majesty's Stationery Office. Tables 4.2, A1.1 and A2.1 have been reproduced from issues of the *Bank of England Quarterly Bulletin*, with the permission of the Bank of England. The graphs in Tables 6.12b and 7.4 were produced using the Data Inspection Package (DIP) on the DEC computer system and Calcomp plotter at the London School of Economics.

1 Introduction to the flow of funds accounting structure

1 A simple balance of payments account

The balance of payments account is one of the most widely used of the economic and financial accounts for the UK, and it is also one which can be illustrated in a very simple form. This makes it a convenient starting point for an introduction to the flow of funds accounts, since the two are closely related.

		UK
Current account (net balance)		+100
Financing account:	(a)	− 60
	(b)	− 40
Sum		0

Table 1.1

We begin with the simple balance of payments account in Table 1.1. This is in two parts, the current account and what we shall call here the financing account. The current account could show exports and imports (visible and invisible), but here we show just the net balance of all these, which is a UK current account surplus of +100. The financing account also could show many different categories, but for our purposes we shall simply divide it into two classes of financing transaction, (a) and (b), with entries of -60 and -40 respectively.

This balance of payments account has two important characteristics. The first is that it distinguishes between the current account and the financing account. The current account covers exports and imports, both of which are income-creating types of transaction (exports creating income at home and imports creating income abroad). The financing account, on the other hand, records transactions which are not income creating in this way. Instead, it can be seen as following out the financing implications of the current account: how a surplus is disposed of or how a deficit is financed.

The second important characteristic arises from the fact that a surplus on current account has to be disposed of through the financing account and a deficit on current account has to be financed through the financing account. This means that, in principle, a surplus (+) occurring on the current account must be exactly balanced by the disposal (-) of this amount in the financing account, so that the balance of payments account as a whole sums to zero. In our example (Table 1.1), category (a) in the financing account might be short term capital and category (b) long term capital; the table then shows the +100 surplus on current account being disposed of in the financing account in the form of lending abroad, -60 in the form of short term capital and -40 in the form of long term capital.

This zero-sum characteristic arises from the conventions on which such an account is constructed. It is a double entry account in which each transaction has two aspects: where the funds came from and where they went to. Thus in recording a transaction the same amount of funds appears twice in the account, once with a + sign and once with a - sign, and hence each transaction must in this form sum to zero. It follows that, in principle, or with perfect information, the balance of payments account will cover all the transactions occurring in a period and it too will sum to zero. (In later chapters we shall deal at some length with the problem of errors in the figures actually available.)

We can now extend this simple balance of payments account for the UK by putting next to it a column containing the balance of payments account for the rest of the world, which we shall call overseas (O's), (Table 1.2):

		UK	O's	Sum
Current account (net balance)		+100	−100	0
Financing account:	(a)	− 60	+ 60	0
	(b)	− 40	+ 40	0
Sum		0	0	0

Table 1.2

The balance of payments account of overseas will, like that of the UK, and for the same reasons, sum to zero in principle. Further, the world is a closed economy; there are no transactions with anyone outside the world, so that the balance of payments of overseas is necessarily the negative image of the balance of payments of the UK. If the UK is in current account surplus of +100, then the only place to which the net exports of 100 can have gone is to overseas, where they must be 100 of net imports, −100. Similarly in the financing account, in row (a), which might be short term capital, −60 shows that the UK has disposed of part of its current account surplus in this form, and this must have been received by overseas in whose column it appears as +60. And in row (b), which might be long term capital, −40 shows that the UK has disposed of the rest of its current account surplus, which must have been received by overseas where it appears as +40. From this it is clear that not only will the columns of such a table sum to zero, but that the rows also will sum to zero. Indeed, what we have really done in Table 1.2 is to take the whole world as a closed economy, which can have no transactions with anyone outside its own boundaries, and subdivided it into two sectors: the UK and overseas. It follows that the transactions of the

UK and overseas must, in principle, exactly offset each other and hence their balance of payments accounts must be negative images of each other.

Up to now we have taken the closed world economy and divided it up into two sectors, the UK and overseas; but, of course, this is only one out of many possible modes of disaggregation. Starting again from Table 1.2, we could equally well leave the UK column unchanged but further disaggregate the overseas column, distinguishing, for example, each of the other EEC countries, giving each of them an individual column like the UK, and again having a residual rest-of-the-world column.

There is no reason why such disaggregation should stop at national level; again starting from Table 1.2 we could leave the overseas column unchanged and disaggregate the UK into its four component regions, England, Scotland, Wales and Northern Ireland, with a separate column showing the balance of payments account of each. This is shown in Table 1.3, where these UK domestic sector columns are numbered 1–4 for convenience. The overseas column is unchanged from Table 1.2, and the purely illustrative figures in the UK domestic sector columns can be seen to add up along each row to the figures in the UK column in Table 1.2. Similarly, each of the UK domestic sector columns in Table 1.3 can be seen to sum to zero, as does the UK column in Table 1.2. The balance of payments of the UK does not appear directly in Table 1.3, but because it is the negative image of the balance of payments of overseas, it can easily be seen by taking the overseas column and reversing the signs of its entries.

	1	2	3	4	O's	Sum
Current account (net balance)	−700	+900	−300	+200	−100	0
Financing account: (a)	+200	−400	+360	−220	+ 60	0
(b)	+500	−500	− 60	+ 20	+ 40	0
Sum	0	0	0	0	0	0

Table 1.3

Finally, there is no reason at all why our disaggregation should be restricted to a geographical basis. We could instead subdivide the UK into domestic institutional sectors, with columns 1–4 in Table 1.3 covering the UK public sector, personal sector, company sector and banking sector respectively. The table would then show a balance of payments type of account for each domestic institutional sector and for the Overseas sector. If we take the Current Account (net balance) row and re-label it Financial Surplus, and replace Sum by the more convenient Σ, we then have a flow of funds zero-sum matrix table for the UK as in Table 1.4.

	Public sector	Personal sector	Company sector	Banking sector	Overseas sector	Σ
Financial surplus	−700	+900	−300	+200	−100	0
Financing account: (a)	+200	−400	+360	−220	+ 60	0
(b)	+500	−500	− 60	+ 20	+ 40	0
Σ	0	0	0	0	0	0

Table 1.4

Having arrived at the flow of funds matrix table, let us go back over the main features which have appeared as we developed it from our starting point of a simple balance of payments account for the UK. Each sector column in the matrix table is a double entry, zero-sum, balance of payments type of account; there is a column for each UK domestic institutional sector and one for the overseas sector which covers the rest of the world. Every transactor and every transaction in the closed world economy can be accommodated somewhere in this matrix table, and we have implicitly assumed that each transactor is consistently classified and assigned to a particular sector column and that every type of transaction is consistently classified and its entries assigned to the appropriate transaction rows. It follows that, for any transaction row, what one sector receives, some other sector(s) must have parted with, so that each transaction row in principle sums to zero. In this way we come to the zero-sum matrix table in which every column and every row sums to zero. This is a framework which can be used to display the flow of funds between sectors, both the national income and expenditure net flows which are shown in the financial surplus row and the capital market flows which appear in the financing account rows.

3 Quadruple entry

We now need to look at two further analytical aspects of this matrix table format. The first of these is a simple extension of the convention that each column in our flow of funds matrix table is a double entry account in which each transaction is recorded by two entries of the same magnitude but opposite sign, so that each column has a zero sum. It follows that in the matrix table a transaction between members of two different sectors will be recorded by a double entry in each of two sector columns, and hence that the flow of funds matrix table is a quadruple entry system in which each transaction is recorded by four entries. Since the two rows containing the entries must be the same for each of the two transactors, the four entries will appear in a rectangular pattern at the intersections of the two relevant sector columns with the two relevant transaction rows (Table 1.5). The two transaction rows may be either the financial

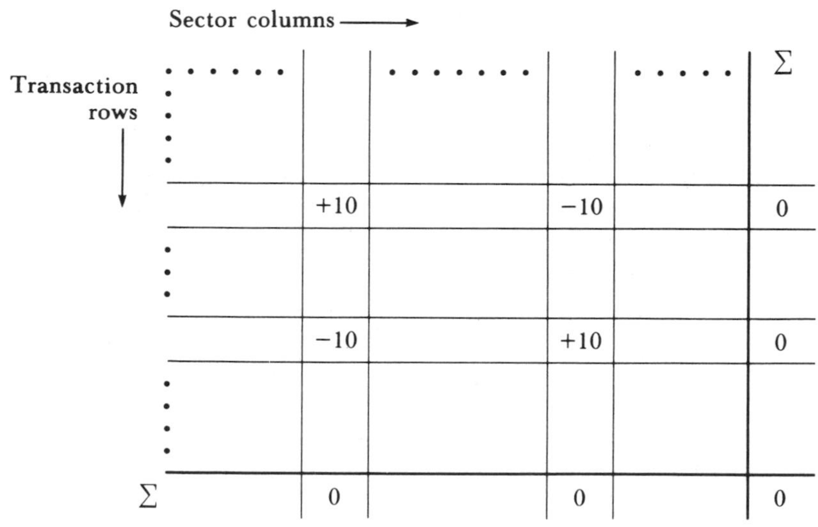

Table 1.5

surplus row and one financing account row (if the transaction is a purchase/sale of current output) or two financing account rows (if it is a transaction which involves only financial claims).

We have already seen that in recording a transaction, in each of the two sector columns the two entries must sum to zero. It will also be seen that in each of the two transaction rows, what one transactor parts with, the other must receive, so that the two entries in each row also must have opposite signs and must sum to zero. Thus in our flow of funds matrix table a transaction is recorded by a quadruple entry which has a zero sum along each row and down each column (Table 1.5). Such an entry will have a magnitude, which is that number, taken regardless of sign, which is entered in the rectangular pattern (the quadruple entry illustrated in Table 1.5 is of magnitude 10) and the signs of the entries on one diagonal will be opposite to the signs of the entries on the other diagonal. In principle the entries in the flow of funds matrix table developed above are the sums, cell-by-cell, of the quadruple entries recording all transactions over a period. Each quadruple entry, and the matrix table as a whole, will sum to zero along each row and down each column. The zero-sum quadruple entry will play a leading role in our analysis of the flow of funds matrix table.

4 The purchasing power view

The second analytical aspect we have to look at relates to the way in which this sign pattern in a quadruple entry is applied in recording any particular transaction. So far our examples have taken it for granted that the signs of entries in the balance of payments or flow of funds accounts are the intuitively simple ones of receipt +/payment –. In fact these examples were chosen because they were simple to understand in this way; but when we come to specific transactions and the way they are recorded, this simple view will no longer suffice.

This is most easily seen by going back to our original single column balance of payments account. First we take case 1 in Table 1.6, in which the 'receipt +/payment –' view is adequate; there we have a transaction with a surplus of +10 on current account being disposed of by lending it abroad as short term capital, –10, and no problem arises. But when we turn to case 2, we have a surplus of +10 on current account which, when it is accumulated in the form of an increase in dollar balances, appears as –10; this minus sign is something of a shock to commonsense. Further, this apparently perverse result will be found to occur both in the balance of payments account and in the flow of funds matrix table, as developed above, whenever a transaction involves a medium of exchange row, which is the case with virtually all transactions. One answer to this problem could be simply

Case 1		Case 2	
Current account:	+10	Current account:	+10
Financing account: short term lending	−10	Financing account: dollar balances	−10

Table 1.6

to say that the accounting convention on which the accounts are constructed requires the signs to come out in this way. This is indeed the case, but such a take-it-or-leave-it answer is not very helpful. Here we shall provide an approach to the sign rules which can be grasped intuitively and readily applied in practice. This is the *purchasing power view* (PPV).

The purchasing power view says that what we are recording in the balance of payments account or in our flow of funds matrix table is not movements of money or any medium of exchange, but purchasing power movements. Signs for particular entries can be defined in terms of these purchasing power movements as in Table 1.7.

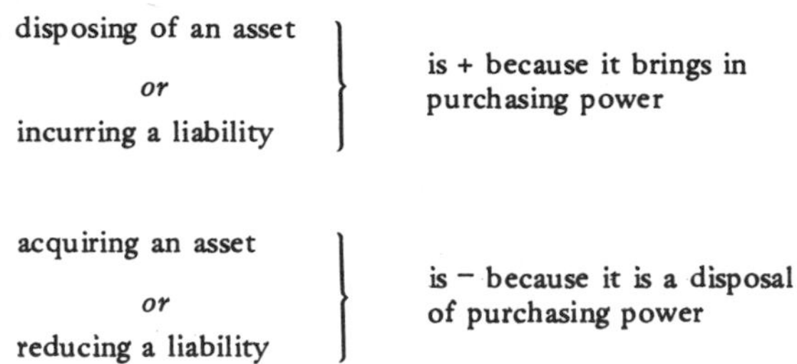

disposing of an asset *or* incurring a liability	is + because it brings in purchasing power
acquiring an asset *or* reducing a liability	is − because it is a disposal of purchasing power

Table 1.7

These rules hold whether we are dealing with entries in the financial surplus row (where output is regarded as an asset) or entries in the financing account, and whether the latter are in a medium of exchange row or any other row.

	Government sector	Personal sector	Company sector	Banking sector
Financial surplus			+ 10 [a]	
Notes and coin		+ 10 [b]		
Bank deposits			− 10 [c]	+ 10 [d]
Bank loans		− 10 [e]		+ 10 [f]
Government debt	+ 10 [g]			

Table 1.8

In Table 1.8 we look at examples of individual cell entries taken from a flow of funds zero-sum matrix table; only selected cell entries are shown (so that these entries will not necessarily sum to zero along each row and down each column) and each is identified by a letter. The purchasing power view would interpret these cell entries as follows:

a Companies have acquired 10 of purchasing power in this cell in the financial surplus row, and they must have acquired it from net sales of current output of 10.

b Persons have acquired 10 of purchasing power in this cell, and it must have come from running down their notes and coin assets by 10.

c Companies have parted with 10 of purchasing power and must have used it to acquire 10 of bank deposits.

d Banks have acquired 10 of purchasing power and must have acquired it from a rise of 10 in their deposit liabilities.

e Persons have parted with 10 of purchasing power and must have used it to pay off bank loan liabilities of 10.

f Banks have acquired 10 of purchasing power and must have acquired it from a reduction in their loan assets of 10.

g Government has acquired 10 of purchasing power and must have acquired it from selling government debt (an increase in its liabilities) of 10.

The key point is that the interpretation always goes straight to the purchasing power movement recorded in the cell concerned and, knowing the row and column of that cell, deduces the relevant part of the underlying liability or asset/output transaction. This deduction is virtually self-evident.

Looking now at a complete transaction in purchasing power terms, in Table 1.9 we have the quadruple entry recording a person spending 10 on the purchase of item Z from a company. (Item Z could be a financial claim, with its row in the financing account, or it could be an item of current output in which case it would be in the financial surplus row). Taking the personal sector column first, the purchasing power view would interpret the entries as showing persons acquiring purchasing power, +10, by disposing of an asset (medium of exchange) and simultaneously disposing of this purchasing power, -10, by acquiring another asset (Z). Then in the company sector column

	Personal sector	Company sector
Z	−10	+10
Medium of exchange	+10	−10

Table 1.9

the company acquires purchasing power, +10, by disposing of an asset (Z) and simultaneously disposes of this purchasing power, -10, by acquiring another asset (medium of exchange). Beginning with the + entry in the medium of exchange row, as we do in this example, will be found to give the more persuasive verbal interpretation for any transaction, and in Table 1.10 the entries are linked in this order by the solid arrows. The relative position of the two rows and two columns concerned is of no significance, and therefore the particular configuration of the solid arrows (forming a hill or a valley, going from left to right or the reverse) is of no significance either. Also in Table 1.10, shown

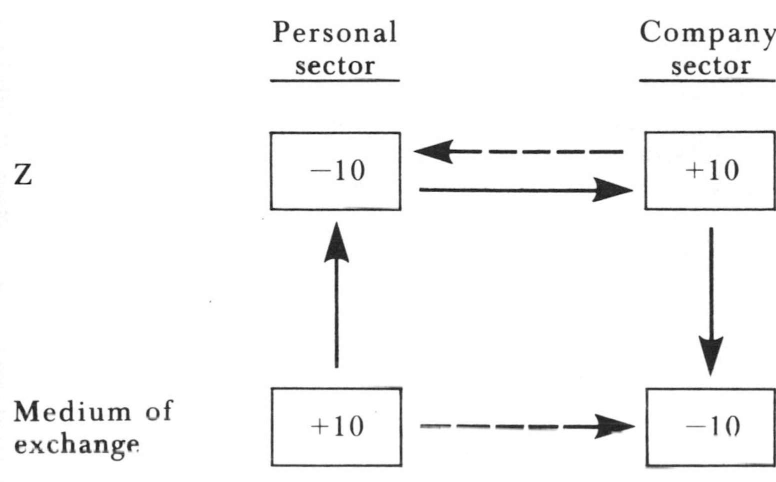

Table 1.10

by the two dashed arrows, are the reciprocal changes in ownership in the transaction. It will be seen in both the medium of exchange and the Z row that it is as if the ownership passes from a + entry to a - entry; it is also clear from the solid arrows of the purchasing power entries and the dashed arrow showing the change in ownership of the medium of exchange, that purchasing power is something significantly different from the medium of exchange. However, medium of exchange can be regarded as having purchasing power as a latent quality, which in the instant of a transaction is activated (+), parted with (-), received (+) and extinguished (-). Looking at Table 1.10, the medium of exchange row contains the initial activation (+) of purchasing power at the point of original ownership of the medium of exchange, and the final extinction (–) of purchasing power at the point of final ownership of the medium of exchange, as if the purchasing power had been carried there by the medium of exchange as its ownership changed. But instead of moving there directly in the medium of exchange row, the circuit of purchasing power entries in Table 1.10 shows that it is as if the purchasing power had moved via the Z row, where we find the intermediate parting with (–) and receiving (+) entries, as if in this row the purchasing power had moved in the opposite direction from, and in exchange for, the ownership of Z.[1]

This then is the purchasing power view; it aims to provide a rationalisation of the sign rules used in the double entry balance of payments account and in the quadruple entry flow of funds matrix table as this has been developed above. In the balance of payments account these sign rules lead to the bald statement 'official reserves (drawing on +/additions to –)' which troubles so many users because it seems arbitrary and counter-intuitive. The object of the purchasing power view is to formulate an approach which can make such a statement intuitively acceptable and which, with a little practice, will be found easy to use.

5 The presentation of the UK flow of funds matrix table

Here we have developed a flow of funds presentation in the form of a zero-sum matrix table (ZSMT). The advantages of this approach are that in such a matrix table a transaction is always recorded by a zero-sum quadruple entry; a formally identical quadruple entry can be used as the unit of variation in such a matrix table, permitting conjectural variation (see Chapter 5) while maintaining at all times the row and column zero-sum restrictions; and the purchasing power view allows easy interpretation of all matrix table cell entries. However, there are certain differences between our zero-sum matrix table and the UK flow of funds matrix table presentation.

Our zero-sum matrix table consists of two components, the Financial Surplus (FS) row and the Financing Account (FA). Together these may be termed the Matrix Table Proper (MTP). This is shown schematically in Table 1.11. When we turn to the UK presentation, we find two main differences from our structure. (1) a set of rows is added which shows how the FS row entries are derived; here we shall call these 'headnote' (HN) rows, and these rows are attached to the FS row to form the capital account (CA) which is to that extent separated from the financing account. (2) the signs in the financing account in the UK presentation are the opposite of those in the financing account in our zero-sum matrix table presentation.

Presentation using PPV signs

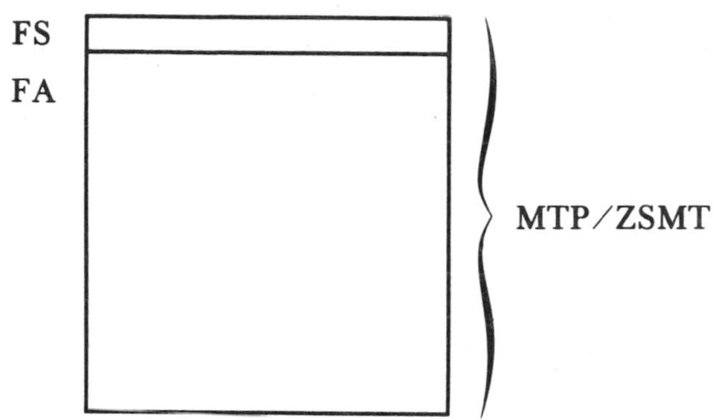

Table 1.11

UK presentation

differences from ZSMT in Table 1.11:

CA
HN
FS

FA

(1) FS row attached to HN rows to form Capital Account

(2) opposite signs in FA.

Table 1.12

The UK presentation is shown schematically in Table 1.12 with these two differences noted on the right hand side.

We now look at these differences from the quadruple entry point of view. In the case of (1), although the headnote rows contain useful information and should be conveniently available to the user, they are not zero-sum rows (this is explained in Chapter 2 sections 3 and 4) and are thus unlike the FS row and the financing account rows which *are* zero-sum rows in all presentations. This means that the headnote rows are not part of our zero-sum quadruple entry system, and to separate the FS row from the financing account and add it to the headnote rows to form the capital account is not logical from the quadruple entry point of view. In the case of (2), having the opposite signs in the financing account means that in the UK presentation a quadruple entry recording a financial transaction, and therefore with all its entries in the financing account, will still be a zero-sum quadruple entry (although with signs which are the reverse of our PPV signs). However, if a transaction affects the FS row (whose signs are the same as in our zero-sum matrix table), then the quadruple entry recording it will not be a zero-sum quadruple entry: its entries will not sum to zero down the columns because of the reversal of the signs in the financing account. This means that, in the UK presentation, the quadruple entry recording a transaction will have different sign characteristics depending upon whether or not it records a transaction requiring entries in the FS row. From the quadruple entry point of view, this shows an inconsistency in signs between the FS row and the financing account in the UK presentation.

The differences between the two presentations are clear, simple and readily allowed for: starting with the UK presentations, it is a trivial rearrangement to ignore the HN rows and to combine the FS row with the financing account to produce the matrix table proper; it is almost equally simple to reverse the signs in the financing account so that we arrive at the ZSMT in which we can use the quadruple entry approach. Indeed, even if we do not specifically intend to use the quadruple entry approach as such, this reversal of the signs in the financing account of the UK presentation can be immediately helpful. Many users have difficulty in making sense of these entries because they find the signs confusing. One effective solution is to switch over to our purchasing power view: mentally reverse the sign of the entry in the UK presentation of the financing account and then apply the purchasing power view to get straight to the underlying change, as explained in section 4 above.[2]

Having set out the clear and simple relationship between our zero-sum matrix table presentation and the UK presentation, in the following chapters we shall use whichever of these is the more appropriate for the matter we are dealing with.

Notes

1 It will be seen that our concept of purchasing power is a form of meta-money. It is as if the buyer of Z uses money to acquire meta-money and uses the meta-money to acquire Z, while the seller of Z parts with it for meta-money and uses the meta-money to acquire money, all in the instant of the transaction. In principle, our flow of funds matrix table records cell by cell the net sums of these activations, transfers and extinctions of purchasing power/meta-money in all the transactions occurring during a period.

2 See also Chapter 4 note 4.

2 The UK flow of funds accounts — I

1 Considerations in the choice of columns and rows

The balance of payments account and the flow of funds account emerge from a common formal structure, but they represent two different lines of development; each of them has its own focus of attention, which is reflected in its choice of rows and sector columns. The UK balance of payments accounts records, from the point of view of the UK, the transactions between the UK and the rest of the world; it can be presented as a single UK column and the balance of payments of the rest can readily be derived as the negative image of this UK column, as in Table 1.2. The UK flow of funds matrix table, on the other hand, is equally concerned with flows between domestic sectors. It therefore has a number of UK domestic sectors and an overseas sector, but no column for the UK as a whole; such a column showing the UK balance of payments can be derived as the negative image of the overseas sector column, as in Table 1.3.

This difference in their focus of attention is also revealed in the choice of transaction rows. To begin with, the balance of payments account derives the UK current account net balance from exports and imports, while the flow of funds account derives UK domestic sector financial surpluses from saving and investment (the two procedures are formally equivalent, see section 4 below, particularly identity (3)). Similarly, in the financing account, the flow of funds account distinguishes a number of rows which relate solely to domestic financing flows and which have no counterpart in the balance of payments account. Indeed, even in the transaction rows which do cover overseas transactions, the classifications in the two accounts are quite different, although being derived from the same underlying body of data, they are reconcilable (see Appendix 8).

In setting up a flow of funds matrix table some decision has to be made on the number of rows and columns it is to contain. No point of principle is involved in this; it is simply a matter of the trade-off between (a) available detail and (b) compactness which allows a significant picture to emerge clearly. Even if the data were to be available, a matrix table with dozens of columns and perhaps two hundred rows in the financing account would be too detailed and diffuse for any useful picture to emerge clearly and too large to be readily rearranged by a user for his own purposes. On the other hand, a matrix table with only three sector columns and three financing account rows would certainly be compact but would obscure so much significant detail that again no useful picture would emerge. Even with unlimited detail, therefore, there is for any user some optimal size of the matrix table; in fact some very desirable detail is not available.

As examples of the different decisions that can be made on the most suitable size of the matrix table, the Bank of England until 1981 produced a flow of funds matrix table with six institutional sector columns and ultimately with 24 transaction rows in the financing account. This represented one practical judgement on the best compromise between available detail and compactness, the aim being to provide a body of data which could be used as the basis for a commentary on recent developments in the UK. Over the same period, the Central Statistical Office produced a flow of funds matrix table with seven institutional sector columns and ultimately with 41 transaction rows in the financing account. This reflected the different aim of providing sufficient detail to allow the user to adapt the data to his own particular requirements.

In the UK flow of funds accounts there is, in addition to the matrix table, a whole range of supporting tables. These give longer time series for each sector column separately, together with useful rearrangements or further details of the financing account entries. Such supporting tables (which are described briefly in Chapter 3 section 5) are very helpful for following changes over time in particular cell entries or for looking at the position of an individual sector. But here we shall take the view that it is more important to concentrate upon the matrix table, because it is the need for consistency in the matrix table which conditions the whole of the flow of funds accounting framework, and because it is the matrix table which reveals most clearly the interdependence of cell entries and allows us to see this in terms of a quadruple entry accounting system.

We now have to turn to the sector columns and transaction rows used in the presentations of the UK flow of funds matrix table. Simply to set out the detailed coverage of the individual columns and rows would be tedious and not very useful. Instead we shall look only at the leading features of the columns and rows used, to provide an introduction to the detailed definitions available in the official sources which are set out in Chapter 3 section 5.

2 UK flow of funds accounts: sector columns and presentations

The institutional sector columns distinguished in the UK flow of funds matrix table have changed very little over the years. The basic six sectors (together with the abbreviations we shall use later on) are:

UK domestic sectors:	Public sector	(Pub)
	Personal sector	(Pers)
	Industrial and commercial companies sector	(ICC)
	Banking sector	(Bkg)
(recently re-named:	Monetary sector	(Mon))
	Other financial institutions sector	(OFI)
Rest of the world:	Overseas sector	(O's)

There have been only two variations on this pattern.[1] From the beginning, one presentation subdivided OFI into two:

OFI	Life assurance and superannuation funds	(LASF)
	Other	(OFI′)

and more recently Pub was divided into three sub-sectors:

Pub	Central government	(CG)
	Local authorities	(LA)
	Public corporations	(PC)

This sectorisation is largely self-explanatory, and aims at homogeneity of transactors within sectors and distinct differences between sectors. This seems to be achieved to a reasonable degree, but there are obviously problems. For example, the Personal sector includes not only households but also unincorporated businesses (such as accountants, lawyers, Lloyds underwriters, farmers etc) and non-profit-making bodies such as charities. One would expect the behaviour of these to differ considerably from that of households. The Industrial and Commercial Companies sector is another which could with advantage be sub-divided; while there are several different ways in which this could be done (e.g. oil and non-oil companies), lack of data is likely to be the problem in most cases. Other financial institutions, referred to in some tables as Financial Institutions Other than Banks (FIOB), also represent a very mixed group, and the subdivision noted above into LASF and OFI′ could therefore be helpful. However, the terminology does involve some unnecessary ambiguity about 'other' financial institutions (avoided here by distinguishing between OFI and OFI′), although this does not seem to have caused any difficulties. This is a case in which a supporting table provides useful further sectorisation which would hardly be justified in the matrix table. Finally, we have seen that the Public sector has recently been sub-divided into central government, local authorities and public corporations. One could well expect each of these to behave differently, but the direct policy influence which central government exercises over the other two groups is a reason for retaining a single Public sector. As we shall see, it is possible to get the best of both worlds in this case.

A quite different kind of change which has occurred has been the reallocation of certain transactors between sectors. One of these was the transfer of steel companies from ICC to Pub when they were nationalised in 1967; another was the recognition of five finance houses as banks and their transfer from OFI to Bkg in 1972. More important was the transfer of a number of institutions to the newly created Monetary sector (Mon) which replaced Bkg from the beginning of 1982.

Column structure of presentations of the UK matrix table

Matrix table presentation	Institutional sectors						Error column		
up to March 1981:									
BEP[1]	Pub	Pers	ICC	Bkg	OFI	O's	annual: qtrly:	none RE	
CSOP(NIE)[2]	Pub	Pers	ICC	Bks	LASF OFI′ (bracketed)	O's	annual:	Un none	(up to 1970) (from 1971)
CSOP(FinS)[3]	Pub	Pers	ICC	Bks	OFI	O's	annual: qtrly:	Un RE	(up to Mar 1971) (from Apr 1971)
from April 1981:[4]									
OP(BE)[5]	CG LA PC Pub (bracketed)	Pers	ICC	Bkg[6]	OFI	O's	annual: qtrly:	RE RE	
OP(NIE)[7]	CG LA PC (bracketed)	Pers	ICC	Bks[6]	LASF OFI′ (bracketed)	O's	annual:	none	
OP(FinS)	CG LA PC	Pers	ICC	Bks	OFI	O's	annual: qtrly:	none none	

All dates in this table are publication dates.

Notes:
1 See Appendix 2, Table A2.1 for the row headings in this presentation.
2 See Appendix 2, Table A2.2 for the row headings in this presentation.
3 This omitted the capital account and was not a full matrix table; otherwise its row headings were the same as CSOP(NIE).
4 Annual matrix tables are available in BEP, CSOP and OP forms for 1979 and 1980.
5 See Appendix 1, Table A1.1.
6 Re-named Mon from beginning of 1982.
7 See Appendix 1, Table A1.2.

Table 2.1

The flow of funds accounts for the UK began to appear regularly in their present developed form in 1963-64,[2] and from then until March 1981 the matrix table appeared in three presentations, each of them showing developments in detail over this period. The first was the Bank of England presentation (BEP) published in the *Bank of England Quarterly Bulletin (BEQB)*; the annual version of this covered each of the three latest years in one matrix table (see Appendix 2, Table A2.1 for the final form of the BEP row headings). The other two were both Central Statistical Office presentations (CSOP); one appeared in the annual *National Income and Expenditure* (NIE), the 'National Income Blue Book', and the other in the monthly *Financial Statistics* (FinS), and we shall call them CSOP(NIE) and CSOP(FinS) respectively (see Appendix 2, Table A2.2 for the final form of the row headings in these presentations). From April 1981 all three presentations moved to a new common format which we shall call the Official Presentation (OP); we shall distinguish the Bank of England version, OP(BE), (see Appendix 1, Table A1.1), and the two CSO versions which appear in the same two sources as above, which we shall call OP(NIE), (see Appendix 1, Table A1.2), and OP(FinS). The column structure of these six presentations is set out in Table 2.1 using the above abbreviations. (Later it may be of some interest to compare the current UK presentation with the United States flow of funds matrix table, which is briefly described in Appendix 3.)

The sectorisations in Table 2.1 call for only a few comments. It was noted above that there is a case for having Pub as a sector and also a case for having its constituents CG, LA and PC shown in the matrix table. OP(BE) tries to solve this conflict by showing both Pub and its constituents; however, this involves implicit double-counting, and there should really be a vertical ruling to warn the user that CG, LA and PC are sub-sectors of Pub, which itself is on the same level as Pers, ICC, etc. (Such a vertical ruling has since been inserted.) Table 2.1 also covers the error columns. The view taken here is that it is important to have an explicit error column in the matrix table, since otherwise the user is not alerted to the large error column entries often required to make the financial surplus row sum to zero; it is also helpful to remind the user that currently the financing account rows are effectively made to have an error column entry of zero by the method of estimation of some institutional sector column entries (see Chapter 3 section 3). Table 2.1 notes the error column situation for both the annual and quarterly versions of the presentations; it seems unfortunate that the current CSO presentations OP(FinS) and OP(NIE) omit an error column. In an earlier version the error column was called Unallocated (Un), but in recent years, where shown, it has always been called Residual error (RE). Since residual error has a particular significance in the national income accounts, for our own purposes here we shall simply call the error column Error (E).

The order of the institutional sector columns in Table 2.1 is only for illustration and is not the same as that used in any of the presentations. It is easiest to consult the particular matrix table concerned to see the column order used; however, it may be helpful to note that:

1. the NIE column order was the same, *mutatis mutandis,* before and after April 1981. This column order differs from:
2. the FinS column order, which also was the same, *mutatis mutandis,* before and after April 1981.
3. the Bank of England column order has, since April 1981, conformed to the FinS column order; before April 1981 the BE column order was different from all those above.

Some of the presentations have higher level groupings of sectors such as Private, Public and Overseas; these too are best appreciated by looking at the matrix tables concerned.

3 UK flow of funds accounts: the capital account

We turn now to the rows in the UK flow of funds matrix table. We begin with the capital account, in which the financial surplus/deficit row entries are derived; ignoring for the moment minor differences in row terminology, this is done in the following way:

Capital account

	Line
Saving	1
Taxes on capital and capital transfers	2
less:	
Gross fixed capital formation at home	3
Increase in value of stocks and work in progress	4
= Financial surplus +/deficit –	5

All BE and NIE presentations use this format, but OP(FinS) leaves out 'less:' (which is needed to show clearly that the entries in rows 3 and 4 have had their signs reversed), enters these row entries with their original signs and relies upon a note to the table to indicate that these signs have to be reversed in order to derive the financial surplus/deficit row entries. This is very unhelpful because it means that at first sight the capital account column entries do not add up; the format used in the other presentations and illustrated above is much to be preferred. Since a deficit can be regarded as a negative surplus, from now on we shall refer simply to the financial surplus (FS) row, and to a sector's financial surplus (which may, of course, be positive or negative).

This derivation of the FS row entries is not quite as straight-forward as it looks. Ignoring row (= line) 2 for the moment, we have saving in row 1 and investment in row 3 + row 4. In row 1, however, saving includes stock appreciation, which is a valuation change and not a money flow occurring in the form of transactions, and this stock appreciation (g) also appears in investment as part of row 4. Therefore instead of the usual economic money-flow concept of saving (S) and investment (I), in the flow of funds capital account we are dealing with the different concepts S′ and I′ where S′ = S + g and I′ = I + g. However, since stock appreciation appears in both S′ and I′, it cancels out when we take the difference between the two:

$$S' - I' = S + g - (I + g) = S - I$$

leaving us with the excess of money flow saving over money flow investment, which is what we want. Now adding in net receipts from taxes on capital and capital transfers (row 2) gives each sector's financial surplus (row 5).

We now find ourselves with two quite different types of rows. The financial surplus row and the financing account rows are in principle zero-sum rows. The saving and investment rows, on the other hand, are functionally defined rows which do not have any zero-sum constraint in principle; put most simply, this is because, in row 1, my positive saving does not require you to have negative saving, and similarly for rows 3 and 4. In fact, as noted in Chapter 1 section 5, rows 1 to 4 can be regarded as 'headnote' (HN) rows, by analogy with footnotes, giving useful information on the derivation of the financial surplus row, but to be kept clearly distinct from the financial surplus and financing account rows which make up the flow of funds matrix table proper (MTP), which can be (though it need not be) set out as a zero-sum matrix table.

Row 2, taxes on capital and capital transfers (TCCT) is a special case. This *is* a zero-sum row because the transactions do have a reciprocal nature, being paid by one sector and received by another. Row 2, therefore, could quite consistently be transferred to the matrix table proper from the headnote rows, and whether to transfer it or leave it in the headnote rows depends upon other considerations. The main reason for leaving it in the capital account is that it records unrequited transfers (a large part of them being involuntary) which are quite different in character from the voluntary and requited payments recorded in the financing account of the matrix table. (Here we use TCCT, which is the Bank of England's row title, in preference to Capital Transfers (net receipts) which is the CSO's title for the same row.)

In passing, it is worth looking briefly at the two component parts of TCCT. The first is taxes on capital, which include death duties, capital transfer tax and capital gains tax paid by the private sector to the central government sub-sector of the public sector. The second, capital transfers, has two components: (a) various grants paid mainly by central government to local authorities, public corporations and other UK domestic sectors, net of repayments, and (b) payments by the UK public sector to the overseas sector in connection with guarantees under the Sterling Agreements of 1968 and after; such payments occurred only in 1973 and 1974, and we shall ignore them here.

Unlike the simple zero-sum schema of Table 1.3 in Chapter 1, the financial surplus row entries for the institutional sectors never in practice add up to zero on their own because there are estimation errors in the other rows in the capital account. They therefore need the help of an error entry in the financial surplus row to bring this about. This entry can be large and the view taken here is that it should always be shown in the matrix table. This requires an error column, and it is surprising that only half of the ten presentations used in recent years show such an error column (see Table 2.1). More is said about the treatment of errors in the next section. Finally, it is important to note that in the case of the overseas sector there are special problems concerning the capital account entries, and these also are dealt with in the next section.

4 The national income accounting background

Here we will go rather further into the national income accounting system which lies behind the capital account in the flow of funds accounts. It starts with a set of identities which relate income, consumption, saving, investment, exports and imports, all of these being measured as current money flows per period of time.

$$C + I + X - M \equiv Y \qquad \ldots(1)$$

Identity (1) can be interpreted as showing how income is generated by expenditure on current output; it defines a sector's income (Y) as being identical with that sector's expenditure on consumption (C) *plus* its expenditure on investment (I) *plus* its exports (X) *minus* its expenditure on imports (M). One way of looking at identity (1) for any sector (which for convenience we shall call the domestic sector) is to see domestic sector expenditure (C + I) as generating income *either* inside the domestic sector *or* outside it in what we shall call external sectors. The domestic sector expenditure which generates income in external sectors is expenditure on imports (M) from external sectors; deducting this from total domestic sector expenditure (C + I − M) leaves us with domestic sector expenditure which creates domestic sector income. Symmetrically, expenditure by external sectors on domestic sector output creates income in the domestic sector; this is domestic sector exports (X). Adding together these two components of domestic sector income and re-ordering them gives us total domestic sector income C + I + X − M as in identity (1).

$$Y \equiv C + S \qquad \ldots (2)$$

Identity (2) is simpler and can be interpreted as showing how income is disposed of; it defines income as being identical with consumption *plus* saving (S). Deducting identity (2) from identity (1) gives us:

$$I - S + X - M \equiv O$$

and

$$S - I \equiv X - M \qquad \ldots (3)$$

These national income accounting identities are definitionally true at every level: for the world as a whole (in which case we have a closed economy with X and M both equal to zero and S ≡ I) or for any part of the world economy, whether a group of national economies, a single national economy or any domestic sector within a national economy. Identity (3) also shows that, at every such level, the balance of payments on current account (X − M) and the financial surplus (S − I) are identical. The use of one term at the level of the national economy and the other at the level of sectors within that economy is purely a matter of convention.

As interpreted earlier, identities (1) to (3) deal with expenditure and income arising from trading transactions; however, particularly in the case of a domestic sector, we would expect to find also current transfer expenditure and current transfer income. For example, taxes on income and expenditure are current transfer expenditure by the private sector and current transfer income for the public sector; conversely, state old age pensions and other welfare payments are current transfer expenditure by the public sector and current transfer income for the private sector. Looking at these current transfers in terms of identities (1) to (3) above, we can regard current transfer receipts by the private sector as being analogous to private sector exports: a rise in these current transfer receipts can then appear as a rise in X and Y in (1), a rise in Y and S in (2) and a rise in X - M and S - I in (3). Similarly, we can regard current transfer expenditure by the private sector as being analogous to private sector consumption expenditure on imports: a rise in these current transfer expenditures can then appear as a rise in C and an offsetting rise in - M in (1), a rise in C and an offsetting fall in S in (2) and a fall in X - M and S - I in (3). Thus current transfers can be fitted without difficulty into accounting identities (1) to (3), and from now on we shall regard these identities as covering both current trading transactions and current transfer items (but not transfers relating to capital).

At this point it is useful to distinguish two forms of these identities, which we shall term the classification form and the estimation form. The classification form of an identity defines the population of entities involved and relationships between them (as in identities (1) to (3) above), the individual entities themselves (C, I, X, etc) being explicitly defined elsewhere or implicitly defined in an identity as a residual. When we estimate values for the various components of an identity for a particular sector and period, there are inevitably errors, and as estimated the identity will no longer add up correctly; however, since we know that in principle — in the absence of errors — it must add up correctly by definition, we add in an error entry (e) and the identity then continues to hold in its estimation form. For present purposes it is sufficient to recognise these two forms of the identities we are concerned with, and to leave the context to indicate which is appropriate and where an error entry is needed to maintain the identities.

As we saw in the preceding section, presentation of the capital account includes a TCCT row for taxes on capital and capital transfers as well as including capital appreciation (g) in both saving and investment. However, in what follows we shall keep to the simpler national income accounting framework outlined above and culminating in identity (3), as this is clearer and the substance of the argument is not affected.

We now go on to consider the ways in which the entries in the financial surplus (FS) row can be derived. For this purpose we set out two illustrative sets of capital accounts, Treatment 1 and Treatment 2, in Table 2.2. In these there are just three domestic sectors denoted by D_1, D_2, D_3 and their column entries have the subscripts 1, 2, 3 respectively. Overseas sector entries have the subscript O. A sum of row entries will be shown by summing the subscripts (so that, for example,

Treatment 1

	domestic economy						
	D_1	D_2	D_3	O's	E	Σ	
S	S_1	S_2	S_3	S_0		$S_{1+2+3+0}$	(= S_W)
					$+e'$	$+e'$	(= error)
−I	$-I_1$	$-I_2$	$-I_3$	$-I_0$		$-I_{1+2+3+0}$	(= $-I_W$)
=FS	$S_1 - I_1$	$S_2 - I_2$	$S_3 - I_3$	$S_0 - I_0$	$+e'$	0	(= FS_W)

Treatment 2

	domestic economy						
	D_1	D_2	D_3	O's	E	Σ	
S	S_1	S_2	S_3	$-X_{UK} + M_{UK}$		S_{1+2+3} $-X_{UK} + M_{UK}$	(= S_{UK} FS_{UK})
					$+e$	$+e$	(= error)
−I	$-I_1$	$-I_2$	$-I_3$			$-I_{1+2+3}$	(= $-I_{UK}$)
=FS	$S_1 - I_1$	$S_2 - I_2$	$S_3 - I_3$	$-X_{UK} + M_{UK}$	$+e$	0	(=FS_W)

Table 2.2

$S_1 + S_2 + S_3 = S_{1+2+3}$); we shall also have the subscript UK (for the UK domestic economy) and W (for the world). It will be seen that $S_{1+2+3} = S_{UK}$, $-I_{1+2+3+0} = -I_W$ etc. We have already noted that the two treatments omit the TCCT row and stock appreciation; in addition, for compactness they show investment in a single row and in the form −I instead of 'less I'. They also have an explicit error (E) column and sum (Σ) column.

It is worth recalling that in the previous section we saw that:

$$S' - I' = S + g - (I + g) = S - I$$

where g is stock appreciation. Whether we work in terms of saving and investment both including or both excluding stock appreciation, Treatments 1 and 2 both hold true. For simplicity, therefore, we have no prime subscripts in the two Treatments and we leave the user to consistently include or exclude stock appreciation as suits his purpose. To match strictly the presentation of the capital account in the flow of funds matrix table, stock appreciation should be included.

Looking first at Treatment 1, this shows the preferred situation in which we have direct estimates for each of the entries S_1, S_2, S_3, S_0 in the S row and $-I_1$, $-I_2$, $-I_3$, $-I_0$ in the −I row. The entries in the Σ column for the S row and the −I row are then world S (S_W) and world −I ($-I_W$) respectively. In principle these two must sum to zero, as we have already seen from identity (3): for the world as a whole, X and M must both be equal to zero and therefore $S - I \equiv O$; thus the entries in the Σ (= world) column in the capital account must sum to zero. However, when we are using estimates of these entries we need an error entry (+e′) to ensure this zero sum. For compactness, we shall attribute all the errors in the capital account to the S row, so that this error entry can be placed in the E column and the S row, but dropped out of line with the other S row entries to remind us of its particular character here. For each sector column, the entry in the FS row is derived from the sum of entries in the S and −I rows. As we have seen, the entries in the Σ column in the capital account definitionally sum to zero; the entries in the FS row are simply a re-ordering of the entries in the Σ column and the FS row also definitionally sums to zero.

In Treatment 2 we have to deal with the fact that in practice there are no direct estimates of saving and investment for the overseas sector, S_0 and $-I_0$. However, we have from identity (3):

$$S_0 - I_0 \equiv X_0 - M_0$$

We also know that, in a closed world economy subdivided into only two sectors, domestic and overseas, the balance of payments on current account for one sector must be the negative image of that for the other sector:

$$X_0 - M_0 \equiv - (X_{UK} - M_{UK})$$

From these two,

$$S_0 - I_0 \equiv - X_{UK} + M_{UK}$$

The term on the right hand side is the negative image of the balance of payments on current account of the domestic economy (which we have already seen is identical to the financial surplus of the domestic economy, FS_{UK}), and since we do have an estimate of the balance of payments on current account of the domestic economy, we can use its negative image as an estimate of the net magnitude of $S_0 - I_0$. This is placed in the FS row/O's column, and also as a window-dressing entry in the O's column/S row, so that for the O's sector the FS row entry is still equal to (though not derived from) the sum of the S row entry and the −I row entry (the latter being zero). Again, we need an error entry (e) to make the Σ column sum to zero, and this will also make the FS row sum to zero since the latter contains a re-ordering of the same terms.[3] However, this procedure means that the S row no longer sums to world S, nor the −I row to world −I, because it is as if a term which is the counterpart of $-I_0$ in Treatment 1 had been deducted from the −I row and added to the S row. This makes the sum of the −I row, which should be a world total, equal to $-I_{UK}$ and the sum of the S row equal to $S_{UK} - FS_{UK}$, a complementary composite term of no special significance.

A comparison of Treatment 1 and Treatment 2 can clarify matters, but in the absence of direct estimates of S_0 and I_0, there is nothing that can be done about this awkward situation which is implicit in the capital account of all the full matrix table presentations with one exception. This exception is CSOP(NIE), (see, for example, CSO *National Income and Expenditure* 1980 p.81); there the CSO uses Net Acquisition of Financial Assets (NAFA) as the title for what we shall continue to call the financial surplus (FS) row. In this presentation again there are no direct estimates of S_0 and I_0 and as in Treatment 2 we have to use $-X_{UK} + M_{UK}$, which is $-FS_{UK}$, as our estimate of FS_0 to be placed in the FS row/O's column. However, this presentation, unlike all the others, does not place this same term as a window-dressing entry in the S or −I rows. This means that the entries in the FS row include $-X_{UK} + M_{UK}$ while the entries in the Σ column are the same except for the omission of $-X_{UK} + M_{UK}$; it follows that the FS row and the Σ column cannot both sum to zero, no matter what error entry is used. A further consequence is that the Σ column entries for the S and −I rows now appear as S_{UK} and $-I_{UK}$ respectively. This gives a deceptive appearance of consistency when in fact this presentation of the capital account is internally inconsistent.[4]

As a help in following this rather tangled trail through these presentations of the capital account, the main findings are summarised in Table 2.3:

	FS of domestic sectors	FS of overseas sector	Sum of S row	Sum of −I row
Treatment 1	derived from S−I	derived from S−I	S_W	$-I_W$
Treatment 2 full presentations except CSOP(NIE)	derived from S−I	estimated by $-FS_{UK}$ (window-dressing entry of $-FS_{UK}$ in S row)	$S_{UK}-FS_{UK}$ (no clear significance)	$-I_{UK}$
CSOP(NIE)	derived from S−I	estimated by $-FS_{UK}$ (no window-dressing entry in S row; capital account is inconsistent)	S_{UK}	$-I_{UK}$

Table 2.3

5 CSO identity schemas

Against this background we now look at the identity schemas put forward by the Central Statistical Office (CSO) as the analytical foundations of their presentation of the capital account. Apart from their unhelpful practice of sometimes transposing rows and columns relative to the statistical presentations which they were intended to illuminate, these schemas are open to a number of objections.

We begin with the CSO schema *(Financial Statistics Explanatory Handbook* 1979, p.7) shown here in Table 2.4. This schema is in classification form, that is, with no error entries; in order to make it comparable, *mutatis mutandis*, with our Treatment 2 above (which is in estimation form), we ignore the E column and e entries in Treatment 2. We also need to note that the CSO uses Balance from Income and Expenditure account (Y − C) and Gross Capital

	CAPITAL ACCOUNT								FINANCIAL ACCOUNT
	Balance from Income and expenditure account		Gross capital formation		Net capital transfers		Net acquisition of financial assets		Changes in financial assets and liabilities
Domestic Sector 1	$(Y_1 - C_1)$	–	I_1	+	T_1	=	$NAFA_1$	=	$A_1 - L_1$
Domestic Sector 2	$(Y_2 - C_2)$	–	I_2	+	T_2	=	$NAFA_2$	=	$A_2 - L_2$
Domestic Sector 3	$(Y_3 - C_3)$	–	I_3	+	T_3	=	$NAFA_3$	=	$A_3 - L_3$
Overseas	$(M - X)$			+	T_0	=	$NAFA_0$	=	$A_0 - L_0$
NATION	$Y - C - X + M$	–	I	+	Nil	=	Nil	=	Nil

Y_i = income, including current transfers
C_i = expenditure on consumption, plus current transfers
I_i = physical investment (as opposed to investment in financial assets)
T_i = capital transfer receipts less disbursements
A_i = changes in financial assets
L_i = changes in liabilities
} in Sector i

X = exports
M = imports
} visible trade and invisibles

$\sum Y_i = Y \quad \sum C_i = C \quad \sum I_i = 1 \quad \sum T_i = 0 \quad \sum (A_i - L_i) = 0$

The expression in the 'Nation' row can be rearranged to illustrate 2 basic identities in national income accounting, as follows:—

$Y = C + I + X - M$, which expresses the equality of gross national product measured from the income and expenditure sides

and

$Y - C - X + M = I$, which expresses the equality of saving and investment across the whole economy

Source: *CSO, Financial Statistics Explantory Handbook* 1979 p. 7.

Table 2.4

Sector and national accounts

	Domestic sector 1	Domestic sector 2	Domestic sector 3	Nation	*plus* Overseas	*equals* World
Capital account						
Balance from income and expenditure account (saving)	(Y_1-C_1)	(Y_2-C_2)	(Y_3-C_3)	$(Y-C)$ }	$(M-X)$	Nil
deduct: Gross domestic capital formation	I_1	I_2	I_3	I }		
add: Net capital transfers	T_1	T_2	T_3	T	T_0	Nil
equals: Financial surplus/deficit	FS/D_1	FS/D_2	FS/D_3	FS/D	FS/D_0	Nil
equals: **Financial account**						
Changes in financial assets and liabilities	A_1-L_1	A_2-L_2	A_3-L_3	$A-L$	A_0-L_0	Nil

Y_i = income } including
C_i = current expenditure } current transfers
I_i = physical investment (as opposed to investment in financial assets)
T_i = capital transfer receipts less disbursements
FS/D_i = Financial surplus/deficit
A_i = changes in financial assets
L_i = changes in liabilities
(all the above: in Domestic Sector i)
X = exports of goods and services and other UK credits } excluding
M = imports of goods and services and other UK debits } capital transfers

$$\sum Y_i = Y \quad \sum C_i = C \quad \sum I_i = I \quad \sum T_i = T \quad \sum FS/D_i = FS/D \quad \sum (A_i - L_i) = A - L$$

The first two rows of the nation and overseas columns can be expressed as the following identity:

$(Y-C) - I + (M-X) \equiv 0$, which can be manipulated to illustrate two basic identities of national income accounting as follows:

$Y \equiv C+I+(X-M)$, which expresses the equality of gross national disposable income measured from the income and expenditure sides (*gross national disposable income = gross national product + net current transfers from abroad*)

and

$Y-C \equiv I+(X-M)$, which expresses the equality of national saving and investment (the latter consisting of domestic capital formation and net investment abroad).

Source: ***CSO, Financial Statistics Explanatory Handbook 1983 p. 8.***

Table 2.5

Formation (I) where Treatment 2 uses saving (S) and investment (I) respectively; we have already seen that NAFA corresponds to our FS, and Net Capital Transfers (T) is the same as our TCCT, which is not included in Treatment 2. Here we shall continue to use the terminology of Treatment 2.

If we now look at the Σ column entries in Treatment 2, we see that they are sectorally heterogeneous, three relating to the UK domestic economy and one (in the FS row) relating to the World. This column therefore cannot validly be labelled either Nation or World, but only Total or Σ. The corresponding (bottom) row in the CSO schema, however, is labelled Nation; simple inspection is enough to show that this must be wrong.

In *Financial Statistics Explanatory Handbook* 1980 the CSO schema appeared in a substantially revised form which, except for trivial amendments, has remained unchanged since then. This new schema, taken from the 1983 edition (p. 8) is reproduced in Table 2.5; it has a correct Nation column and its Total column is now labelled World. While this schema is valid in its own terms, unfortunately it does not match the current presentation of the capital account. Taking only the OP(FinS) and OP(NIE) presentations, these both follow Treatment 2 above in having $-X_{UK} + M_{UK}$ in both the FS row and the S row of the Overseas sector column, producing the same sectorally heterogeneous entries as in the Σ column of Treatment 2, which then is not a World column. The CSO schema in effect combines the S and −I rows at this point, so that their entries S_{UK}, $-FS_{UK}$ and $-I_{UK}$ which otherwise would appear individually in the Σ column now net out to zero, and allow the Σ column to be titled World.

The view taken here is that it is not really helpful to manipulate entries in this way to make the Σ column into a World column. Treatment 1 shows the circumstances in which this occurs naturally, while Treatment 2 shows that if the information on S and −I for the overseas sector is not available, we cannot avoid having a sectorally heterogeneous set of entries in the Σ column of the capital account. It is better to recognise and accept this rather than to strain after a tidy World column at the expense of a schema which ceases to match the statistical presentations of the capital account.

In the bottom lines of the notes in Table 2.4 the CSO illustrates one of '2 basic identities in national income accounting' which 'expresses the equality of saving and investment across the whole economy'. This identity appears in Table 2.4 in the form:

$$Y - C - X + M = I$$

This can be readily re-written in terms of the Σ column entries (excluding e) in Treatment 2, and it then becomes:

$$S_{UK} - FS_{UK} \equiv I_{UK} \quad \text{... (4)}$$

In Table 2.5 the CSO revises its identity to:

$$Y - C \equiv I_D + X - M$$

which as before can be re-written:

$$S_{UK} \equiv I_{UK} + FS_{UK} \quad \text{... (5)}$$

Looking at national income accounting from the economic point of view, we have identity (3) above:

$$S - I \equiv X - M \quad \text{... (3)}$$

which tells that only for the world as a whole, when X - M is zero by definition, is $S \equiv I$ across the whole (world) economy; for any open domestic economy there is no necessity for S to equal I. This economic viewpoint is not the only one, and in accounting terms there is nothing against having a terminology in which saving and investment have to be equal for the domestic economy. But then we find the CSO achieving this in (4) by having a conventional definition of investment and defining saving ($S_{UK} - FS_{UK}$) to always be equal to this investment, while it achieves it in (5) by reverting to a conventional definition of saving and defining investment ($I_{UK} + FS_{UK}$) to always be equal to this saving. Of the two, that in (5) seems the more satisfactory, and it is in line with the usage in the US flow of funds matrix table (see Appendix 3). The important thing is to be clear about which terminology is being used at any particular time. Here we always follow the economic usage embodied in identities (1) to (3) above unless otherwise stated.

The CSO has a further schema (*Financial Statistics Explanatory Handbook* 1983, p. 28) which is concerned with the error entries in the capital account (Table 2.6). This also is comparable with our Treatment 2, with both of them being in estimation form and the CSO's residual error (RE) corresponding to our error entry e. The World column in this schema contains a nil entry for World S and no entry at all for World I, which must be wrong. However, it is the error column we are concerned with. There, as in Treatment 2, the error entry in the FS row is repeated in the S row, as is necessary for the capital account to be internally consistent. The current CSO presentations of the full matrix table do not contain an error column, so we

Sector unidentified transactions and the residual error

	Domestic sector i	Nation	*plus* Overseas	*plus* Errors/ omissions	*equals* World
Capital account					
Balance from income and expenditure account	$(Y_i - C_i)$	$Y - C$	$(M - X)$	RE	Nil
plus Net capital transfers	T_i	T	T_o	Nil	Nil
less Gross domestic capital formation	I_i	I_D			
equals Financial surplus or deficit	FS/D_i	FS/D	FS/D_o	RE	Nil
equals					
Financial transactions account					
Transactions in financial assets and liabilities	$A_i - L_i$	$A - L$	$A_o - L_o$	Nil	Nil
plus Unidentified items	U_i	U	U_o	RE	

U_i = *Unidentified transactions* items in account of domestic sector i
U_o = Unidentified transactions items in balance of payments accounts (ie the *balancing item*)
RE = *Residual error* in the gross national income and expenditure accounts

} These entries are placed in the financial account only by convention

Source: *CSO, Financial Statistics Explanatory Handbook* 1983 p. 28.

Table 2,6

cannot see if its entries match those in the schema. However, the earlier version of CSOP(NIE) which was used for the years 1964-69 did have an Unallocated column, and this had an error entry in the FS row but did not have it in any other capital account row; the same is true with the current Bank of England presentation, OP(BE), which has a residual error column. The result in both cases is that the FS row entries will sum to zero in the Σ column, but the Σ column entries for the other capital account rows will not sum to zero in the FS row. This is an exact parallel with the inconsistency in CSOP(NIE) noted above in the comparison between Treatments 1 and 2 and shown in Table 2.3.

Notes

1 There have been some changes in sector titles over the years. ICC initially appeared as non-financial companies, OFI as non-bank financial institutions, and LASF as insurance companies and superannuation funds. Bkg was called Banks (Bks) until recently in some presentations (see Table 2.1); from the beginning of 1982 this sector was re-defined and re-named the Monetary sector (Mon), the change of name being applied retrospectively. Many of our examples later on will be drawn from periods when it was still called Bkg and we shall then use that title.

2 The regular publication of flow of funds matrix tables for the UK began with the three-year matrix table for 1960-62 which appeared in BEQB Sept 1963 and thereafter in June each year. Annual matrix tables for a single year began with the one for 1963 which appear in NIE 1964 (published in August 1964). Quarterly matrix tables first appeared in *Financial Statistics* Dec 1964 (with an introductory note on p. 106 of that issue).

3 On the relationship between e′ in Treatment 1 and e in Treatment 2, see Appendix 4.

4 In examining the structure of the capital account, it is sufficient here to use the examples in Treatments 1 and 2 as our points of reference. However, the capital account can be analysed as a quadruple entry system, although one with different characteristics from the zero-sum quadruple entry system introduced in Chapter 1. This different quadruple entry system is looked at in Appendix 7.

3 The UK flow of funds accounts — II

1 UK flow of funds accounts: the financing account

In looking at the capital account we have seen how the financial surplus row entries are arrived at sector by sector. A sector with a positive financial surplus must have used this surplus to acquire financial assets or to pay off financial liabilities. Similarly, a sector with a negative financial surplus — a financial deficit — could only have spent its way into deficit if it could somehow acquire funds in excess of its current income, for example, by running down its financial assets or by borrowing and thus increasing its financial liabilities. The whole purpose of the flow of funds accounts is to set out the data which throws light on the complex web of relationships between income, expenditure and financial transactions, sector by sector; this brings us to the account in which these financial transactions are recorded. In the current official presentation of the matrix table the name given to this account by the Bank of England is Changes in Financial Assets and Liabilities, while the CSO calls it Financial Transactions Account. Here we shall simply call it the Financing Account (FA).

The capital account has only a few rows and has undergone no significant changes over the years. The financing account, on the other hand, began in two different presentations (BEP and CSOP) each of which underwent many small changes over the years, culminating in a complete revision to the current single official presentation (OP) in April 1981. This new version has 42 transaction rows (excluding the

Total and Unidentified/Balancing Item rows) in the financing account. Looking at this presentation in Appendix 1 will show the row titles and will also show that the rows are arranged in groups and sub-groups as shown in Table 3.1.

	Liabilities of:			
	Sector	Sub-sector	Rows	Notes
Group 1	Pub	CG	6 – 18	financing of PSBR
		LA	19.1 – 19.4	
		PC	20.1 – 20.2	
Group 2	Mon		21.1 – 21.3	deposit liabilities
	OFI		22 – 23	
Group 3	O's		24.1	liabilities of borrowers from banks & OFI, and from Pub; trade etc credit
	ICC & Pers		24.2 – 29	
Group 4	ICC & O's		30 – 32	ICC & O's securities; long term liabilities of LASF
	LASF		33	
	Misc		34	
Group 5	O's & ICC		35 – 36	direct and other international investment
	Misc		37	

Table 3.1

These groups and sub-groups reflect two forms of ordering. The first is by the sector which has the particular claim as a liability (the liability sector). The second is by the liquidity of the particular claim (which itself is not a simple concept), starting with the most liquid; this liquidity ordering appears both within groups and over the table as a whole. The first two groups in Table 3.1 are consistently defined by the liability sector: Pub in group 1 (with CG, LA and PC sub-sectors) and banks and OFI in group 2. Group 3 is not so consistent; it is primarily based on O's, ICC and Pers as liability sectors with loans from banks and OFI, and credit from PC. However, it also includes other credit which is extended between these three sectors, so that there they are asset sectors also. Within these groups and sub-groups liquidity ordering can be seen in several places. In the remaining two groups the situation is less clear. Group 4 focuses on O's, ICC and OFI as liability sectors, but there is a considerable element of them also being asset sectors within the group. It is also possible to see the group as reflecting liquidity ordering on a larger scale, since the dominant LASF claims are generally less liquid than most of the preceding claims. Finally group 5 deals mainly with longer term investment transactions between ICC and O's, each in turn being the liability sector, so that again liquidity ordering is apparent. Rows 29, 34 and 37 appear at the end of their respective groups and row 38, accruals adjustment, is the last transaction row of all. These positions seem to reflect the miscellaneous nature of the first three and the peculiar nature of the last, rather than either of the two forms of ordering seen elsewhere in the financing account. Altogether, it is clearly not feasible to apply either of these two forms of ordering consistently throughout, but the way in which they are applied does give a structure to the rows which is helpful to the user.

If we compare this row structure in the official presentation (OP) with the earlier Bank of England and CSO presentations (BEP and CSOP), then we find that CSOP had 41 transaction rows in the financing account against 42 in OP, but had a less ordered row structure by the liability sector and liquidity criteria. BEP, on the other hand, had only 24 rows and partly for that reason had a clearer structure than CSOP. In fact, for many general purposes these earlier presentations remain readily usable. This is of some importance, because at the time of writing (late 1983) the OP matrix table has not been published for years before 1979 or quarters before 1980 Q4; while the data for earlier periods is available on print-out, it is not in matrix table form. The earlier presentations of the matrix table, therefore, still retain some value. (It is worth noting that there does not so far appear to be any published reconciliation between the row categories of the current OP matrix table and those of the earlier BEP and CSOP versions.)

For one particular purpose the row structure of the current OP matrix table is clearly superior to its predecessors; this is for following out the financial consequences of the public sector borrowing requirement (PSBR), which in turn reflects the importance attached to this in current policy. All the nineteen rows relating to public sector liabilities and the financing of the PSBR are shown together in group 1 in the current presentation.

2 Sign rules in the flow of funds matrix table

In looking at the capital account there were no problems with the signs of entries, which in the FS row emerged as one would intuitively expect: financial surplus +/deficit –. However, when we come to the financing account, as we have already seen in Chapter 1 section 5, there are two possible sign rules which can be followed. This is most easily seen by using two examples of entries which could appear in a sector column:

1 the sector has a FS of + 100 which it uses to acquire net financial assets (+ 100);
2 the sector has a FS of + 100 which it disposes of (– 100) by acquiring net financial assets.

The first of these follows the sign rules used in all the statistical presentations of the matrix table by the Bank of England and the CSO; there a FS of +100 is balanced by, or is equal to, an acquisition of +100 of net financial assets. It takes what for obvious reasons can be called the assets view of the entries in the financing account. The second follows the sign rules used in the financing account of the zero-sum matrix table developed in Chapter 1, which takes the purchasing power view (PPV) of cell entries; in this the FS brings in purchasing power (+100) and that purchasing power is then disposed of (–100) in acquiring net financial assets in the financing account, so that the financing account entry offsets the FS entry and the two entries sum to zero. The simple difference between these two alternative sign rules, therefore, is that they have opposite signs for the entries in the financing account.

The signs for the cell entries in the financing account of the Bank of England and CSO presentations we shall call here assets view (AV) signs. These are: for assets a rise is shown + and a fall –; liabilities are treated as negative assets so that for liabilities a rise is shown – and a fall +. In the Bank of England presentations these sign rules appear at the head of the financing account and in the CSO presentations they appear as a footnote to the matrix table. In table form:

Assets view (AV) signs:		rise	fall
	assets	+	–
	liabilities	–	+

If we now take these AV signs as our starting point, the two alternative sign rules illustrated above can be set out in identity form as their entries would appear in a sector column of the matrix table proper[1] as follows:

	sector column entries	
Conventional format (CF):	$FS \equiv FA_{a+b} + E$	... (1)
Zero-sum format (ZSF):	$FS - FA_{a+b} - E \equiv 0$	... (2)

Table 3.2

Here we continue with our schematic example of a financing account with only two rows, a and b, and in any sector column FA_{a+b} denotes the sum of the entries in these two rows using AV signs. These two identities match the two examples given above, with the addition of E for the error row. Identity (1) in Table 3.2 represents the row format with AV signs as used by the Bank of England and the CSO, and we call this the conventional format (CF). We simply re-arrange the terms in identity (1) to give us identity (2), which represents the row format with PPV signs used in the zero-sum matrix table developed in Chapter 1, and we call this the Zero-Sum Format (ZSF). Comparing CF with ZSF, there is no difference in the sign of the FS entry, but in the financing account entries, the sign of FA_{a+b} in CF has been reversed into $- FA_{a+b}$ in ZSF, and the AV signs in CF have been reversed into the PPV signs in ZSF. The sign of the E entry has also been reversed.[2] Identities (1) and (2) can each be implicitly embodied in a row layout as they would each appear in the matrix table proper, with a numerical example for a single sector column; this is done in Tables 3.3a and 3.3b respectively. The format used is shown by CF or ZSF in the top left hand corner in each case; this labelling will also be followed later on where required.

CF

		Sector A
FS		+ 100
FA:	a	+ 60
	b	+ 30
E		+ 10

Table 3.3a

ZSF

		Sector A
FS		+ 100
FA:	a	− 60
	b	− 30
E		− 10
Σ		0

Table 3.3b

It will be seen that the cross-ruling in each sector column appears at the same relative position as the ≡ symbol in identities (1) and (2) respectively. These row layouts are discussed in more detail in section 4 below.

3 Treatment of errors

All the current UK presentations of the flow of funds matrix table have an unidentified transactions row, but only the Bank of England presentation, OP(BE), also displays what it terms a residual error column; this column is implicit in the OP(NIE) and OP(FinS) presentations even though it is not displayed. Here, as above, we shall denote this row and column by E (for error). In the Bank of England presentation there is a characteristic pattern of error entries in the matrix table proper, and in Table 3.4 this is illustrated schematically in a zero-sum format matrix table.

The first thing to note in this table is that each row in the financing

ZSF

	1	2	3	4	O's	E	Σ
Financial surplus						$+e_t$	0
Financing account: (a)						0	0
(b)						0	0
E	e_1	e_2	e_3	e_4	e_5	$-e_t$	0
Σ	0	0	0	0	0	0	0

Table 3.4

account has a zero entry in the E column; this is because the entries (not shown here) in these rows for the identified sectors already sum to zero. This may occur for any one of several different reasons, for example:

(a) There may indeed be precise figures for the net sectoral changes in holdings of a particular class of claims. This is most likely to be the case where there is a relatively small number of bilateral transactions between a small number of transactors. One example would be Net government indebtedness to the Banking Department (row 11); another would be Other non-marketable government debt (row 14), which involves only six transactors.

(b) Institutions reporting the change in a type of claim outstanding may themselves allocate this change between other sectors. The allocation may contain errors, but it will still produce zero-sum entries for the identified sectors in that row, which will then have a zero E column entry. An example would be sterling time deposits with the banking sector (row 21.2).

(c) There may be good figures for the change in the total amount of a claim outstanding, but independent and less good figures for the sectoral allocation of that change, so that there is a discrepancy between the two. However, it may be possible to make some reasonable judgement as to which sector is most likely to account for this discrepancy, and this becomes the residual sector to which the discrepancy in this row is allocated. An example would be British Government Securities (row 8), where the total change is exactly known and the Personal sector is judged to be the residual sector; again, this leads to a set of zero-sum entries for this row in the identified sector columns and to a zero entry in the E column.

(d) Finally, there is the other limiting case where no usable figures are available for the change in the total amount of a claim outstanding or for its sectoral allocation; an example would be the types of trade credit other than those covered in rows 25, 26.1 and 26.2. Lack of information means that we have to omit the other types, which is equivalent of attributing to them a row of zero entries, including one in the E column.

These cases are arranged in order of increasing unsatisfactoriness, but every one leads to a zero-sum set of entries in the identified sector columns and so to a zero entry in the E column. In cases (b) and (c) we are increasingly relying upon judgement in making sectoral allocations, but it can reasonably be argued that so long as there is some basis upon which to work, such judgement should be exercised.[3] It can also be argued that the user should be told the size of such potential E column entries and how they have been allocated (see Chapter 6 section 1).

Table 3.5 shows the rows (or parts of rows) in the current UK presentation in which there is a residual sector (r) or, in the case of notes and coin (row 6) a pair of joint residual sectors. As might be expected, it is Pers and ICC which are most often the residual sector. It will be seen from the footnotes to this table that some of the residual sectors reflect adjustments made to the matrix table entries. One of these adjusts for the weekly cycle of notes and coin passing between Pers and ICC (footnote 1); the others adjust for the effect of the level of turnover of bank deposits (reflected in items in transit in the banking sector's balance sheet) upon bank sterling sight deposits and bank sterling lending (footnotes 2 and 3).

It is an open question whether it is better to present the financing account entries cleaned-up as at present, or to show explicitly any discrepancies as entries in the E column (as was done on a small scale up to March 1970, see footnote 3) perhaps with the compiler's preferred allocations in footnotes. The former certainly presents a clearer picture to the user; the question is whether its clarity could be misleading.

The situation we have seen above in the financing account can be contrasted with that in the headnote rows of the capital account; there the sectoral entries have to be directly estimated and are subject to errors of unknown magnitude, as are the non-zero row totals. This means that the financial surplus row entries for the identified sectors contain errors, but that there is no real basis for dealing with this problem in a judgemental way such as exists in the case of the financing account rows. This difference between the two classes of data and the ways in which they can reasonably be treated leads us to the error pattern

Residual cells in the current UK matrix table

	sectors					
	line	Mon	OFI	ICC	Pers	O's
Notes and coin	6			r[1]	r[1]	
Market treasury bills	7			r		
British government securities	8				r	
National savings	9				r	
Tax instruments	10			r		
Northern Ireland central government debt, of which:	12					
Treasury bills				r		
other					r	
Local authority debt:						
Temporary	19.1				r	
Foreign currency	19.2		r			
Sterling securities	19.3				r	
Other sterling debt	19.4				r	
Deposits with banking sector:						
Sterling sight	21.1	r		[2]		
Sterling time	21.2	r				
of which sterling CD				r		
Foreign currency	21.3	r				
of which for.curr. CD						r
Bank lending (excluding Pub):						
Sterling	24.2	r		[3]		
Credit extended by retailers	25				r	
Identified trade credit:						
Public corporations (dom)	26.1			r		
Loans for house purchase:						
Building societies	27.1				r	
Unit trust units	30				r	
UK company securities	31				r	
Overseas securities	32				r	
Misc overseas instruments	37			r		

1 17% ICC, 83% Pers, adjusted for day of the week and proximity to Easter.
2 The ICC figure is adjusted by 60% of net debit transit items.
3 The ICC figure is adjusted by 40% of net debit transit items.

Table 3.5

Reliability gradings in the financial accounts

	Central government	Local authorities	Public corporations	Monetary sector	Other financial institutions	Industrial and commercial companies	Personal sector	Overseas sector
Financial surplus or deficit	C	C	C	D (Monetary sector and other financial institutions combined)		D	D	D
Notes and coin	A			B		D	D	D
Market Treasury bills	A	B	C	B	B	D		C
British government securities	A	B	C	B	B	D	D	C
National savings	A	A	B		A	A	A	
Tax instruments	A		C	B	B	C	B	
Net government indebtedness to banking department	A			A				
Northern Ireland central government debt	A			B	C	D	D	
Government liabilities under exchange cover scheme	A	A	A					
Other non-marketable debt	A		A		A			
Issue department's transactions in commercial bills	A					A		
Government foreign currency debt	A			A				A
Other government overseas financing	A							A
Official reserves	A							A
Local authority debt:								
Temporary	B	B	D	C	B	D	D	C
Foreign currency		B		B				B
Sterling securities	B (Sterling securities and other sterling debt combined)	B	C	B	B	D (Sterling securities and other sterling debt combined)	D (Sterling securities and other sterling debt combined)	C
Other sterling debt		B	D	C	B			C
Public corporations debt:								
Foreign currency			B	B			D	B
Sterling	A	C	B	B	C	C	D	C
Deposits with monetary sector:								
Sterling sight	C	C	C	C	C	C	C	C
Sterling time	B	B	B	B	B	B	B	B
Foreign currency	C	C	C	C	C	C	C	C
Deposits with building societies					B	B	B	B
Deposits with other financial institutions	B	B			B	B	B	B

Bank lending (exc. public sector):								
Foreign currency	C	C	C	C	C	C	C	C
Sterling	C	C	C	C	C	C	C	C
Credit extended by retailers			B			C	C	
Identified trade credit:								
Domestic	B		D		D	D	D	
Import and export	B		C		B	C	C	C
Loans for house purchase:								
Building societies					B	B	B	
Other	B	B	B	C	B		C	
Other public sector lending	B	B	B		B	C	C	B
Other lending by financial institutions					C	C	C	
Unit trust units					B		B	
UK company securities	B		B	B	B	D	D	D
Overseas securities	B			B	B	D	D	D
Life assurance and pension funds	A				D		D	
Miscellaneous domestic instruments	B	B			C	C	C	B
Direct and other investment abroad				B	C	C		C
Overseas direct and other investment in UK				B	C	C		C
Miscellaneous overseas instruments	C		C	B	D	D		D
Accruals adjustment	D	D	D	C	C	D	D	
Total financial transactions	C	C	C	B	C	D	D	D

Source: CSO, *Financial Statistics Explanatory Handbook* 1984 p. 18.

Table 3.6a

displayed in Table 3.4: zero entries in the E column for the financing account rows and a typically non-zero entry in the E column for the FS row ($+e_t$, which is the residual error in the gross national product account). Moving on to the E row, sizeable entries are normally required to make the sector columns sum to zero (e_1 to e_5, of which e_5 is the negative image of the balancing item in the UK balance of payments[4]). But since the E column must, like the identified sector columns, sum to zero, the sizeable E row entries must require an entry in the error column ($-e_t$) which is the negative image of the FS row entry in the E column ($+e_t$).

At first sight this looks rather like sleight-of-hand, but it can be made intuitively clear using an example. Take any zero-sum pattern of FS row entries including the E column entry $+e_t$; further, let the entry in every cell in the financing account be zero. Then the E row must be the negative image of the financial surplus row, and it will therefore have $-e_t$ in the E column. Now suppose that we replace the zero entries in the financing account with recorded entries which take the standard form noted above and sum to zero along the rows for the identified sectors. Such entries would not alter the financing account zero entries in the E column and therefore would not alter the entry $-e_t$ in the E row/E column, which remains determined by the entry $+e_t$ in the FS row/E column. The zero-sum recorded entries in the financing account rows can only require zero-sum changes in the E row entries e_1 to e_5 in order to maintain the zero-sum of each identified sector column. They cannot affect the sum of the E row entries e_1 to e_5 nor the E column entry $-e_t$ required to make the E row sum to zero.

Some indication of the likely degree of error in individual cell entries is given in the table on p.18 of CSO *Financial Statistics Explanatory Handbook* 1984 and reproduced here as Table 3.6a. In notes to that table the CSO explains its four gradings, which relate to quarterly figures whose reliability is generally lower than that of annual figures. These gradings are:

- A accounting-type figures, relating to individual institutions mainly in central government.
- B reliable figures, obtained by aggregating statistical returns (and thus prone to coverage and reporting errors).
- C less reliable, but fairly good figures, based on returns but with some degree of estimation, e.g. sampling.
- D figures involving a substantial amount of estimation, or where the coverage is known to be significantly incomplete.

Here we shall try to gain a broader view of reliability by quantifying these gradings and averaging them for transaction rows and sector columns in the matrix table. We do this by simply converting the CSO gradings A, B, C and D into scores of 4, 3, 2 and 1 respectively; the pitfalls in this conversion are obvious enough and will not be elaborated on here.[5]

Quantifying and averaging the gradings in this way gives us the figures in Tables 3.6b and 3.6c (in the latter, for clarity, the gradings are sorted into four columns by the integer part of each grading). Looking first at the sectors, Table 3.6b shows central government at the top of the gradings (3.2) with ICC and Pers at the bottom (both 1.8) and O's rather better (2.2). Table 3.6c looks at the rows and shows how low in the gradings is the FS row (1.4) with the IF (or Total Financial Transactions) row only a little better (1.8). The highest grading (4) occurs only for rows reported by central government.

The presentations of the UK matrix table have over the years given various names to what we have called (and shall continue to call) the E (for error) row and column. The E row has been called Unidentified Items, Unidentified Transactions, Unidentified and, most recently, Balancing Item. The E column was at one time called Unallocated but since then, when displayed, has always been called Residual Error.

In looking at this terminology it is worth considering the nature of the entries in the E row and column. It will be recalled that we earlier defined the magnitude of a quadruple entry as the absolute size of the entry which appears four times in it. If for any transaction the magnitude of the quadruple entry recording it in the matrix table is incorrect (and the limiting case is a magnitude of zero, which means that the transaction has not been recorded at all) the quadruple entry will nevertheless have the usual zero-sum character, and will not lead to any E entries. These will only occur if the four entries are inconsistent with this zero-sum character.

Quantified reliability gradings

	Public sector			Financial companies and institutions				
	Central government	Local authorities	Public corporations	Monetary sector	Other financial institutions	Industrial and commercial companies	Persons	Overseas
column averages	3.2	2.7	2.3	2.8	2.5	1.8	1.8	2.2

Table 3.6b

Quantified reliability gradings

		row averages			
Financial surplus or deficit	5				1.4
Financial transactions account					
Notes and coin	6			2.6	
Market treasury bills	7			2.6	
British government securities	8			2.4	
National savings	9		3.8		
Tax instruments	10			2.8	
Net government indebtedness to Banking Department	11	4.0			
Northern Ireland central government debt	12			2.2	
Government liabilities under exchange cover scheme	13	4.0			
Other non-marketable debt	14	4.0			
Issue Department's transactions in commercial bills	15	4.0			
Government foreign currency debt	16	4.0			
Other government overseas financing	17	4.0			
Official reserves	18	4.0			
Local authority debt:	19				
Temporary	19.1			2.0	
Foreign currency	19.2		3.0		
Sterling securities	19.3 }			2.2	
Other sterling debt	19.4 }				
Public corporation debt:	20				
Foreign currency	20.1			2.5	
Sterling	20.2			2.4	
Deposits with banking sector:	21				
Sterling sight	21.1			2.0	
Sterling time	21.2		3.0		
Foreign currency	21.3			2.0	
Deposits with building societies	22		3.0		
Deposits with other financial institutions	23		3.0		
Bank lending (excluding public sector):	24				
Foreign currency	24.1			2.0	
Sterling	24.2			2.0	
Credit extended by retailers	25			2.3	
Identified trade credit:	26				
Public corporations (domestic)	26.1				1.4
Import and export	26.2			2.3	
Loans for house purchase:	27				
Building societies	27.1		3.0		
Other	27.2			2.7	
Other public sector lending	28			2.4	
Other lending by financial institutions	29			2.0	
Unit trust units	30		3.0		
UK company securities	31			2.1	
Overseas securities	32			2.0	
Life assurance and pension funds	33			2.0	
Miscellaneous domestic instruments	34			2.5	
Direct and other investment abroad	35			2.3	
Overseas direct and other investment in UK	36			2.3	
Miscellaneous overseas instruments	37				1.7
Accruals adjustment	38				1.3
Total financial transactions	39				1.8

Table 3.6c

It follows that Unidentified Transactions cannot be a suitable title for the E row, since transactions which are not identified do not give rise to entries in that row.[6] Unidentified Items and Unidentified are less clear but seem similarly unsatisfactory. Our own term, Error, is acceptable if it is interpreted in the narrow sense of entries required to make columns sum to zero, but it does not necessarily compel this narrow interpretation; the newly arrived Balancing Item coincides with balance of payments terminology and is unobjectionable but rather bland. Perhaps the best title would be Discrepancy (D); it indicates that entries arise because something does not add up as it should; it warns that something is wrong and that is all. This would broadly follow the terminology used in the US flow of funds matrix table (see Appendix 3).

The E column terminology has changed over the years only from Unallocated to Residual Error. The former title has a certain colourless neutrality, but the latter raises some questions. We can distinguish in the matrix table between a null cell and a nil cell; a null cell is one which by definition cannot have an entry (for example, tax instruments (row 10) are not held by local authorities, and the corresponding cell is a null cell). On the other hand some cells could in principle have any entry but are in practice constrained to have a nil entry (for example, notes and coin are certainly held by local authorities but we have no substantive information about the changes in holdings, so that the relevant cell is constrained to be a nil cell). Now, for a financing account row that has a residual sector, is the E column cell a nil cell or a null cell?[7] If we take residual error to mean just what it says, then the only entries in such a column would be the residual error entry in the FS row and the counterpart entry in the E row, and the financing account rows would all have null cells in the residual error column. However, it seems more reasonable to regard the residual sectors as a convenient contrivance rather than as a mandatory procedure, in which the financing account rows would have nil cells (and not null cells) in the E column, which accordingly should have a less constricted title than residual error. Perhaps the best solution, as in the case of the E row, would be to follow the US terminology and use the title Discrepancy for the E column also.

4 Row terminology and hierarchy

Table 3.7 shows (with some simplification of inessentials) the layout and implicit hierarchy of the main rows in the current and earlier presentations of the UK matrix table. All of these are conventional

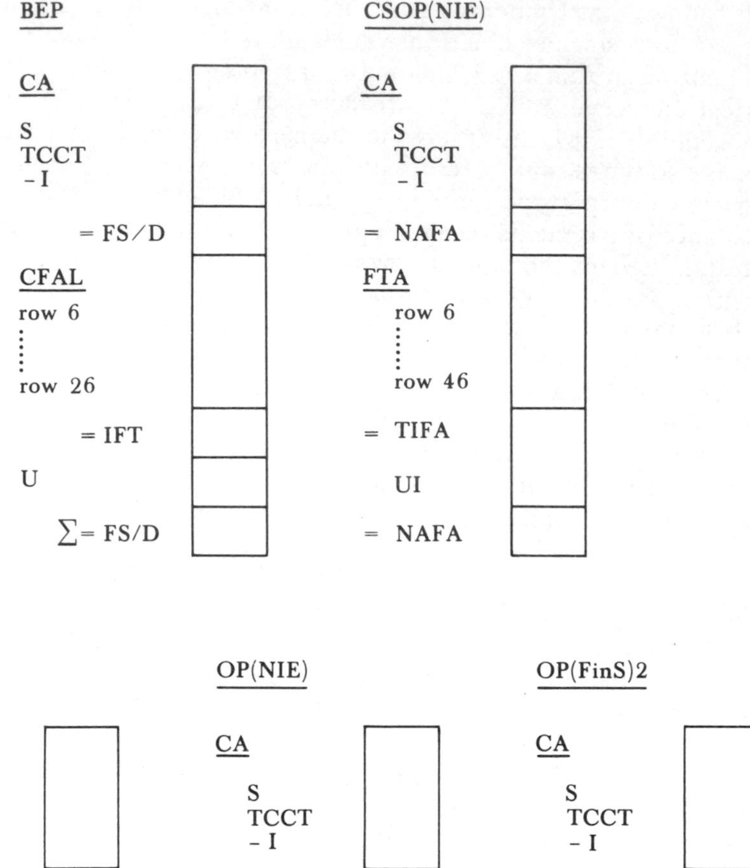

OP(BE)

CA

S
TCCT
- I

= FS/D

CFAL

row 6
⋮
row 38

= FT

U

OP(NIE)

CA

S
TCCT
- I

= FS/D

FTA

row 6
⋮
row 38

= TFT

BI

OP(FinS)2

CA

S
TCCT
- I

= FS/D

FTA

row 6
⋮
row 38

= TFT

BI

Table 3.7

format (CF) presentations, and except for OP(FinS)2 they can be compared with the originals in Appendices 1 and 2. In each case a single sector column of the matrix table displays the cross-rulings used.

We begin in the lower half of the table with the current presentations, OP(BE), OP(NIE) and OP(FinS)2, the latter being a revision (in March 1983) of the previous OP(FinS). All of these start with a capital account (CA), followed by a financing account called Changes in Financial Assets and Liabilities (CFAL) by the Bank of England and Financial Transactions Account (FTA) by the CSO (who have recently shortened it to Financial Account), and end with an error row called Unidentified (U) or Balancing Item (BI), the latter now being standard in all these presentations. All of these titles are distinguished by being in heavy type or, in the case of OP(FinS)2, by having all other rows inset. (In Table 3.7 the inset of a row title is shown by the initials of its title and not by the preceding symbols = or –.) Here we underline the initials of these titles to show that they belong to the highest level in the hierarchy.

There is nothing to say about CA, but when we come to CFAL/FTA, FTA is objectionable because a transaction is recorded by a quadruple entry and FTA does not only cover financial transactions but also the financing entries for non-financial transactions which give rise to entries in the FS row. CFAL, on the other hand, uses a terminology which is quite different from CA, although they are at the same level. It would seem better to call this account the Financing Account (FA), as we have done earlier, which would relate it more clearly to CA.

In the preceding section we have already looked at the terminology of the error row: Unidentified Items (UI), Unidentified Transactions (UT), Unidentified (U) and Balancing Item (BI). Two other points about them now arise. First, in the earlier presentations U and UI could appear to be part of CFAL/FTA, implying that all the errors were attributable to the entries in the financing account. This was an interpretation that the statisticians producing the matrix table would certainly not accept,[8] and the current row hierarchy makes it clear that U/BI are at the same level as CA and CFAL/FTA. The second point follows from this. Although U/BI are clearly shown at this level, these titles do not help to emphasise the fact; in addition there is something unsatisfactory in having one title which refers both to an account and to a row (admittedly the only row) in that account. Perhaps a better treatment would be to replace U/BI by Balancing Account (BA) to place it clearly at the same level as CA and FA, and to have a separate name (Discrepancy (D) as suggested above, for example) for the only row in that account. It is also worth noting that there is no compelling reason to place BA as the last of these three accounts; indeed, a good case could be made for placing it between CA and FA, either with unchanged signs, as a simple reversal of the positions of FA and BA, or with its signs reversed (see identity 1a in note 2). The latter could be taken to imply that the FS row was the main source of E row entries, and many would argue that this is probably the case.

Moving down to the next level, in the current presentations we come to Financial Surplus/Deficit (FS/D), the CA entry total, and to Financial Transactions (FT) and Total Financial Transactions (TFT), the CFAL and FTA entry totals respectively. FS/D is simply a more elaborate version of Financial Surplus (FS) which we have already used to cover both a positive surplus or a negative surplus (= deficit), and which we shall still prefer. In both OP(BE) and OP(FinS)2 the placing of FS/D is acceptable, but in OP(NIE) it is placed in register with CA etc and out of register with TFT which is at the same level as FS/D in the hierarchy of rows; there is no clear reason for this. It will be seen that in the earlier CSOP(NIE), Net Acquisition of Financial Assets (NAFA) was used in place of FS/D; this was objectionable because it used terminology from the financing account for the CA entry total, and this was dropped in favour of FS/D, a terminology more obviously related to CA. In the earlier presentations FS/D or NAFA was repeated as the bottom row in the matrix table, emphasising the fact that IFT + U ≡ FS/D or TIFA + UI ≡ NAFA. This could be helpful, but with the clearer hierarchy in the current presentations, it is not a significant loss. It will be seen in Table 3.7 that the cross-rulings help to emphasise FS/D as the total of entries under CA except in the case of OP(FinS)2 where the lack of a ruling under FS/D appears to be inconsistent with its CF signs.

FT and TFT are at the same level as FS/D in the current presentations; both titles are open to objection on the grounds that, as in the case of FTA above, they imply totals of financial transactions when they really mean totals of financing account entries arising from both financial and non-financial transactions. At an earlier stage OP(BE) used Identified Financial Transactions (IFT) instead of FT; this too was open to objection because the existence of residual sectors in many financing account rows meant that many entries were far from being identified in any useful sense. (The same objection applies to Total Identified Financial Assets (TIFA), the predecessor of TFT, which appeared in CSOP(NIE) earlier.) Perhaps a better title would be Financing Account Total (FAT). Again, the cross-rulings help to emphasise FT/TFT as row totals under CFAL/FTA although here too the lack of an under-ruling in OP(FinS)2 is a little surprising; the lack of a comparable ruling in CSOP(NIE) is more understandable since that version has NAFA as a final total. Finally we come to the lowest level in our hierarchy, the original entry rows in CA and CFAL/FTA. There is nothing to say about them from the point of view of Table 3.7; there have sometimes been trivial differences in the financing account row titles used in the different OP versions, and some unimportant changes in some of these titles.

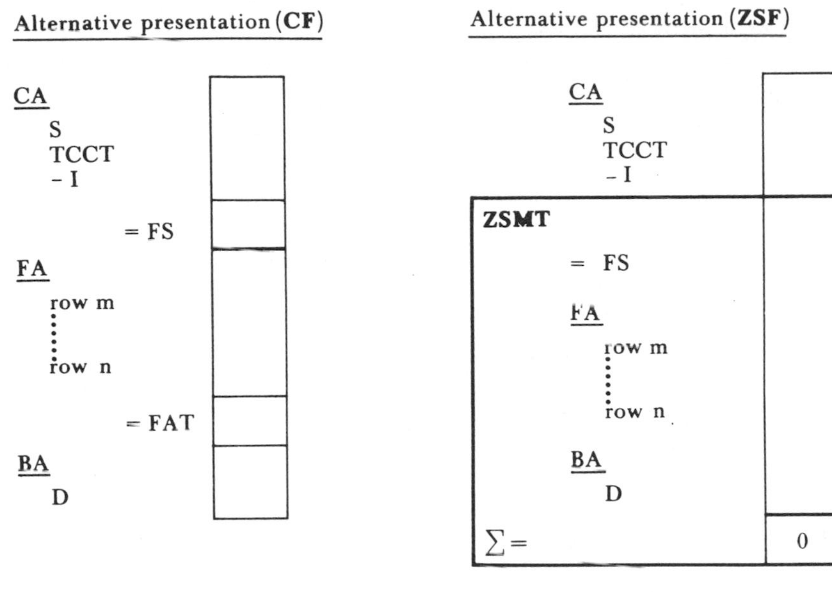

Table 3.8

Table 3.9

For comparison, Table 3.8 presents a CF matrix table similar to those in Table 3.7 but incorporating the various changes suggested above. In its specimen column we use a light cross-ruling at the top and bottom of the column and also to mark off a summation of preceding entries. We use a heavy cross-ruling (below FS) at the point at which the identity sign occurs in the underlying identity (see identity (1) in Table 3.2, and Table 3.3a). A further comparison is given by Table 3.9 which shows a ZSF presentation. There the zero-sum matrix table (ZSMT) is marked-off by a continuous line; in the ZSMT there is a heavy cross-ruling above the Σ entry, again at the point at which the identity sign appears in the underlying identity (see identity (2) in Table 3.2, and Table 3.3b).

5 UK flow of funds accounts: sources

CSO statistical sources

In CSO, *National Income and Expenditure* (annually), the 'National Income Blue Book', the flow of funds accounts are referred to as financial accounts, and in the 1983 edition (the latest one used here) they appear in section 13. This section presents a matrix table for the latest year and also a full range of supporting tables covering annual data for the last eleven years: one for the capital account by sectors, one for each sector (using the matrix table rows with suitable omissions) and two tables on the Public Sector Borrowing Requirement (PSBR) and its financing. Section 16 contains a sectorised table covering current capital and financial transactions for the preceding year.

In CSO,*Financial Statistics* (monthly), Section 1, the flow of funds accounts are now referred to as Financial Accounts. This section gives a full flow of funds matrix table for the latest available quarter together with a summary capital account and tables covering each sector, both containing annual and quarterly data. Later sections in *Financial Statistics* are devoted to each sector and in some cases these include the flow of funds data re-arranged on a sources/uses basis.[9] Finally, each issue contains supplementary tables, which include the first publication of the annual matrix table in May each year; a guide to these supplementary tables appears inside the back cover of each issue.[10]

Notes and definitions on the flow of funds accounts are given in the back of *National Income and Expenditure*, but the fullest ones appear in the annual CSO, *Financial Statistics Explanatory Handbook* (the edition used here is that for February 1984) pp.15 – 28. This also includ a useful introduction (pp.3–9) and commentary on many aspects of the financial accounts (pp. 10–14). More recent changes in definitions etc are noted in Supplements to the Explanatory Handbook at the back of each issue of *Financial Statistics.*

A reconciliation between the annual financial accounts figures and those in the UK balance of payments accounts for 1982 (the latest available at the time of writing) is given in matrix table form in *Financial Statistics* October 1983, Supplementary table S22 (see also the note on this table, op. cit. p.150). This reconciliation is looked at in Appendix 8 below.

Bank of England statistical sources

Each issue of the *Bank of England Quarterly Bulletin* (*BEQB*) contains in its statistical annex the latest quarterly flow of funds matrix table (unadjusted and seasonally adjusted) together with supporting tables (seasonally adjusted) for the Pub, ICC and Pers sectors, to which a table for OFI has recently been added. Starting with June 1983, the June issue contains an annual article on sector financing which includes the annual matrix table for the two latest years and a commentary on the most recent of these; it also includes an additional six supporting tables in the statistical annex, which then covers all the domestic sectors on a liabilities/assets or borrowing requirement/financing basis and the O's sector on a private/public sector transactions basis (all seasonally adjusted), as well as having other tables.

Before 1983 this annual June article in *BEQB* contained all the supporting tables as well, and this was also the case with the earlier Bank of England presentation before April 1981. Longer runs of these earlier figures will be found in Bank of England, *United Kingdom flow of funds accounts: 1963-1976* (1978, referred to below as *UKFOFA*) Part 5; these are not given in matrix table form but by individual sectors. Annual figures for the period before 1963 will be found in Bank of England, *An introduction to flow of funds accounting: 1952-70* (1972).

Notes on definitions and seasonal adjustment appear in the June article on sector financing in *BEQB*. The most detailed notes on the earlier presentation will be found in *UKFOFA* Part 6.

Some further reading

A notable survey of the literature on all aspects of flow of funds is:

A D. Bain, 'Flow of funds analysis: a survey', *Economic Journal* December 1973.

There are many books and articles describing financial flows and the financial system, and attempting some informal explanation; a book which does this for an earlier period, using a clear flow of funds framework is:

Christopher Johnson, *Anatomy of UK Finance 1970-75*, Longman, 1976.

A more general view of the factors in sector behaviour is given by:

Graeme S. Dorrance, *National Monetary and Financial Analysis*, Macmillan, 1978.

A study which goes more deeply into the financing behaviour of one UK sector is:

A.D. Bain, Day and Wearing, *Company financing in the United Kingdom - a flow of funds model*, Martin Robertson, 1975.

The most advanced attempts at modelling the financial sector, all embodying a flow of funds matrix, will be found in the macro-econometric models of the Treasury, the Bank of England and the London Business School (see the brief comments in Chapter 4 section 3). Technical manuals are available on all of these.

Official articles relating to the UK flow of funds accounts, sectoral balance sheets and integrated stock/flow accounts are likely to appear in *BEQB* or in CSO, *Economic Trends,* monthly (which usually carries two or three articles, on various subjects, at the back). A search for further writings will find earlier references in the items cited above; more recent material (which continues to be sparse) can be looked for in:

The Banker (monthly), which has a selective annotated list of books and articles at the back, although this does not cover the scattering of articles which have appeared in *The Banker* itself.

Economic Journal (quarterly), see Book Notes (under classification 220).

Journal of Economic Literature (quarterly), see the annotated listing of books (under 220) and articles and abstracts (under 223).

Notes

1 It should be noted that we use the row title to stand for the entry in that row and a particular sector column. From now on we shall generally leave the context to show whether we are dealing with the matrix table proper (the FS row and the financing account) or the full UK presentation including what we have called the headnote rows.

2 It is worth noting that in identity (1) in Table 3.2, the E row entry could be moved to produce:

$$FS - E \equiv FA_{a+b} \qquad \text{... (1a)}$$

This would still have AV signs for the FA entries, but the sign of the E row entry would be reversed.

3 In publications up to March 1971 both CSO presentations had an Unallocated column and this did contain entries required to make some financing account rows sum to zero. In the case of CSOP(NIE), for example, there were 8 such financing account rows in the matrix table for 1963, 3 in each of the tables for 1964-67 and one each in those for 1968 and 1969; thereafter the Unallocated row was dropped from this presentation, although in CSOP(FinS) it was replaced by a Residual error column which had only zero entries for the financing account rows. BEP always had zero-sum entries for the

institutional sectors in the financing account rows except for the two rows covering UK company and overseas securities: capital issues (row 23) and other transactions (row 24). Both of these were non-zero-sum rows although added together sector by sector they would form a zero-sum row. In the BEP quarterly matrix table, the only one with a Residual Error column, there was no entry for either row in that column; this could indicate either that the two rows were implicitly being taken together, or that the Residual Error row was indeed intended to contain only the residual error entry in the FS row and its counterpart entry in the Unidentified row.

4 The UK balance of payments account and the flow of funds matrix table in Table 3.4 both use ZSF presentation, and the entries in the O's column of that matrix table are simply the UK balance of payments figures with the signs reversed, so that e_5 is the balancing item in the UK balance of payments account with its sign reversed. The CSO schema in Table 2.6 above has explicit headnote rows, but otherwise matches Table 3.4, but with CF presentation so that the entries in the financing account have the opposite signs from those under ZSF. It follows that $+U_0$ in Table 2.6 is the balancing item in the UK balance of payments account with its sign unchanged, even though it appears in the O's sector column. See also Appendix 8.

5 In averaging these gradings, the D (= 1) shared by Mon and OFI in the FS row has been allocated to OFI.

6 See Chapter 6 section 1 for some further development of the quadruple entry approach to entries in the E row and E column, and elsewhere in Chapter 6 for other aspects of these entries.

7 It is worth noting that both OP(NIE) and OP(FinS) place a sign for nil (or less than half the final digit shown), a light bar and a minus sign respectively, in every cell without a numerical entry, making no distinction between nil and null cells. OP(BE) shows many nil cells with a light bar, but also many blank ones, and one is tempted to regard the latter as null cells. However, these blank cells include the notes and coin (row 6)/local authorities cell and the Northern Ireland central government debt (row 12)/O's cell (neither of which can be a null cell) as well as the official reserves (row 18)/Pers cell (which certainly is a null cell). One can only conclude that the usage is not consistent, and gives no guidance on whether the blank cells in the financing account rows/residual error column are being regarded as nil or null cells.

8 See, for example, the note at the bottom of the CSO schema reproduced in Table 2.6.

9 This sources/uses basis is a re-arrangement of rows, with some additional categories distinguished, and for the financing account

amounts to dividing rows into sector liabilities/sector assets. It should be distinguished from the sources/uses format for sector sub-columns which is used in the US flow of funds accounts and is described in Appendix 3 below.

10 Information about CSO data available on computer print-out and Bank of England data available on tape is given under Data Service on the inside front cover of *Financial Statistics.*

4 Introduction to the use of the flow of funds accounts

1 Flow of funds and complementary data

The great improvement in financial statistics in the UK dates from the recommendations of the Radcliffe Report (1959), which included the setting up of flow of funds accounts. Since the financing account had to be built up from separate figures from the individual sources, the flow of funds accounts became the point at which all the component figures had to fit together. This emphasised the necessity for a systematic and consistent basis on which all the figures should be collected, something that had been lacking before. It required a consistent classification of rows and sector columns, and consistency in the time periods covered by the data; with these went the need for a high degree of coverage, together with sufficient detail to distinguish the flows which seemed likely to be most significant. These requirements are reflected in the present flow of funds accounts.

A whole set of flow of funds accounts – matrix tables and supporting tables – for the UK, with annual figures from 1952 and quarterly figures (seasonally adjusted and unadjusted) from 1963, forms an impressive body of data. It is easy to feel that such a battery of statistics should provide the material for the explanation of financial behaviour. But in fact it represents the detailed record of only the transaction flow dimension of the system. Explaining/interpreting/rationalising the pattern of these flows can be expected to require additional financial information such as stock data on financial claims and terms data covering prices/rates of return, tax factors and capital rationing relating to these claims (not to mention all the non-financial data on real stocks and flows, prices,etc). Here we shall consider briefly just this financial information which is complementary to the flow of funds accounts.

Stock data

One way of looking at financial flows is to regard them as attempts to eliminate discrepancies between desired and actual levels of the related stocks. The hierarchy of decisions relating to such stocks and flows, the mode of adjustment (which could be confined to the financing account or could spill over into the capital account) and the constraints upon these processes, all can be expected to differ between sectors and between the different types of claim involved. Further, it is worth remembering that such adjustment processes can be seen as generating *desired* transaction flows in a period, which could well differ from the *actual* transaction flows achieved in that period, which could well differ from the *estimated* transaction flow figures recorded in the flow of funds accounts for that period, which themselves are quite likely to be replaced by *revised* estimates as time passes. Nevertheless, if we take this stock adjustment view, then the explanation of the pattern of cell entries in the flow of funds accounts will require stock data in the form of domestic sector balance sheets covering financial claims and real assets.[1] (For a somewhat different view on the case of the UK company sector see Bain, Day and Wearing, op. cit., particularly pp. 4–5).

When we look at the stock data it is useful to distinguish between marketable claims and fixed-value claims. Marketable claims are created with specific characteristics (for example, equities; long-dated government fixed interest stocks; short-dated Treasury bills, commercial bills and certificates of deposit). They are sold initially by the sector creating them and from then on may be bought and sold by other transactors (until their maturity date, if any), all of these transactions being done at the market price/rate for each type of claim, which commonly varies from day to day.

Fixed value claims, on the other hand, have a fixed money value. Some of these claims are transferable – sight bank deposits, notes, coin – and make up the stock of money used for transactions. Others are not transferable themselves, but may on certain terms or on maturity be converted into transferable claims; examples of these are bank term deposits or building society shares. Only the default of the borrower alters the money value of these fixed value claims.

One way in which stock data can in principle be related to the flow of funds accounts is set out in Table 4.1. This table shows in illustrative

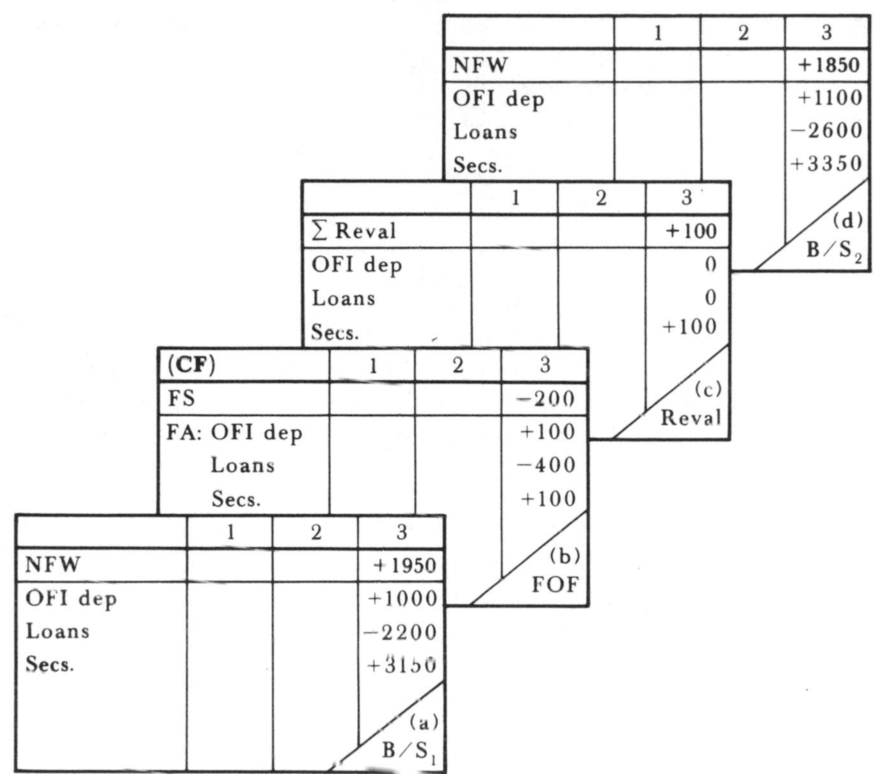

	1	2	3
NFW			+1850
OFI dep			+1100
Loans			−2600
Secs.			+3350
			(d) B/S$_2$

	1	2	3
Σ Reval			+100
OFI dep			0
Loans			0
Secs.			+100
			(c) Reval

(CF)	1	2	3
FS			−200
FA: OFI dep			+100
Loans			−400
Secs.			+100
			(b) FOF

	1	2	3
NFW			+1950
OFI dep			+1000
Loans			−2200
Secs.			+3150
			(a) B/S$_1$

Table 4.1

form four financial accounts, labelled (a) to (d) in their bottom right-hand corners, all using the same sector columns (1, 2, 3) and the same financing account rows; for clarity only three specimen rows have been identified, and example entries are shown only for sector 3. For the moment we shall consider only financial items, ignoring real assets. Account (a) is a statement of claims at time 1, all shown at their values ruling at time 1. It shows the balance sheet, suitably rearranged as a column, for each sector and it is labelled B/S$_1$ in the lower right-hand corner. With assets +/liabilities −, if the account were complete we would see that for any claim/row the same amount of claims would appear as liabilities for some and assets for others, with the row summing to zero. But for any sector column, the sum of its financial assets and liabilities is unlikely to equal zero and we shall therefore have a net financial wealth (NFW) row which we place at the top; this NFW row, like the others, will sum to zero.

Account (b) is the flow of funds matrix table (FOF). Here it uses the conventional format (shown by CF in the top left hand corner) with assets: rise +/fall −, liabilities: rise −/fall +. It shows the changes in the stock of claims occurring due to transactions in the period, by sector and by type of claim. It also shows the financial surplus row, which is the link between these financial accounts and the national income accounts. As we have already seen, all the rows in this account will sum to zero. Account (c) shows revaluations; in the case of marketable claims these arise from changes in price over the period, and here we show an entry for the securities row. For fixed-value claims entries would only appear in this account in the case of a default. Here again we use the top row to show the total revaluations (Σ Reval) for each sector; in principle the entries in each row in this account will sum to zero. Finally we come to account (d), the balance sheet at time 2, with all claims shown at values ruling at time 2. B/S_2 in its turn will be the opening balance sheet for the next period.

It is instructive to take each cell entry in (a) and follow it through the changes recorded in accounts (b) and (c) to the entry in account (d). The same can be done with the entries in the top row in each table. Taking our example of sector 3, if we assume that it has only the entries shown in Table 4.1, then it is easy to see that in account (a), NFW_1 is + 1950; in account (b), FS is shown as − 200; in account (c), Σ Reval is + 100; and these add up in account (d) to NFW_2 of + 1850. The reason for keeping all the rows in register across this set of accounts is to make it easy to follow the entries through in this way.

So far as the estimation of the entries in the four accounts (a) to (d) is concerned, the situation in practice varies depending upon the particular claim concerned. Two examples will suffice. In the case of fixed-value claims, a large part of these are the liabilities of financial intermediaries which provide reasonably good balance sheet figures on a sectoral basis for accounts (a) and (d). With the entries in account (c) only arising from defaults, which are typically known to be zero, we can then deduce the appropriate row entries for account (b). On the other hand, for marketable claims such as stock exchange securities, we may have estimates of the row entries for (a), (b) and (c), the latter being estimated by the use of price indices, from which we can deduce the entries for (d).

Turning briefly to real assets, it is clear that we can extend all the accounts in Table 4.1 to cover these. For example, we could add real asset rows to accounts (a) and (d), corresponding rows showing net expenditure on real assets to (b), which would match the real investment entries in the flow of funds capital account with their signs reversed, and corresponding rows for the revaluation of real assets (including depreciation) in (c). Unlike the rows for financial claims, none of these would have to sum to zero; for this reason alone it would be desirable to keep the two clearly separate.

The Bank of England has used a presentation for integrated stock/flow accounts which, for any sector, is the equivalent of taking its column from each of the four accounts in Table 4.1 and setting these out next to each other period by period. The resulting pattern of row headings is:

.... B/S_1	Cash flow	Revaluations	B/S_2	Cash flow	Revaluations	B/S_3 ....

The heading 'cash flow' is the Bank of England's terminology. It is not satisfactory since these tables use conventional format (CF) signs, in which, for example, a purchase of assets is shown +, so that the one thing such an entry does not show is cash flow. A more accurate heading would be 'transactions'.

A problem then arises over the row structure. For an integrated set of matrix tables, such as that illustrated in Table 4.1, the row structure has to be uniform across all sectors and across all matrix tables. However, when we look at a particular sector on its own (as in the Personal sector balance sheets referred to above, or the Personal sector supplementary table in *BEQB* March 1984, Statistical annex Table 19.4, for example), we find that the rows are re-ordered into sector liabilities and sector assets, with considerable differences in the two cases, each intending to be helpful in revealing the sector's behaviour. Clearly the aim must be to have a system of integrated stock/flow accounts which allows the data to be presented in these ways, each of which has its value, while providing a full reconciliation between them. It should also help users to find their way around the accounts, and allow them to adapt the data in new ways.

Terms data

Since rates of return (interest rates and yields), capital rationing and tax arrangements can be expected to influence financial (and real) flows, it would be useful to have a comprehensive range of such terms data coordinated with the rows recording the sectoral stocks and flows of the related claims. At present there is really no such coordination.

Beginning with rates of return (which are always a reward to one party and a cost to the other), there are three general points to be made:

1 It is usually *relative* rates of return which can be expected to influence financial flows, rather than absolute rates of return.
2 The data we have for rates of return refers to *actual* or *realised* rates; in practice it is quite often *expected* rates (relative to current actual rates or relative to other expected rates) which are the relevant ones for decisions, and therefore the ones which will affect flows. In the case of international flows this means that expected exchange rates may also be relevant. In fact we have no direct data on any of these expected rates.
3 There is the vital distinction between a *nominal* rate of interest and a *real* rate of interest. The (expected or realised) real rate of interest is the nominal rate adjusted for the (expected or realised) change in the price level. (As a crude example, a 10 per cent p.a. nominal rate of interest and a 6 per cent p.a. expected rate of rise in the price level produces a 4 per cent p.a. expected real rate of interest). In a world in which capital markets are imperfect, both nominal and real interest rates can be expected to influence decision

The widest range of terms data for the UK is to be found in *Financial Statistics.* Taking the issue for January 1984 as an example, in section 13 there are 41 individual series for prices and rates of return on British government securities (gilt-edged), 22 for company securities, 14 for short term (mainly money market) rates up to 3 months, including the London clearing bank base rate and the Finance House base rate, 1 for National Savings Bank investment account, 11 for local authority market rates, 33 Public Works Loan Board rates, 4 for certificates of tax deposit and 6 for building societies. In addition, Supplementary Table S7 (which appears quarterly) has annual and quarterly averages for six of the more important of these rates.

Looking through this range of data, two things stand out. First, looked at as data complementary to the flow of funds accounts, it is a very ill-balanced selection. There is a large amount of data on gilt-edged and company securities, but for banking sector lending there is only the London clearing bank base rate. It is true that the *Financial Statistics Explanatory Handbook* (1982) included rates for some official lending schemes, but its remark that 'Most lending is between 1 per cent and 5 per cent higher than base rate' (p. 116) only serves to underline this weakness. (In the 1983 edition even this quantification was eroded into the statement that 'the size of the margin over base rate depends on the nature and status of the customer' and this was repeated unchanged in the 1984 edition.) There is a similar lack of rates on finance house lending and on instalment credit extended by retailers. For building societies, three of the rates are Building Societies Association recommended or advised rates, but the other three are annual averages of no clear meaning (see *Financial Statistics Explanatory Handbook* 1984 p. 116, notes to Table 13.12).

Second, it seems clear that the reason for having such an ill-balanced selection of rates is reliance upon data which can easily be picked up from market information, mostly reported in the press (including commercially produced indices) or which is the by-product of public sector administrative activity. A small amount – average rates and calculated gilt-edged rates – consists of the secondary processing of this material. But there appears to be no primary rate of return data which is collected because of its likely importance, only data which is collected because it is already easily available. It is hardly surprising, therefore, that rates of return on important classes of financial claim are very poor or do not appear at all in *Financial Statistics.*

Turning to other terms, these too can be expected to affect (directly or indirectly) financial flows; indeed, this is their object. Looking back at controls on the balance sheets of the banks, special deposits were well documented in regular statistical series in *BEQB*, but supplementary special deposits less so, since there was no regular series on the IBELs ceiling to which they related. There were no official time series covering the pre-1971 bank lending controls or the related controls affecting finance houses, or the qualitative requests on bank lending.[2] More recently, monetary targets are regularly (but poorly) graphed in CSO *Economic Trends* (monthly) but details have to be followed up in 'Economic Events' at the front of each issue or in *BEQB.*

Exchange controls on overseas capital flows ended in October 1979, but before that they were tightened and relaxed on various occasions; there appear to be no series which would act as indicators of these episodes. There have been changes in the tax treatment of interest on house mortgages, on bank borrowing by persons and on capital gains. Of these, only those on capital gains on gilt-edged stocks are dealt with in *Financial Statistics Explanatory Handbook* 1984 p.113.

This brief survey of some of the main weaknesses in the rate of return and other terms data reveals considerable room for improvement in the data itself and in its co-ordination with the flow of funds accounts.

2 An approach to using the flow of funds matrix table

The would-be user is faced with a difficult task when he comes to the flow of funds matrix table for the first time. Here we suggest a simple approach for gaining familiarity with the matrix table using Table 4.2. This is adapted from the OP(BE) matrix table for 1980 (see *BEQB* June 1982 p. 256) by leaving out the sub-sectors of the public sector. Since we are simply using it as an example, its date is not important;

Table D
Financial transactions: annual matrix 1980

£ millions

	Line	Public sector	Monetary sector	Other financial institutions	Industrial and commercial companies	Personal sector	Overseas sector(a)	Residual error
Capital account								
Saving	1	+ 3,859		+4,296	+15,199	+24,680	– 3,058	
Taxes on capital and capital transfers	2	– 456		– 202	+ 383	+ 275	—	
less:								
Gross fixed-capital formation at home	3	–12,333		–4,999	–15,644	– 6,995		
Increase in value of stocks and work in progress	4	– 724		+ 51	– 1,488	– 232		
Financial surplus+/deficit–	5	**– 9,654**		**– 854**	**– 1,550**	**+17,728**	**– 3,058**	**–2,612**
Changes in financial assets and liabilities								
Assets: increase+/decrease–								
Liabilities: increase–/decrease+								
Notes and coin	6	– 406	– 318	—	+ 361	+ 363	—	
Market Treasury bills	7	– 355	+ 430	+ 35	+ 16		– 126	
British government securities	8	–10,672	+ 1,528	+ 5,590	+ 133	+ 1,905	+ 1,516	
National savings	9	– 1,378		—		+ 1,378		
Tax instruments	10	– 266	– 18	– 43	+ 330	– 3		
Net government indebtedness to Banking Department	11	+ 864	– 864					
Northern Ireland central government debt	12	– 6	+ 10	—	—	– 4		
Government liabilities under exchange cover scheme	13	—						
Other non-marketable government debt	14	+ 151		– 151				
Issue Department's transactions in commercial bills	15	+ 403			– 403			
Government foreign currency debt	16	+ 769	– 543				– 226	
Other government overseas financing	17	– 121					+ 121	
Official reserves	18	+ 291					– 291	
Local authority debt:								
Temporary	19.1	– 494	+ 98	+ 400	– 50	+ 42	+ 4	
Foreign currency	19.2	+ 47	– 25	—			– 22	
Other listed securities	19.3	+ 146	+ 141	– 84		– 222	+ 19	
Other long-term	19.4	– 1,794	+ 1,468	+ 247	+ 6	+ 68	+ 5	
Public corporation debt:								
Foreign currency	20.1	+ 429	– 154	—			– 275	
Other	20.2	+ 103	– 101	– 121	—	– 10	+ 129	

	Line							
Deposits with banks:								
Sterling sight	21.1	+ 243	− 676	+ 27	− 278	+ 711	− 27	
Sterling time	21.2	+ 95	−12,516	+ 1,342	+ 2,520	+ 5,530	+ 3,029	
Foreign currency	21.3	+ 49	−31,805	− 261	+ 771	+ 367	+30,357	
Deposits with building societies	22			− 7,140	− 22	+ 7,175	− 13	
Deposits with other financial institutions	23	—		− 809	− 1	+ 807	+ 3	
Bank lending (excluding public sector):								
Foreign currency	24.1		+31,426	+ 107	− 1,229	− 151	−30,153	
Sterling	24.2		+11,892	− 739	− 5,616	− 2,774	− 2,763	
Credit extended by retailers	25	− 3			+ 75	− 72		
Identified trade credit:								
Public corporations (domestic)	26.1	− 699			+ 573	+ 126		
Import and export	26.2	− 561		+ 250	+ 394		− 83	
Loans for house purchase:								
Building societies	27.1			+ 5,722		− 5,722		
Other	27.2	+ 708	+ 490	+ 469		− 1,667		
Other public sector lending	28	− 123		+ 11	+ 119	+ 4	− 11	
Other lending by financial institutions	29	—		+ 811	− 374	− 437		
Unit trust units	30			+ 9		− 9		
UK company securities	31	+ 206	− 241	+ 2,373	− 885	− 2,319	+ 866	
Overseas securities	32	—	+ 906	+ 2,453	+ 1,718	− 516	− 4,561	
Life assurance and pension funds	33	− 313		−11,045		+11,358		
Miscellaneous domestic instruments	34	—	+ 9	− 289	+ 198	+ 82	—	
Direct and other investment abroad	35		+ 240	+ 179	+ 2,037		− 2,456	
Overseas direct and other investment in United Kingdom	36		− 103	− 14	− 3,189		+ 3,306	
Miscellaneous overseas instruments	37	+ 302		− 16	+ 672		− 958	
Accruals adjustment	38	+ 1,433	− 20	− 731	− 961	+ 279		
Identified financial transactions	39	**−10,952**	**+ 1,254**	**− 896**	**− 3,085**	**+16,289**	**− 2,610**	
Unidentified transactions	40	+ 1,298	−1,212		+ 1,535	+ 1,439	− 448	−2,612

— nil or less than £½ million.

(a) It has not been possible to incorporate in this table the revised balance of payments estimates which were released in June.

Source: adapted from *Bank of England Quarterly Bulletin* June 1982 p. 256.

Table 4.2

for a more recent and complete OP(BE) matrix table, see Appendix 1, Table A1.1, or a more recent issue of *BEQB*.

The approach suggested here can be stated briefly in the form of three rules:

(a) Treat the FS row entries as a set of balance of payments current account balances where 'one sector's surplus is another sector's deficit', and each sector's FS row entry is the balance between its aggregate income and expenditure (with a relatively small adjustment for taxes on capital and capital transfers, TCCT).
(b) Treat each sector column in the matrix table as a balance of payments statement for that sector.
(c) Treat each financing account row as a capital market channel along which sectors lend and borrow from each other.

It is a corollary of these rules that, when looking at any particular cell entry, one should think of it in terms of its sector column, applying rule (b) above, and its row, applying rule (a) or (c) as appropriate. These rules also help to act as a reminder of the row and column constraints which have to hold at all times.

Starting with rule (a) and looking at Table 4.2, the largest absolute entry in the FS row is +17,728 for Pers (£ million being understood here and in what follows). If Pers is to have a surplus of this size then, since the row must sum to zero, one way or another, other sector entries must show the counterpart deficits and in fact we find: Pub, −9,654; O's, −3,058; ICC, −1,550; Mon + OFI, −854 and a residual error of −2,612. Ignoring the residual error for the moment, this pattern of sectoral entries could be interpreted as showing that Pers was deliberately running a large surplus (for example, because it felt its stock of net financial assets was too low) and that Pub was helping to accommodate this by running a deficit which was over half as large in absolute terms. If the Pub deficit were lower, then either the deficits of other sectors would have to be greater or the surplus of Pers would have to be lower, or some combination of these. If this led each of the domestic sectors to reduce its expenditure in order to improve its financial surplus, then one would expect a decline in domestic economic activity which would allow this to occur to some extent, with a worsening of the position of O's as its counterpart. The large Pub deficit can therefore be seen as a policy response helping to insulate other domestic sectors from the efforts of Pers to run a high surplus; it will also help to insulate O's.

The presence of the large residual error of −2,612 in the FS row reminds us of one reason why it is as well to be tentative in drawing conclusions from such figures. It indicates that, as they stand, the sector FS entries are internally inconsistent due to errors and omissions, and require a residual error entry of -2,612 to make the FS row sum to zero (i.e. this net amount of -2,612 needs to be distributed in some unknown gross way between the other FS row entries). But there is another reason also: figures are liable to be revised, sometimes by substantial amounts; more will be said about this in Chapter 7 section 2.

Turning now to the capital account and the derivation of the FS row entries for the UK domestic sectors, we have already seen that both S (row 1) and - I (row 3 + 4) include stock appreciation and that these offset each other so far as the FS entries are concerned. (For the UK as a whole, the 'highly uncertain' estimate of stock appreciation for 1980 was 6,456, of which 5,061 was attributed to ICC; see *National Income and Expenditure* 1982 Table 12.4). Looking at the figures for S and - I in Table 4.2, it will be seen that while these are of similar magnitude for Mon + OFI and for ICC, they are very different for Pub and Pers. Thus in the FS row, Mon + OFI and ICC both have relatively small deficits of -854 and -1,550 respectively, Pub has a large deficit of -9,654 and Pers has a large surplus of +17,728. If we deduct stock appreciation from S, we get what might be called cash flow saving; we then find that both Mon + OFI and ICC have financial deficits of 15 to 20 per cent of their cash flow saving. This is very different from the situation in the two predominantly non-commercial sectors Pub and Pers. Pub has a financial deficit equal to about 280 per cent of its cash flow saving while Pers has a financial surplus equal to about 74 per cent. (For some purposes the saving of Pers can be divided into committed and discretionary saving; see *Financial Statistics* supplementary table S23, now in the October issue each year, and the notes on that table in *Financial Statistics Explanatory Handbook* 1984, p. 122.)

The capital account gives a clear framework linking S, - I and FS entries sector by sector. It is not difficult to list the influences on S and - I sector by sector, but here we can only say that it is quite another matter to find any simple and reliable basis for explaining the changes in sectoral S and - I. The FS row entry in the RE column has already been noted as an additional problem. It will be seen that the TCCT entries are relatively very small for all domestic sectors, and we saw in Chapter 2 that the S row entry in the O's column is only a window-dressing entry.

We now come to the sector columns and rule (b). We begin by deriving Table 4.3 from Table 4.2 by:

1 excluding rows 1 to 4 and restricting Table 4.3 to the matrix table proper;
2 excluding all cell entries under 1,500; thus we have only selected

CF £ billion	Line	Pub	Mon	OFI	ICC	Pers	O's	RE
FS	5	−9.7			−1.6	+17.7	−3.1	−2.6
British government securities	8	−10.7	+1.5	+5.6		+1.9	+1.5	
LA debt: Other long term	19.4	−1.8						
Bank deposits: Sterling time	21.2		−12.5		+2.5	+5.5	+3.0	
: Foreign currency	21.3		−31.8				+30.4	
Deposits with building societies	22			−7.1		+7.2		
Bank lending: Foreign currency	24.1		+31.4				−30.2	
: Sterling	24.2		+11.9		−5.6	−2.8	−2.8	
House purchase loans: Building socs	27.1			+5.7		−5.7		
: Other	27.2					−1.7		
UK company securities	31			+2.4		−2.3		
Overseas securities	32			+2.5	+1.7		−4.6	
Life assurance and pension funds	33			−11.0		+11.4		
Direct/other investment abroad	35				+2.0		−2.5	
Overseas direct/other investment in UK	36				−3.2		+3.3	
Identified financial transactions	39	−11.0			−3.1	+16.3	−2.6	
Unidentified transactions	40				+1.5			−2.6

Table 4.3

cell entries and the row and column constraints cannot be expected to apply.

We make use of Table 4.3 because we now have to deal with many more cell entries, and concentrating initially upon the much smaller number of heavyweight entries brings out the main structure of flows more clearly.[3]

With rule (b) we treat each sector column in the matrix table as a balance of payments statement for that sector; having already looked at the derivation of its FS entry, we now go through the financing account entries to see how its financial surplus was disposed of or its financial deficit was financed. Taking Pers in Table 4.3 as our example, we have already interpreted its FS entry of 17.7 (£ billion = £ thousand million being understood here and in what follows) as indicating that it wished to raise its holding of net financial assets by this amount. Assuming that this 17.7 surplus is a true figure, it must be disposed of in the financing account. However, looking at the Pers column entries in the financing account shows quite a complex situation.

In 1980 Pers acquired 26 of financial assets: 1.9 of British government securities (row 8), 5.5 of sterling time deposits with banks (row 21.2), 7.2 of deposits with building societies (row 22) and 11.4 of claims on life assurance and pension funds (row 33). These uses of funds were financed from its financial surplus and from its financing account sources of funds (the latter, under the conventional format (CF) used in the UK matrix table, all having negative signs[4]), which either raised its liabilities or reduced its other financial assets. These financing account sources were: -2.8 of bank borrowing in sterling (row 24.2), -5.7 of building society borrowing (row 27.1), -1.7 of other borrowing for house purchase (row 27.2) and -2.3 of sales of UK company securities (row 31). This simultaneous rise in deposits with, and borrowing from, banks and building societies confirms what we already know perfectly well: that Pers is not a homogeneous sector, and an important part of the explanation of its financing account entries is likely to depend upon the behaviour of its different sub-groups. Persons at different stages of their financial life-cycle are likely to form significant sub-groups of this kind, but it is not easy to see how such sub-groups with shifting populations could in practice be identified statistically. Nevertheless, the rise in assets with life assurance and pension funds does account for about two-thirds of the FS entry of Pers (although one could regard part as being financed by the net sale of UK company securities as persons switch from direct holdings to life insurance assets – a process that seems to have been going on for many years).

There are signs of the same kind of non-homogeneity if we look at the financing account entries in the ICC sector column, although there, perhaps, a more striking feature is the large unidentified entry. Mon and OFI provide a contrast, for their combined FS entry is well below the level for it to appear in Table 4.3, while the financing account entries are large and reflect the role of the two sectors as financial intermediaries.

Although only two entries appear in the unidentified transactions row in Table 4.3, looking back at Table 4.2 shows that there are entries in this row for all sectors (including residual error), and that the entries for Pub (where one might expect errors/omissions to be minimal), Mon + OFI and Pers are not far below the >1.5 magnitude required for inclusion in Table 4.3. There are some reasons for believing that the FS row entries are responsible for much, even most, of the unidentified transactions row entries. However, in the last resort it is an implicit definition of these entries that they are those about whose sources we can only guess, and they are a reminder of the limitations of the data we have.

In looking at Pers, we first took the financing account rows which in 1980 were uses of funds for Pers, followed by those which were sources (either through raising liabilities or reducing assets). While this may be satisfactory for a single year or quarter, over time a cell entry may swing from being a source of funds in one period to being a use in another. If we look at the Bank of England's supporting table for Pers (*BEQB* March 1984, Statistical annex, Table 19.4) we find a more structured re-arrangement of the financing account rows into borrowing (= financial liabilities of Pers) and financial assets of Pers. The aim in both cases is the same: to bring out the significant features of a sector's financing behaviour. The Bank of England's supporting tables for the other sectors (*loc. cit.*) are re-arranged in comparable ways with the same aim.

We turn now to rule (c) and the treatment of financing account rows as capital market channels along which funds are borrowed and lent between sectors. Looking along a typical row (and remembering that we are using a CF presentation – see Table 4.6 in note 4), it is easy to see which sectors used funds (+) and so provided a source of funds (–) for other sectors. But one of the most important features of these capital market flows is the high proportion which passes through the hands of financial intermediaries. For this reason it is not enough to look at the financing account rows one at a time; we need also to look at them in terms of the activities of the main groups of financial intermediaries. This typically consists of collecting funds along one or more financing account rows and lending them out along one or more other rows. Table 4.4 contains the same heavyweight entries as Table 4.3 and identifies the main flows of funds through financial intermediaries, marking them with four sets of arrows labelled (A) to (D).

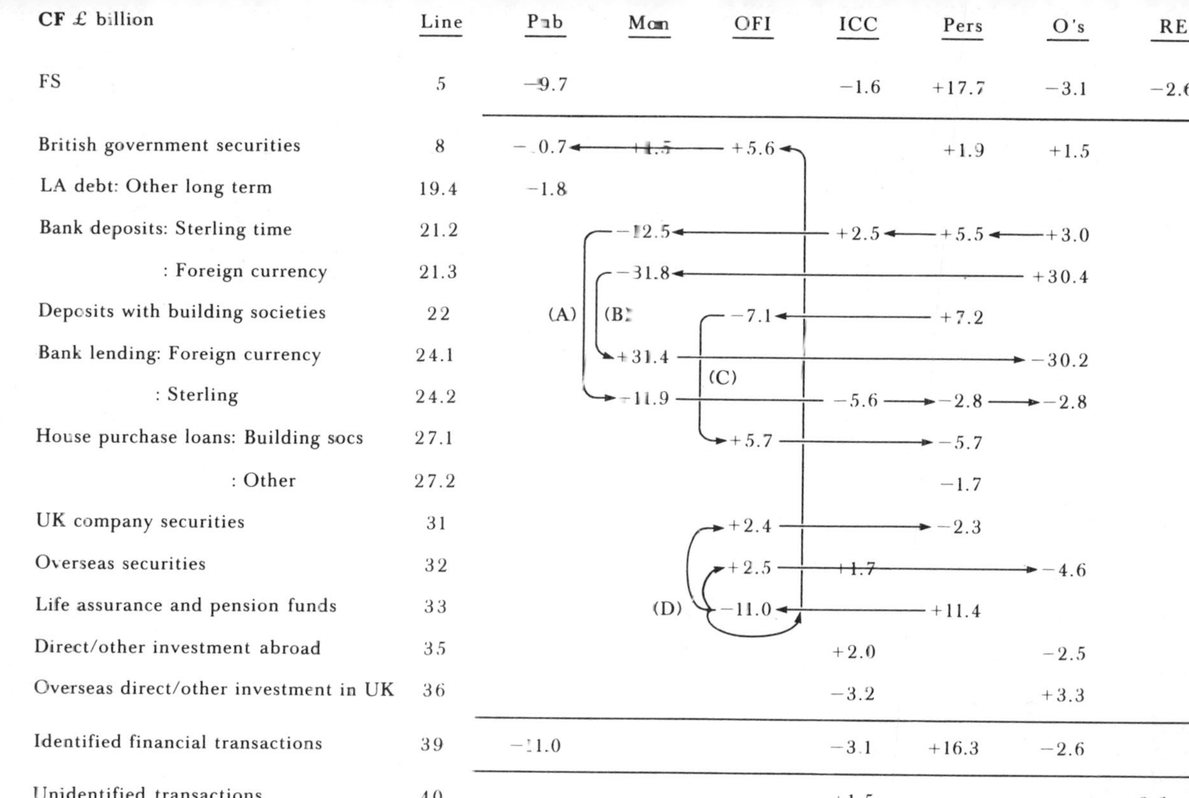

CF £ billion	Line	Pub	Mon	OFI	ICC	Pers	O's	RE
FS	5	−9.7			−1.6	+17.7	−3.1	−2.6
British government securities	8	−0.7	+1.5	+5.6		+1.9	+1.5	
LA debt: Other long term	19.4	−1.8						
Bank deposits: Sterling time	21.2		−12.5		+2.5	+5.5	+3.0	
: Foreign currency	21.3		−31.8				+30.4	
Deposits with building societies	22			−7.1		+7.2		
Bank lending: Foreign currency	24.1		+31.4				−30.2	
: Sterling	24.2		+11.9		−5.6	−2.8	−2.8	
House purchase loans: Building socs	27.1			+5.7		−5.7		
: Other	27.2					−1.7		
UK company securities	31			+2.4		−2.3		
Overseas securities	32			+2.5	+1.7		−4.6	
Life assurance and pension funds	33			−11.0		+11.4		
Direct/other investment abroad	35				+2.0		−2.5	
Overseas direct/other investment in UK	36				−3.2		+3.3	
Identified financial transactions	39	−11.0			−3.1	+16.3	−2.6	
Unidentified transactions	40				+1.5			−2.6

Table 4.4

(A) shows banks (= Mon) collecting funds in the form of sterling time deposits from ICC, Pers and O's along row 21.2 and lending them out to the same three sectors (although in different proportions) along row 24.2.

(B) shows banks taking in foreign currency deposits from O's along row 21.3 and re-lending the funds to other members of O's along row 24.1.

(C) shows the building societies (part of OFI) taking deposits from Pers along row 22 and lending some 80 per cent of these funds to other members of Pers along row 27.1.

(D) shows life assurance and pension funds (also part of OFI) acquiring funds from Pers along row 33 in return for various forms of life assurance and pension arrangements; in this case the funds are shown as being used partly along row 32 in acquiring overseas securities from O's, partly along row 31 in acquiring UK company securities from Pers, but chiefly along row 8 in acquiring British government securities from Pub.

There is a significant difference between cases (A) to (C) above and case (D). In cases (A) and (B) the rows are defined in terms of the intermediary activities of the group of institutions which form the Mon sector, while in case (C) the rows are defined in terms of the intermediary activities of the building societies, a sub-group of OFI. Each of these rows is therefore clean of entries arising from the activities of other financial intermediaries. In case (D) the life assurance and pension funds (LAPF) are also members of OFI, but while row 33 is effectively defined in terms of the intermediary activities of LAPF (except for a very small component under Pub, which can be seen in Table 4.2), so that the entry of −11.0 in row 33/OFI is a clean entry for LAPF, the entries in the OFI column and in rows 32, 31 and 8 relate to all members of OFI and are not clean entries for LAPF. In fact the LAPF component is dominant in each of these entries, amounting to about 72 per cent, 109 per cent and 78 per cent respectively,[5] so that case (D) does give a broadly acceptable picture of the intermediary activities of LAPF. These cases illustrate some of the advantages of co-ordination between row and column definitions in the matrix table.

Although Table 4.4 contains only entries greater than 1.5, if we look at the entries joined by the arrows in each of cases (A) to (D), the matching between uses (+) and sources (−) of funds (as measured by taking the smaller as a percentage of the larger) along each row and in the sector column of the institutions concerned, is typically over 90 per cent. (In case (D) this measure is not really applicable to rows 32, 31 and 8.) The importance of these financial intermediation entries can be gauged from the fact that, after minor adjustments,[6] they cover

87 per cent of the absolute sum of the financing account entries (excluding the IFT row 39) in Table 4.4. If we go back to Table 4.2 and conduct the same exercise on all readily identifiable financial intermediation entries relating to Mon and OFI, the corresponding figure is 80 per cent. It is worth noting that Table 4.4 does not include the two medium of exchange rows, notes and coin (row 6) and deposits with banks: sterling sight (row 21.1), and it can be seen from Table 4.2 that all their entries are well below the heavyweight level. The reason is obvious enough; although effectively all transactions involve the use of medium of exchange and therefore lead to pairs of entries in one or other of these two rows, it is virtually an implicit definition of medium of exchange that the vast bulk of these gross entries will offset one another leaving us with the quite small net entries seen in Table 4.2.

In cases (A), (B) and (C) the arrows show how financial intermediation appears to take funds through a 'U' turn in the sector column of the intermediary concerned, and this is a useful pattern to keep in mind. However, this pattern does depend upon the relative position of the sector columns concerned, and as can be seen in case (D), where about half of the funds collected from the right hand side along row 33 are disposed of to the left along row 8, intermediation can also take funds through what can be described as a 'Z' turn. Further, the extent to which financial intermediaries appear to concentrate their activities in a small number of rows and columns is itself related to the row and column definitions used in the matrix table.

We have already noted that the RE column entry in the FS row reveals problems for the interpretation of the institutional sector entries in that row. An additional problem arises from revisions to the figures in the matrix table. As an example of this, the matrix table for 1980 in Table 4.2 (which appeared in June 1982) contains large revisions from the original table for 1980 which appeared in June 1981. These include revisions of over 1 billion in every entry in the FS row (including RE) except that for O's, and (net) revisions of around 1 billion in the IFT row (row 39) entries for Pub, OFI, ICC and Pers. In these two rows, the sum of these absolute revisions amounts to 17 per cent of the sum of their absolute entries shown in Table 4.2. Experience shows that we can expect further significant revisions in succeeding versions of this matrix table; more is said about revisions in Chapter 7.

3 Further aspects of the flow of funds accounts

The approach suggested above provides no more than a starting point for gaining a grasp of the flow of funds matrix table; it is essentially a process of systematically working through the rows and columns, using the figures for a single year, to get some structured idea of the pattern and relative magnitudes of the cell entries. The obvious next step would be to look at the changes in the matrix table entries over a number of past periods, and to begin linking these changes with the complementary statistical data (on financial stocks, interest rates, etc) and non-statistical information (on government policy etc). This is very much more easily said than done, because the amount of data to be dealt with immediately becomes very much larger, and the whole enterprise soon exceeds the capacity of any individual to handle it adequately even in the informal ways we have considered so far.

The response to this problem is best seen by looking at what has happened in the past decade or so. The Treasury needs to understand the past behaviour of the UK economy as a basis for forecasting its future course and the policy trade-offs that it offers. In the past the Treasury used a large econometric model of the UK economy which together with forecasts on world trade was used to forecast in detail the main macro-economic variables; these included the balance of payments on current account and figures for saving and investment for each of the UK domestic sectors, and hence the FS row entries in the flow of funds matrix table. This macro-economic forecast used to be followed by a second stage, the forecasting of the financing account entries in the matrix table. This was done jointly by the Treasury and the Bank of England, and the whole detailed procedure had to rely heavily upon economic judgement to supplement a number of single equation econometric forecasts of some cell entries and simple extrapolation forecasts for others. With changes of assumption and further adjustments to cell entries, the process would be iterated a number of times until an acceptable set of forecast entries was achieved in the balanced matrix table.[7]

This procedure was open to criticism on two grounds: first, it was insufficiently systematic, relying as much as it did on partial relationships, economic judgement and ad hoc adjustment; second, there was a lack of direct interaction between financial variables and the real economy. With the aim of overcoming these two weaknesses, the next stage was the extension of the macro-model to incorporate the financial sector, embodying the flow of funds matrix in the model and bringing in a range of financial feed-backs. This is now the position in the Treasury model, and in the macro-models which have been developed by the Bank of England and the London Business School. So far no study seems to have been published on the effectiveness of this modelling of the financial sector; some users seem to feel that up to now it has achieved only a rather moderate degree of success. If resources on this scale have managed to make only limited progress in understanding/forecasting the financial behaviour of the sectors in the UK economy, there would seem to be rather poor prospects for less well-supported efforts.

However, at a more restricted and less rigorous level, flow of funds studies are carried out by those concerned with the capital market and financial investment. Such studies are likely to use the flow of funds data in a selectively more aggregated form; they often begin with forecasts of the pattern of financial surpluses and then attempt to forecast the supply and demand for funds along certain main capital market channels and the resulting flows and changes in interest rates/ security prices.

The flow of funds accounts, therefore, can be used at different levels. They provide a body of sectorised and classified financial flow data, although one with the considerable imperfections already noted; the approach suggested above can use this data to gain what might be termed a descriptive understanding of the financial flows in the UK economy. Informal methods of interpretation, making use of complementary data, can often allow provisional explanations of features revealed in the flow of funds matrix table,[8] and the same data can be used in limited studies of individual sectors and particular financial markets. Using the flow of funds accounts in these ways can be expected to add something to our understanding of the financial system; at present it seems that to go further we must enter the realm of econometric models of the whole economy.

Notes

1 For some time the CSO and the Bank of England have been working on balance sheet data for the UK domestic sectors. The CSO has produced sectoral balance sheet data for end-years (C.W. Pettigrew, 'National and sector balance sheets for the United Kingdom', *Economic Trends,* Nov 1980) and the figures for the personal sector are now being regularly updated each year (see *Financial Statistics,* Feb 1984, Supplementary table S12). It also regularly produces end-quarter figures for the financial liabilities and assets of the UK non-bank private sector; these were introduced in the article 'Financial wealth of the non-bank private sector', *Economic Trends* July 1981; the figures are published in *Financial Statistics,* beginning with a long series going back to 1966/4 (in August 1981, Supplementary Table E) and currently as Supplementary Table

S15 each quarter. The latest CSO article on integrated accounts is M. Marland, 'The reconciliation of personal sector transactions and wealth', *Economic Trends,* June 1983.

The Bank of England has produced quarterly integrated balance sheet/flow accounts from 1963 for the banking sector, for investment trust companies and for insurance companies. This last series of integrated stock/flow accounts is illustrated by data for the four quarters of 1976 in *BEQB* Sep 1978, pp. 371–6, which includes useful comments and notes.

2 For an attempt to produce this type of data for an earlier period see R.F.G. Alford, 'Indicators of direct controls on the UK capital market 1951–1969', in M.H. Peston and B. Corry (eds), *Essays in Honour of Lord Robbins* (1972).

3 Excluding the headnote rows 1 to 4 in Table 4.2 reduces it to the matrix table proper (MTP), always remembering that the IFT row 39 is simply a sub-total or *aide-mèmoire* row which does not contain any original entries. In this MTP, taking original entries (and thus excluding those in IFT row 39) regardless of sign, the total of heavy-weight entries displayed in Table 4.3 (and 4.4) amounts to 86.5 per cent of the total of all entries in the corresponding MTP in Table 4.2. This is shown in Table 4.5:

absolute entry magnitude (£bn)		number of entries	sum of absolute entries (£bn)	%
> 1.5		41	305.7	86.5
⩽ 1.5		147	47.6	13.5
	Σ	188	353.3	100.0
	blank cells	118		
	total cells	306		

Table 4.5

In Table 4.2 the MTP contains 44 rows and 7 columns (including the UT row and the RE column, but excluding the IFT row 39), giving a total of 308 cells; however, the Mon and OFI cells are combined in the FS and UT rows, reducing the total to 306. Of the 118 blank cells, 42 are the cells in the financing account rows and the RE column. The 147 cells with entries ⩽ 1.5 in magnitude include 13 cells containing a bar, indicating an entry of nil or less than £½ million.

Rather than defining a convenient floor magnitude for heavyweight entries and allowing the percentage of all absolute entries covered in the resulting heavyweight MTP to emerge (as we have done above) it would be more satisfactory, though more work, to specify this percentage and allow it to define the floor magnitude for heavyweight entries. Working to a given percentage should provide a broad degree of comparability between the resulting heavyweight MTPs for different years.

4 When we are looking at particular cell entries, rather than constantly spelling them out as a rise/fall in liabilities/assets, it is convenient to have a more general term. Under the zero-sum format (ZSF) matrix table we can talk about a cell entry as showing the

	ZSF		CF	
	sign	source or use of purchasing power	sign	source or use of funds
FS:				
surplus	+	source	+	source
deficit	−	use	−	use
FA:				
assets: rise	−	use	+	use
fall	+	source	−	source
liabilities:				
rise	+	source	−	source
fall	−	use	+	use

Table 4.6

acquisition/+ or disposal/– of purchasing power or, what is the same thing, as being a source/+ or use/– of purchasing power. In the conventional format (CF) used in the UK matrix table, we shall now use the term funds synonymously with purchasing power under ZSF. This is shown in Table 4.6, where, for example, a rise in assets under ZSF has a – sign and is a use of purchasing power, and under CF has a + sign and is a use of funds.

It will be seen that under ZSF, we consistently have sources/+, uses/–; under CF this consistency no longer holds, and while for the FS row we have sources/+, uses/–, for the financing account rows we have sources/–, uses/+. This sources/uses terminology based on the signs of cell entries needs to be distinguished from the sources/uses terminology used in the US flow of funds matrix table, where sources are defined as changes in liabilities and uses as changes in assets (see Appendix 3).

5 These percentages have been derived from the more detailed figures for LAPF for 1980; see Table J, *BEQB* June 1981, p. 221.

6 The minor adjustments are the allocation to the financial intermediation cell entries of –5.6 in row 8/Pub and –2.5 in row 32/O's.

7 See 'Financial forecasts in the United Kingdom', *BEQB* June 1977 pp. 188–196

8 Informal interpretation is not without its hazards: it can produce more than one possible explanation of the same phenomenon; an explanation may be followed by revision of the figures which removes the feature which has been so painstakingly explained; finally, it can easily slip into what may be called the 'bad old Board of Trade method' (BOBOTM). This consists of taking a table of figures and turning them directly and uncritically into a verbal narrative. Explanation can often be in the form of a narrative, but a narrative which is no more than the translation of a table from figures into words is not an explanation. Further, BOBOTM may, through its ordering of the narrative, imply an order of events and a causal sequence for which there is no justification, while concentration upon turning a particular table into words may lead to the neglect of relevant complementary data.

5 Some applications of the quadruple entry approach

1 Manipulation of zero-sum matrix tables

The manipulation of the entries in a zero-sum flow of funds matrix table usually has as its object the modelling of some actual or possible set of transactions. Such manipulation is faced with the need to maintain the zero-sum character of the matrix table which, in the accounting system we are using, is a necessary condition for consistency. The obvious way of doing this is to recognise that the flow of funds matrix table is a quadruple entry system, and to restrict manipulation changes to the addition of quadruple entries to the matrix table so that its zero-sum condition is maintained at all times. The constraint of having to use only quadruple entry changes may be hampering and inconvenient but, in the accounting system we are using, it is simply a consequence of the necessity to be consistent. Here we shall explore some aspects of the use of quadruple entries for the manipulation of the zero-sum flow of funds matrix table.[1]

The entries in a zero-sum matrix table can be regarded in principle as the cell by cell sum of the very large number of quadruple entries which record all the transactions occurring in the period concerned. But the entries in a zero-sum matrix table can also be built up from a very much smaller number of what may be termed composite quadruple entries; these do not (except by chance) relate to any actual transaction, but are used simply as instruments for manipulating the entries in a zero-sum matrix table. To show how this can be done, we shall start by setting out a systematic procedure, or algorithm, for taking a specified set of zero-sum entries (using those in the 4 x 4 zero-sum matrix table in Table 5.1a for our example) and using composite quadruple entries to duplicate this set of entries in a previously empty (all zero-entry) 4 x 4 matrix table, so producing Table 5.1b. From this we can derive a general formula for the minimum number of composite quadruple entries which will always enable us to construct any specified complete set of zero-sum entries in a matrix table.

The construction process we use is systematic in two respects. First, it uses a systematic procedure for selecting cells for adjustment. It begins with the top row of the matrix table and selects the cells in order from left to right; it then moves to the second row and again selects the cells in order from left to right and so on. This we shall term sequential cell selection. Second, in each selected cell it adjusts the entry to the desired level by adding to the matrix table a composite quadruple entry with certain systematic characteristics.

In such a composite quadruple entry (which from now on we shall just refer to as a quadruple entry) we term the top left entry the adjusting entry, and use it to adjust the entry in the selected cell; the diagonally opposite, bottom right, entry we term the trailing entry. The position of the cell entry to be adjusted determines the position of the adjusting entry in the matrix table, and the adjustment required determines the magnitude and the sign pattern of the quadruple entry. However, the trailing entry could normally fall in any one of a number of different cells. Here we shall define two systematic positions for the trailing entry out of a number of possible ones. In the first case it would always be as near as possible to the adjusting entry, so that we would always have a compact quadruple entry, one with all its entries in continguous cells. In the second case the trailing entry would always fall in the bottom right hand cell in the matrix table, and this we shall term an extended quadruple entry. Here we shall use extended quadruple entries in our construction process (the comparable construction process using compact quadruple entries is shown in Appendix 5).

In what follows we shall refer to each cell in the matrix table by its row number and column number, so that r_2 c_3 means the cell in row 2 and column 3. We shall refer to the location of a quadruple entry by the position of its adjusting entry and its trailing entry (since these determine the position of the other two entries), for example: r_1 c_3/ r_3 c_4. As we add quadruple entries to the previously empty matrix table, where only one entry falls in a cell so that it becomes the cell total, we shall show it in heavy type. In a cell which receives more than one entry, these will be shown in sequential order (left to right and/or top to bottom) in light type with the final cell total in heavy type.

We now begin the systematic process of constructing, in a previously empty matrix table, the complete set of zero-sum entries shown in Table 5.1a and thus producing matrix Table 5.1b; we use sequential cell selection and extended quadruple entries.

1 We select cell r_1 c_1 in our empty matrix table; from Table 5.1a we can see that this cell is to contain the entry -5; we therefore specify the extended quadruple entry r_1 c_1/r_4 c_4 to have this entry in cell r_1 c_1; this determines all the other entries in this quadruple entry, which we now add cell by cell to the empty matrix table.
2 We select cell r_1 c_2 in the previously empty matrix table and follow the same procedure as above, adjusting its entry from zero to the desired entry of +3.
3 We select cell r_1 c_3 and proceed as above. This completes all the entries in row 1 which (as can be seen from Table 5.1b) now has the same entries as row 1 in Table 5.1a.
4 We select cell r_2 c_1 and proceed as above.

and so on until we have the complete set of entries shown in Table 5.1b. The numerical entries from this procedure, using the rule stated above for setting out successive cell entries and cell totals, can be readily followed through in Table 5.1b.

	1	2	3	4
1	-5	+3	−1	+3
2	+4	+2	−7	+1
3	−1	−1	+12	−10
4	+2	−4	−4	+6

Table 5.1a

	1	2	3	4
1	-5	+3	−1	+5−3+1 =+3
2	+4	+2	−7	−4−2+7 =+1
3	−1	−1	+12	+1+1−12 =−10
4	+5 −4 +1 =+2	−3 −2 +1 =−4	+1 +7 −12 =−4	−5+3−1 +4+2−7 −1−1+12 =+6

Table 5.1b

At stage 3 above, the third quadruple entry achieved the desired entries in both cell r_1 c_3 and cell r_1 c_4. This follows from the zero-sum character of the desired entries (shown in row 1 of Table 5.1a) and the zero-sum character of the three entry pairs falling in row 1 from the first three quadruple entries. This is shown in Table 5.1c, where it will be seen that these three entry pairs produce the desired cell totals in columns 1, 2 and 3, and the required zero entry in the Σ column. It follows that the cell total in column 4 must also be the desired one. The same argument will hold for the other rows in the matrix table.

		col 1	col 2	col 3	col 4	Σ
row 1	entry pairs:	− 5			+ 5	0
			+ 3		− 3	0
				− 1	+ 1	0
	desired cell totals:	− 5	+ 3	− 1	+ 3	0

Table 5.1c

On exactly analogous grounds, in any column, a quadruple entry which adjusts a cell in the penultimate row will also produce the required entry in the final row; and the quadruple entry which adjusts the entry in the penultimate row and the penultimate column will produce the three required entries in the final row and the final column. This can be seen in the bottom right matrix of Table 5.1d, and is the basis for a distinction between the dependent entries shown by the stars in the bottom row and right hand column and the other independent entries; this location of the dependent entries is simply a consequence of the sequential cell selection procedure we are using.

The procedure we have used above can easily be generalised to the case of constructing a specified zero-sum matrix table of r rows and c columns. All the specified entries in a row can be achieved using c − 1 quadruple entries, and the matrix table entries can be completed by doing this for the top r − 1 rows. Any specified zero-sum matrix table can therefore be constructed using (r − 1) (c − 1) quadruple entries. Referring back to the bottom right matrix in Table 5.1d, it will be seen that (r − 1) (c − 1) is also the number of independent cell entries in that matrix; taking this 4 x 4 case we therefore have:

$$(r-1)(c-1) = rc - r - c + 1 = 9 \quad \text{(independent cell entries)}$$

$$r + c - 1 = 7 \quad \text{(dependent cell entries)}$$

adding these equations

$$rc = 16 \quad \text{(total cell entries).}$$

The process we have shown above starts from an original zero-sum matrix table and adds to it (cell by cell, using (r – 1) (c – 1) quadruple entries) what we can term an alteration zero-sum matrix table to produce a resultant zero-sum matrix table. The construction process used for our example is conveniently simple because the original matrix table had only zero entries, so that the resultant matrix table was the same as the alteration matrix table and the process amounted to an exercise in duplicating the alteration matrix table, which was found to require (r – 1) (c – 1) quadruple entries. But it is clear that the same procedure can be used to add any alteration zero-sum matrix table to any original zero-sum matrix table to produce a resultant zero-sum matrix table. (It can easily be seen that if our procedure is presented with a non-zero-sum alteration matrix table, it cannot add it to a zero-sum matrix table). The procedure set out above is, therefore, generally applicable in the manipulation of zero-sum matrix tables, and any set of zero-sum changes can always be achieved using no more than (r – 1) (c – 1) quadruple entries.

One question that can be asked is whether desired alterations in a zero-sum matrix table can be achieved with fewer than (r – 1) (c – 1) quadruple entries, for example, if some cell entries do not need to be altered, or if four of the changes desired are such as to allow a single quadruple entry to achieve them simultaneously. This question runs into semantic difficulties, turning upon the question of whether not-using a quadruple entry is the same as using a quadruple entry of zero magnitude. Here we will simply say that, if we follow the procedure set out above, making alterations to the cell entries in a zero-sum matrix table will always require us to take (r – 1) (c – 1) *decisions* (explicit or implicit) about adjusting cell entries by adding quadruple entries to the matrix table.

If we take a particular set of alterations which we wish to add into a zero-sum matrix table, then the procedure set out above using sequential cell selection and extended quadruple entries means that there is a unique set of extended quadruple entries which will achieve this. Similarly, sequential cell selection and compact quadruple entries also means that there is a unique set of compact quadruple entries which will achieve this particular set of alterations. The uniqueness in each case requires the rigid specification of the quadruple entries which are to be used in the procedure. However, if we maintain sequential cell selection but replace these rigid specifications by the less rigid requirement that any cell entry, once adjusted, must not subsequently be disturbed, then one specified set of alterations in a

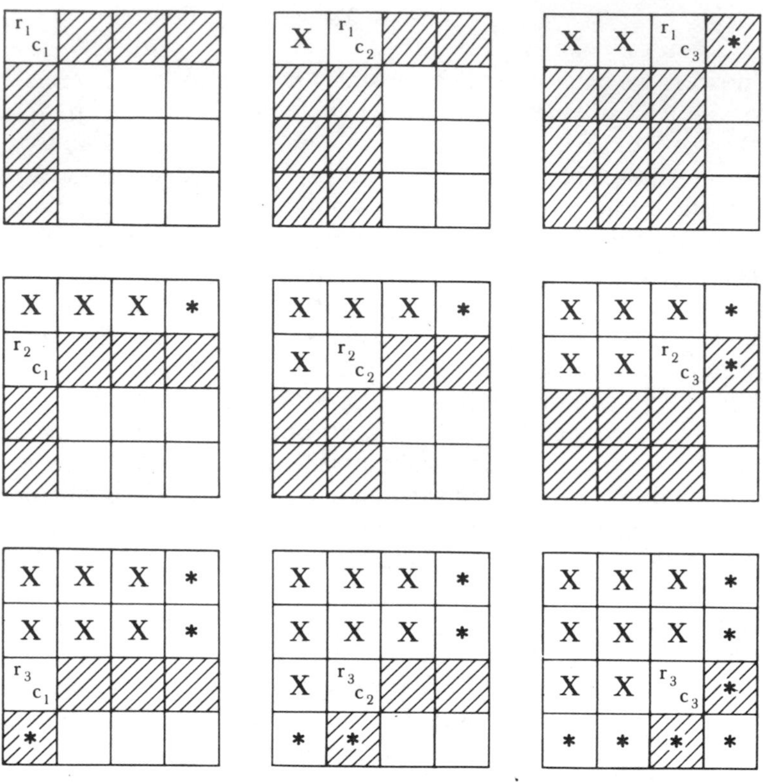

Table 5.1d

zero-sum matrix table can be achieved by a number of different sets of quadruple entries, and an expression can be derived for this number in terms of r and c.

To do this we start from the sequential cell selection process illustrated in Table 5.1d. There the top left matrix table shows the adjustment of cell r_1 c_1, and the unshaded cells show the possible positions that could be taken up by the trailing entry of the quadruple entry we use for this. The top centre matrix shows the next adjustment, to cell r_1 c_2; the quadruple entry used for this must not disturb cell r_1 c_1 (now marked X to show it has already been adjusted), and so its trailing entry can fall only in the smaller number of unshaded cells shown. The last matrix table in the top row shows the adjustment of cell r_1 c_3 and by the same type of argument shows the still smaller number of unshaded cells in which the trailing entry of this quadruple entry can fall. The * in cell r_1 c_4 shows that it contains the dependent entry for this row, which is adjusted to the required level at the same time as cell r_1 c_3. The remaining matrix tables in Table 5.1d are to be interpreted in a similar way.

The number of unshaded cells available for the trailing entry at each stage of the process shows the number of different possible quadruple entries that could be used at that stage. The product of these numbers of unshaded cells over all stages of the process shows the total number of different sets of (r – 1) (c – 1) quadruple entries which can be used. It will be seen that starting from the bottom right matrix in Table 5.1d, the number of rows containing unshaded unadjusted cells in each column of matrix tables, reading from bottom to top is 1, 2, r – 1, and that the number of columns containing unshaded unadjusted cells in each row of matrix tables, reading from right to left, is 1, 2, c – 1. The number of unshaded unadjusted cells in the array of matrix tables is therefore given by the following corresponding array of terms:

(r – 1) (c – 1)	(r – 1).2	(r – 1).1
2. (c – 1)	2.2	2.1
1. (c – 1)	1.2	1.1

To find the product of all the terms in this array, we note that the left hand components of the terms in each column multiply out to (r – 1) ! and with c – 1 such columns this comes to:

$$[r-1]\,!^{(c-1)}$$

The right hand components of the terms in each row multiply out to (c – 1) ! and with r – 1 such rows this comes to:

$$[c-1]\,!^{(r-1)}$$

The product of these two terms gives us:

$$[r-1]\,!^{(c-1)}\,[c-1]\,!^{(r-1)}$$

for the number of different possible sets of (r – 1) (c – 1) quadruple entries which can alter all the cell entries in an r X c zero-sum matrix table, using sequential cell selection and the specification that the quadruple entries used must not disturb any cell entry once it has been adjusted to the desired level.

It is now possible to go one step further by dropping the requirement of sequential cell selection from the zero-sum matrix table adjustment process used above, so that we can take the cells for adjustment in random order; the only requirement then is that the quadruple entries we use must not disturb a cell entry once it has been adjusted. In this case we can run up against the possibility of obstruction – the random selection of cells for adjustment may be such that, before all cells have been adjusted, no further quadruple entries can be added to the matrix table without disturbing a cell entry which has already been adjusted.

As a simple preliminary test of this possibility, twenty of our 4 X 4 zero-sum matrix tables were put through an adjustment process using random numbers to choose the row/column numbers defining each successive cell to be adjusted by the adjusting entry of successive quadruple entries; in each case the remaining three entries were distributed only subject to the requirement that they did not disturb any cell entry which had already been adjusted. Out of these twenty cases, four ran into obstruction before the adjustment process was completed. Since the possibility of obstruction (and therefore the need for more than (r – 1) (c – 1) quadruple entries in the adjustment process) cannot be ruled out for any size of zero-sum matrix table, random cell selection has, as one might expect, inherent disadvantages compared to sequential cell selection in the process of adjusting cell entries.

Besides allowing obstruction patterns of adjusted/unadjusted cells to arise from this crude Monte Carlo type of test, it is also possible to deliberately set up such patterns in matrix tables of any size (above a certain minimum). Inspection of a number of such cases suggests at first sight a relationship between some of these cell patterns and those in some lower-order Hadamard matrices. This is pursued further in Appendix 6.

2 Conjectural variation using quadruple entries

Suppose that we have a flow of funds zero-sum matrix table for a past period, and that the forecast for the coming period is that there will be no change in any of the entries. Suppose also that the policy-makers wish to explore the possible effects on the forecast accounts for the coming period of a policy which directly changes the entry in one financing account cell (the target cell) by a given amount (the policy impact), let us say –50. Using the quadruple entry approach, the simplest first step is to add to the forecast matrix table, cell by cell, a quadruple entry of magnitude 50 in such a way that –50 falls in the target cell, producing the policy impact we wish to consider. This means that three other cell entries must change in addition to the target cell entry, and since we could produce the same policy impact by adding to the matrix table a number of quadruple entries with target cell entries adding up to the required policy impact of −50, it is clearly possible that all other cell entries in the matrix table could change. Here we shall look at the number of different possible outcomes in some of these cases.

Starting with our original case of a single quadruple entry of magnitude 50 with an entry of −50 falling in the target cell to provide the required policy impact, how many different configurations are possible for the remaining three components of the quadruple entry? The number of possibilities can be seen by considering how many positions the other, diagonally opposite or trailing, cell entry of −50 can take up. This can be seen from Table 5.2, where the row and

Sector columns

Transaction rows

				y	
	x				
		T			
			z		
w					

Table 5.2

column containing the target cell (T) are shaded. The trailing entry of −50 can fall in any of the r rows except the shaded one (making r − 1) and in any of the c columns except the shaded one (making c − 1); therefore we have the familiar magnitude (r − 1) (c − 1) for the number of cells in which it can fall. In Table 5.2 with r = 10 and c = 6 this amounts to 45 possible cells of which four examples (w, x, y, z) are shown. Each of the cell pairs T,x T,y etc show where the negative entries lie for their respective quadruple entries; an outline is shown for each of these quadruple entries, the other corners showing the cells in which the positive entries will fall. For each quadruple entry it will be seen that, while the trailing negative entry must fall outside the target cell's shaded column and row, the positive entries on the other diagonal must fall inside the shaded column and row.

This policy impact of −50 produced by one quadruple entry of magnitude 50 could equally well be produced by two quadruple entries of magnitude 25 (each with an entry of −25 falling in the target cell, the two trailing entries of −25 falling in two other separate cells, so that the two quadruple entries of magnitude 25 are always distinguished from one quadruple entry of magnitude 50) and so on for five of magnitude 10, ten of magnitude 5 and twenty five of magnitude 2.

To see how many different permissible outcomes can arise, we have to determine $C\binom{n}{m}$, the number of different combinations of n items taken m at a time, where n = (r − 1) (c − 1) = 45 and m is successively 1, 2, 5, 10 and 25. For this we have to evaluate

$$C\binom{n}{m} = \frac{[(r-1)(c-1)]\,!}{[(r-1)(c-1)-m]\,!m!}$$

for the values of m given above; this is done in Table 5.3.

m	$C\binom{45}{m}$
1	4.5×10^{1}
2	9.9×10^{2}
5	1.2×10^{6}
10	3.2×10^{9}
25	3.2×10^{12}

Note: the mantissa is rounded to one decimal place in the last three cases

Table 5.3

The total number of different permissible outcomes is the sum of the entries in the $C\binom{45}{m}$ column, and this is a very large number even for the small matrix table and the limited range of cases considered so far.[2, 3] If we allow the policy impact to be made up of entries with different magnitudes, which do not have to be integral values but can be multiples of some smaller unit (though with some *minimum sensibile* floor), and which do not all have the same sign, then the number of permissible outcomes will grow in a typical combinatorial explosion.

This emphasises two features of the application of the quadruple entry approach to conjectural variation: at every stage this approach enforces the consistency required by the accounting system we are using, and even with consistency enforced in this way, it reveals the enormous number of permissible outcomes we may have to face in even the simplest case of a conjectural change in one cell entry. The problem facing anyone trying to forecast the effects of even this elementary change is to use their knowledge of the working of the economic and financial system to narrow down this potentially enormous range of permissible outcomes to a manageably small range of likely outcomes.

3 Syndrome entries

An individual transaction is recorded in the flow of funds accounts by an (individual) transaction quadruple entry. However, in using the flow of funds accounts we are normally concerned with a homogeneous group of such transactions occurring between transactors in each of two institutional sectors; we therefore sum, cell by cell, over such a homogeneous group of transactions and deal with the resulting (aggregate) transaction quadruple entry. It is then possible to go further by taking the view that two or more different groups of transactions can, in certain circumstances, be expected to occur in association. Then summing the (aggregate) transaction quadruple entries, cell by cell, for these different but associated transactions will produce what we shall term a syndrome entry.

The usefulness of a syndrome entry depends upon two things. First, the association of the transactions involved must be realistic and relevant for the purpose in hand and, second, the construction of a syndrome entry must allow the netting out of cell entries in the underlying (aggregate) transaction quadruple entries, so reducing (often by up to a half) the number of entries to be handled. Given these, the fact that a syndrome entry has the same zero-sum character as the quadruple entries from which it is derived means that we then have a realistic and relevant set of netted out entries which can be used as a building block for conjectural variation exercises in a flow of funds zero-sum matrix table, and one which will maintain the zero-sum condition at all times. The general idea behind syndrome entries is therefore perfectly straightforward, and here we shall set up only one example.

Suppose that one regular type of capital outflow from the UK involves O's reducing trade credit to UK firms, taking out these funds in foreign exchange, and forcing the UK firms to borrow from the banks to replace the withdrawn trade credit. This set of associated transactions can be embodied in a syndrome entry as shown in Tables 5.4 to 5.7.

Table 5.4 shows in four zero-sum matrix tables the four separate (aggregate) transaction quadruple entries involved; each quadruple entry is identified by a superscript (a, b, c, d), and a brief description of the transaction is given below it. The entries in this table are readily interpreted using the purchasing power view introduced in Chapter 1 section 4. The Bk Dep (bank deposit) row has been made larger to take the greater number of entries that fall in it, and outlined for clarity. Table 5.5 shows these four quadruple entries, each still identified by its superscript added cell by cell into a single matrix table, while Table 5.6 shows the same quadruple entries but in outline form and labelled as before. Finally Table 5.7 shows what we shall term the syndrome entry outline, in which the quadruple entries have been summed, cell by cell, netting out many of them and with the remaining ones joined up to form the outline. This syndrome entry outline can easily be linked up with the entries in Table 5.5 and gives an easily recognised pattern to the entries which do not net out; it will have an entry at each corner (but not where the outline simply crosses itself) and these entries will all have the same magnitude, but their signs will alternate corner by corner round the outline (as they do in a quadruple entry). Because of this, the single entry (+10) placed at the top left hand corner of the syndrome entry outline determines all the entries at the other corners.

In our example of a syndrome entry the netting-out process reduces the number of cell entries to be dealt with from sixteen to eight. This netting out occurs in the row recording the medium of exchange and indeed such netting-out is virtually an implicit definition of a medium of exchange. In our example the entries in the bank deposit row all net out to zero; where this is not the case there must have been either a net transfer of a given volume of bank deposits between non-bank sectors or, if there is one net entry in the banking sector column, a change in the volume of bank deposits.

In Tables 5.4 to 5.7 the Banking sector is in the right hand column, and this gives rise to the 'L' shaped element in the syndrome entry outline when financial intermediation through the banks is involved (the 'U' turn picture of financial intermediation given in Chapter 4 section 2 occurring along the foot of the 'L'). In our example there is also a mirror image element of this kind because the Public sector, with its column on the left hand side, acts as a financial intermediary for

ZSF

	Pub	O's	ICC	Bkg	Pub	O's	ICC	Bkg	Pub	O's	ICC	Bkg	Pub	O's	ICC	Bkg
FS																
FA:																
TC		$+10^{a}$	-10^{a}													
Bk. Dep.		-10^{a}	$+10^{a}$		-10^{b}	$+10^{b}$			$+10^{c}$			-10^{c}			-10^{d}	$+10^{d}$
Bk. Loans															$+10^{d}$	-10^{d}
PSD									-10^{c}			$+10^{c}$				
For. Exc.					$+10^{b}$	-10^{b}										

(a) O's withdraws 10 of trade credit (TC) from ICC

(b) O's uses this 10 of sterling to buy foreign exchange (For. Exc) from Pub

(c) Pub uses this 10 of sterling to redeem 10 of public sector debt (PSD) held by Bkg

(d) ICC borrows 10 from Bkg to replace 10 of TC withdrawn by O's

Table 5.4

	Pub	O's	ICC	Bkg
FS				
FA:				
TC		$+10^{a}$	-10^{a}	
		-10^{a}	$+10^{a}$	
Bk. Dep	-10^{b}	$+10^{b}$	-10^{d}	$+10^{d}$
	$+10^{c}$			-10^{c}
Bk. Loans			$+10^{d}$	-10^{d}
PSD	-10^{c}			$+10^{c}$
For. Exc.	$+10^{b}$	-10^{b}		

Table 5.5

Pub	O's	ICC	Bkg

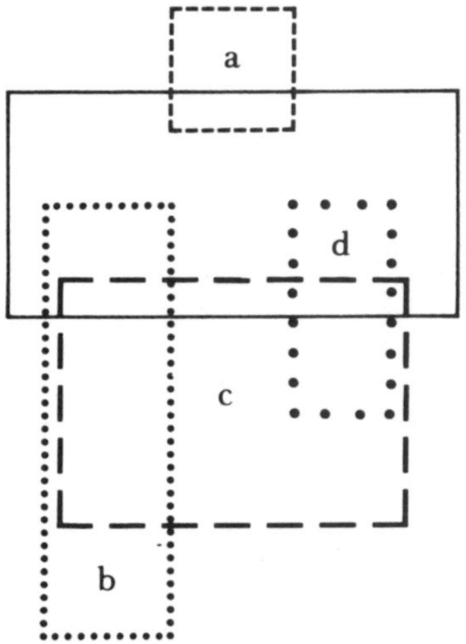

a

d

c

b

Table 5.6

Pub	O's	ICC	Bkg

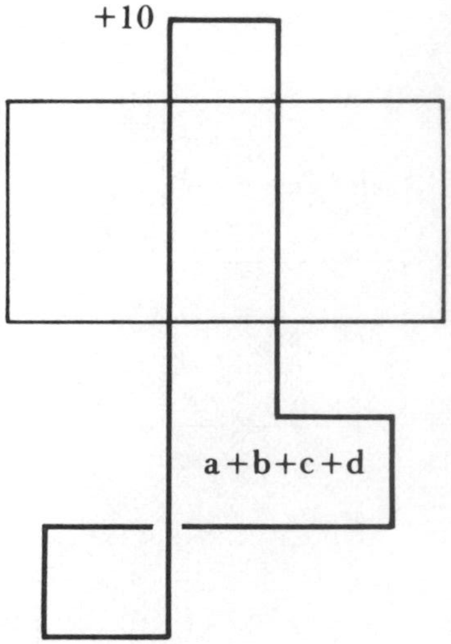

+10

a+b+c+d

Table 5.7

transactions between sterling and foreign exchange. Such patterns can be useful to keep in mind, but it has to be remembered that they depend upon the particular arrangement of rows and columns in the matrix tables used here.

So far we have dealt with a case which involves entries with only a single magnitude; but we would also expect to find more complex associations in which transaction a of magnitude 10 is associated with transaction b_1 of magnitude 4 and b_2 of magnitude 6 and so on. There is no problem in building up the more complex syndrome entries for such cases, but they will require at least one syndrome entry outline for each magnitude involved, and the point may come where the use of syndrome entry outlines shows no advantage over direct use of the pattern of netted-out cell entries.

4 Macro-economic models and the flow of funds matrix table

In a consistent macro-economic model, the events in the model which give rise to entries in the flow of funds matrix table will do so in the form of (composite) quadruple entries; equally, many quadruple entries can (with suitable assumptions) be interpreted as recording events in a macro-model. Here we shall look at some examples which illustrate, at the simplest level, the connections between some macro-models and the flow of funds matrix table.

Tables 5.8 to 5.11 are all flow of funds zero-sum matrix tables, each with sector columns 1 to 5, a financial surplus row (FS) and a financing account (FA) with transaction rows a to h (these row labels being shown only for Table 5.8 but applying across to the other tables also). We assume for convenience that there are only zero error entries and we therefore omit error rows/columns, which allows us to use e for an ordinary transaction row; the Σ rows/columns are omitted to avoid congestion. Each table is assumed to have a full complement of cell entries (the underlying entries) and can be regarded as a (correct) no-change forecast table. Here we take all these underlying entries for granted and put in only the changes in them, which are shown by the quadruple entries we add to the matrix tables. These changes can then be treated either as changes compared with what actually happened last period or what otherwise would have happened in the forecast period.

Our first example is shown in Table 5.8. We assume here a closed multi-sector domestic economy and an ultimate policy aim of reducing expenditure by sector 2. This policy is pursued through the intermediate target of a reduction of x (the policy impact) in sector 2's borrowing along the capital market channel shown by row g in the financing account. In the simplest case we represent the effects of this policy action by the addition of a quadruple entry of magnitude x to the matrix table, with −x falling in the intermediate target cell (heavily outlined) and the other three entries falling in row c and column 5 as shown. There are various fiscal and monetary methods by which this policy impact could be achieved, but here we adopt the convenient simplification that it is done through capital market obstruction (such as control on bank lending, hire purchase control or exchange control) which in the past was regularly used in Britain.

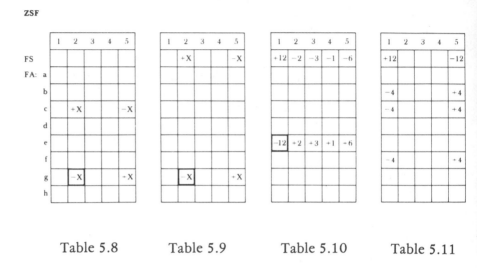

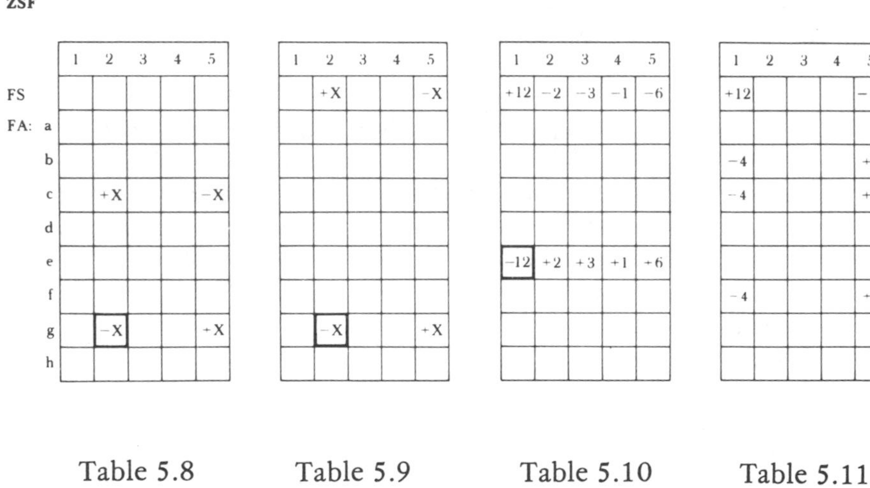

ZSF

	1	2	3	4	5
FS					
FA: a					
b					
c		+X			−X
d					
e					
f					
g		−X			+X
h					

Table 5.8

	1	2	3	4	5
FS		+X			−X
FA: a					
b					
c					
d					
e					
f					
g		−X			+X
h					

Table 5.9

	1	2	3	4	5
FS	+12	−2	−3	−1	−6
FA: a					
b					
c					
d					
e	−12	+2	+3	+1	+6
f					
g					
h					

Table 5.10

	1	2	3	4	5
FS	+12				−12
FA: a					
b	−4				+4
c	−4				+4
d					
e					
f	−4				+4
g					
h					

Table 5.11

How are we to interpret this quadruple entry change? Suppose that along row g sector 2 had been borrowing +100 and sector 5 had been lending the corresponding amount, − 100; the quadruple entry of magnitude x means that sector 2's borrowing is now reduced to 100 − x and sector 5's lending is correspondingly reduced to − 100 + x. Along row c, suppose that sector 2 had been borrowing +50 and sector 5 lending the corresponding amount, − 50; the quadruple entry shows that sector 5 has now increased its lending to − 50 − x and that sector 2 has increased its borrowing correspondingly, + 50 + x. An alternative way of looking at this quadruple entry is to see sector 2 having to repay x of its borrowing along row g (−x), with sector 5 receiving this repayment (+x) and using it along row c to re-lend this amount (−x) to sector 2 which receives it (+x). The economic interpretation of this quadruple entry is that it shows a case of capital market substitution; policy action to reduce borrowing/lending along one capital market channel (row g) has been exactly offset by borrowing/lending along another channel (row c).

If the aim of policy is to reduce the expenditure of sector 2, then this must mean ensuring that the capital market obstruction imposed by policy is not offset in this way. This could be (and was) done by obstructing all of a group of substitute channels simultaneously so that the effect would be forced on to expenditure. This is illustrated in example 2, in Table 5.9, where we assume that row g covers all of a group of substitute capital market channels; for present purposes row g then becomes the only relevant financing account row so that the matrix table in Table 5.9 is effectively reduced to two rows, the FS row and row g.

The economic interpretation of this quadruple entry is that sector 2 is forced to reduce its expenditure on goods and services by x, the amount it can no longer borrow along row g because of the capital market obstruction policy, with a consequent rise in its financial surplus of +x. Sector 5, on the other hand, is prevented from acquiring financial assets of x by lending along row g and instead increases its expenditure on goods and services by x, reducing its financial surplus by this amount.

If we do not specify the initiating change (as we did in example 2) then we could have another example, 2a, by interpreting Table 5.9 as showing a decision by sector 5 to bid up for x more funds in the capital market in order to spend x more on goods and services, 'crowding out' sector 2 (although the mechanism by which this is achieved is not specified) which therefore has to borrow and spend x less. (In this case we do not have to assume that row g has no substitute rows.) This implies that example 2 is the reverse of this 'crowding out' case, in which, as sector 2 is forced to reduce its borrowing and spending by the capital market obstruction policy, sector 5 'floods in' to restore the level of domestic expenditure. Simple monetarist models, which assume that income is rigidly determined by a given money stock in the short run, seem to envisage such 'crowding out' and 'flooding in'. (It should be remembered that if we are assuming the money stock to be given in such a model, the entries in the financing account need to be consistent with this.) These alternative interpretations of a single quadruple entry remind us that *ex post* changes recorded in the flow of funds accounts, or the national income accounts, taken by themselves typically leave open the question of the causal mechanism that is at work.

We now go on to example 3, an elementary Keynesian balance of payments model with a constant exchange rate and constant prices. We assume a capital market obstruction policy which reduces by 12 the entry in the target cell (row e/column 1 in Table 5.10) with the aim of reducing by 12 the expenditure of sector 1, and hence the expenditure of the whole domestic sector, in order to improve the balance of payments on current account with sector 5, the overseas sector. Again, we assume no substitution between row e and any other capital market channel, so that row e is the only relevant financing account row.

When sector 2 finds that it can borrow 12 less than it intended to along row e, it reduces its expenditure which raises its financial surplus/reduces its financial deficit. Part of this fall in expenditure will be on imports from the overseas sector, reducing overseas sector income (but we assume that this and similar falls are too small to have any consequential effects on the exports of domestic sectors). The rest of the fall in sector 2's expenditure will be on its 'imports' from other domestic sectors; this will reduce the income of these other domestic sectors and lead them to reduce their expenditure (but by less than their fall in income) so that their financial surpluses fall. This reduction in expenditure will further reduce imports and domestic sector incomes and so on. This inter-sectoral multiplier process will go on until sector 1 has succeeded in reducing its borrowing along row e by 12 and raising its financial surplus by 12. The financial surpluses of the other domestic sectors will have fallen but by less than the rise in the financial surplus of sector 1, so that the financial surplus of the domestic sector, its balance of payments on current account, will have risen and that of the overseas sector will have fallen correspondingly. In Table 5.10 a numerical example of this outcome is shown by four quadruple entries with magnitudes of 2, 3, 1 and 6, each having the top right negative entry in the FS row for sectors 2, 3, 4 and 5 respectively; the bottom left negative entry in each case falls in the target cell, row e/column 1. For sector 1 the outcome is that imposed by the capital market obstruction policy, -12 in row e and +12 in the FS row; for the rest of the domestic private sector (sectors 2, 3, 4) the FS row entries fall in total by -6, giving a rise in the balance of payments on current account for the whole domestic sector of +6, and a corresponding fall in the FS row entry for the overseas sector, sector 5, of -6.

As in the case of example 2, if we no longer specify the initiating change to be the imposition of a capital market obstruction policy, we can interpret the entries in Table 5.10 in another way, as example 3a. There sector 1 could be the government sector and its +12 entry in the FS row could arise from budgetary policy action (lower government expenditure and/or higher tax revenue) in order to achieve the same objective as before: as improvement in the balance of payments on current account through a reduction in domestic expenditure. The outcome would be the same as before and would occur through the same intersectoral multiplier process. (Here again we need no longer assume that row e has no substitute rows.)

Example 4 is a simple illustration of the 'Godley thesis' (or New Cambridge, as it was often called), put forward several years ago by the

Cambridge Economic Policy Group.[4] It is related to the preceding case of a budgetary change in a Keynesian model (example 3a), but New Cambridge embodied a different view of the behaviour of the UK private sector: it was assumed to run a constant financial surplus. Given the zero sum of the FS row in the matrix table, this immediately implies that a change in the UK government sector financial surplus will change the financial surplus of the whole UK domestic sector by the same amount (compared with only half this amount in example 3a) and cause an equal and opposite change in the financial surplus of the overseas sector. This is illustrated in Table 5.11, with sector 1 as the UK government sector, sector 5 as the overseas sector and sectors 2, 3 and 4 making up the UK private sector. We have simply chosen three quadruple entries of magnitude 4 to model UK budgetary policy action which leads to a rise in the FS of the UK government of +12, a corresponding fall in the FS of overseas and no change in the FS of the private sector. There are no restrictions on the financing account entries, which appear here in three different rows. The conclusion drawn from New Cambridge for policy was that a UK balance of payments on current account target could be most effectively pursued by adjusting the financial surplus of the UK government sector through budgetary policy. The reliability of this policy conclusion depends, of course, upon the stability of the UK private sector financial surplus; in fact it has proved to be much less stable since the early 1970s than it had been over the preceding two decades.

The flow of funds matrix table allows the explicit coverage of transactions which affect the money supply, a strategic variable in most macro-economic models; here we give some examples of this. In Table 5.12 we use a zero-sum matrix table with just two sectors Pub (or government) and Pri (private), and two financing account rows, M′ (money) and Bonds, each of which is the liability of Pub. In its most elementary role, Pub would keep its income and expenditure constant and equal and would simply control M′ by buying bonds from Pri using newly created M′ to pay for them, or the reverse. The first of these is illustrated by the quadruple entry in 5.12 (a). This implies that at some earlier period Pub must have run a deficit financed by bonds, and this is illustrated in 5.12 (b).[5] It also implies that as the mix of M′ and Bonds held by Pri is changed, expenditure by Pub, though constant in amount, will vary in composition between interest payments and other expenditure. Pub could also have run a deficit and financed it by creating money, as illustrated in 5.12 (c). If we were to add in the headnote rows showing S and − I, then in 5.12 (a) we would see the entries for Pub both at a constant and equal absolute level, giving us the zero entry in FS/Pub. As M′ changed, we would expect to see S and − I for Pri changing in the same direction (a symptom of the changes in income

ZSF

	(a) Pub	(a) Pri	(b) Pub	(b) Pri	(c) Pub	(c) Pri
FS			− 2	+ 2	− 2	+ 2
FA: M'	+ 2	− 2			+ 2	− 2
Bonds	− 2	+ 2	+ 2	− 2		

Table 5.12

ZSF

	(a) Pub	(a) Pri	(a) Bkg	(b) Pub	(b) Pri	(b) Bkg	(c) Pub	(c) Pri	(c) Bkg
FS							− 2	+ 2	
FA: Bk dep		− 2	+ 2	− 2		+ 2		− 1	+ 1
Bk loans		+ 2	− 2					+ 1	− 1
Bonds				+ 2		− 2	+ 2	− 2	

Table 5.13

and expenditure caused elsewhere in the model by the change in M′), but they too would remain equal in their absolute levels, giving us the zero entry in FS/Pri.

In Table 5.13 we add a banking sector (Bkg) and have three financing account rows: bank deposits (Bk dep = money = M′), bank loans (Bk loans), and Bonds (the liability of Pub) which can be held by Pri and Bkg.[6] We illustrate an increase in M′ due to a rise in bank loans to Pri in 5.13 (a) and a rise due to the purchase of bonds by Bkg from Pub (a rise in another form of bank lending to Pub) in 5.13 (b). Note that, as in the examples in 5.12, the sign of the entry in the cell in the M′ row, and the column for which M′ is a liability, gives the magnitude and the sign of the change in M′. In 5.13 (c) the entry of magnitude 2 shows Pub running a financial deficit of 2 which has as its counterpart an FS entry of +2 for Pri, and this deficit is financed by sales of Bonds by Pub to Pri. This reduces the ratio of M′ to Bonds for Pri which responds by borrowing 1 from Bkg and holding it as M′ to raise this ratio again.

The examples set out above illustrate the way in which, from a starting situation with its underlying entries, events in a text-book macro-economic model can be recorded by a small number of quadruple entries in a simple flow of funds zero-sum matrix table; at the same time, the use of quadruple entries helps to ensure the consistency of the macro-economic model.

Notes

1 Seasonal adjustment is one form of manipulation of quarterly flow of funds matrix tables, and the Bank of England's method is described very clearly in Bank of England, *United Kingdom flow of funds accounts: 1963-1976*, Part 4. This procedure (after prior adjustments) starts by estimating a set of seasonals for each cell series individually, using conventional methods. The resulting seasonals are unlikely to produce seasonally adjusted cell entries which conform to the row and column constraints required by the matrix tables, and they need to be constrained to do so by a further balancing procedure which is essentially arbitrary.

However, starting from our identification of the flow of funds matrix table as a quadruple entry system, and taking the seasonal pattern we are seeking to be a seasonal pattern in recorded transactions, then it is evident that what we are seeking is a seasonal pattern of quadruple entries. From the start, therefore, we should look for seasonal patterns of quadruple entries, subject to the usual constraints for seasonal adjustment, using a search programme of the type common in operations research. Such an approach would avoid any arbitrary balancing procedure and seems to deserve further investigation.

2 In practice, flow of funds matrix tables contain null cells which cannot contain entries (see Chapter 3, end of section 3), and we therefore have to distinguish between the total number of cells in a zero-sum matrix table (rc), the number of null cells (u), the number of operational cells ($p' = rc - u$) and the number of available cells (a') which can be used for combinatorial calculations like those in our example above. We have already seen that in a matrix table without any null cells ($u = 0$, $p' = rc$) the number of available cells is $a' = (r - 1)(c - 1)$. However, in a matrix table with null cells ($u > 0$, $p' < rc$), for any particular target cell there may be null cells in the target cell row or column (although obviously the target cell itself cannot be a null cell). In this case the null cells in the target cell column (u_c) define null rows and the null cells in the target cell row (u_r) define null columns (both with respect to that particular target cell) in which no cells can be available for combinatorial calculations. The number of available cells is then

$$a' = (r - 1 - u_c)(c - 1 - u_r) - u'$$

where u' is the number of null cells falling outside the target cell row and the null rows and outside the target cell column and the null columns (the total number of null cells being $u = u_r + u_c + u_u + u'$ where u_u is the number of null cells falling in null rows or null columns but outside the target cell row or column).

In a matrix table without null cells there is a simple and regular relationship between a' and rc which holds for any target cell. In a matrix table with null cells, however, this relationship no longer holds and for any rc, while a' will always be smaller than in the preceding case, it is liable to change as the target cell is changed.

The presence of null cells does not affect the process of constructing a complete set of matrix table entries, described in section 1 above. We simply regard a null cell as one which, in a complete matrix table, has a zero entry and the special characteristic that it cannot contain any other entry. During the construction process a null-cell-to-be may at some stage contain a temporary non-zero entry, but when the construction process is completed it will always contain a zero entry and it is only then that its special characteristic as a null cell will apply.

3 It can readily be seen that the trailing entry cell in the matrix table process shown in Table 5.1b in section 1 above is homologous with the target cell shown in Table 5.2 in section 2 above, each receiving one entry from all the quadruple entries used in their respective

cases. However, in the case of section 1, the (r - 1) (c - 1) independent cell entries are the objectives of the successive quadruple entries and the entries in the trailing entry cell are the consequence, while in the case of section 2, the entry in the target cell is the objective of the quadruple entries and the entries in the (r - 1) (c - 1) cells which can accomodate the trailing entries are the consequences.

4 See *The Economist*, 22 March 1975, pp. 30–1; J.A. Bispham, 'The New Cambridge and "Monetarist" criticisms of "conventional" policy-making', *National Institute Economic Review*, Nov 1975, pp. 39–48; Cripps, Fetherston and Godley, 'What is left of "New Cambridge"?', *Economic Policy Review*, March 1976, pp. 46–49.

5 The transactions will use M′, so that this quadruple entry is in fact the sum, cell by cell, of two quadruple entries of magnitude 2, one with entries in the FS and M′ rows, the other with entries in the Bonds and M′ rows; the two pairs of entries in the M′ row cells then both net out to zero.

6 In such a simple model it would seem reasonable for Bkg to act simply as a balance sheet, in which case we would have to constrain the entry in the FS/Bkg cell to be zero. The use of quadruple entries then provides the balance sheet constraint: Δ liabilities $\equiv$ Δ assets.

6 Error entries in the UK flow of funds accounts

1 Error entries: the quadruple entry approach

We can gain some insight into errors in the flow of funds matrix table by looking at them in terms of quadruple entries. Suppose that for a particular period we have a published r × c zero-sum matrix table (which we shall term a realistic matrix table). Conceptually we can regard this realistic zero-sum matrix table as being the cell by cell sum of (1) the correct r × c zero-sum matrix table, which has correct entries in every cell in the identified matrix table (which is shown in Table 6.1, labelled IMT and shaded) and zero entries in the E row and E column, and (2) an r × c zero-sum matrix table of corrupting entries which will have many non-zero entries in the E row and E column.

We now divide quadruple entries into three classes which we label by the number of their cell entries which fall in the identified matrix table (Table 6.2).

Class 1 quadruple entries (illustrated by the x entries in Table 6.2) have one cell entry in the identified matrix table and three in the E row/E column.

Class 2 quadruple entries (illustrated by the y entries in Table 6.2) have two entries in the identified matrix table and two in the E row or two in the E column.

Class 4 quadruple entries (illustrated by the z entries in Table 6.2) have all four entries in the identified matrix table and none in the E row/E column.

It can readily be seen that a class 4 quadruple entry can be expressed as the cell by cell sum of two class 2 quadruple entries or four class 1 quadruple entries, and a class 2 quadruple entry can be expressed as the cell by cell sum of two class 1 quadruple entries.

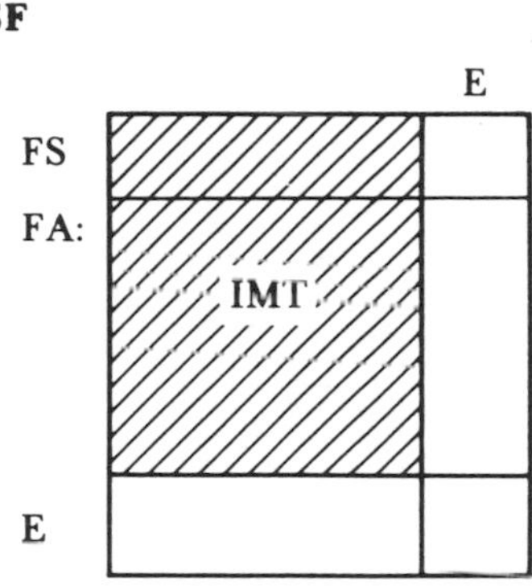

Table 6.1

We have already seen in Chapter 5 section 1 that an r X c zero-sum matrix table can be analysed into, or reproduced by, (r - 1) (c - 1) composite quadruple entries, and that these could be extended or compact quadruple entries. It can now be seen that the extended quadruple entries are class 1 quadruple entries; on the other hand, the compact quadruple entries will have a class dependent upon their location in the matrix table.[1]

Returning now to the realistic, correct and corrupting zero-sum matrix tables introduced above, the correct matrix table contains entries which are the cell by cell sums of the very large number of class 4 quadruple entries which record all transactions in the period; it can in effect be analysed entirely into composite class 4 quadruple entries (from note 1 above it will be seen that this can be done using (r - 2) (c - 2) such entries). It is likely that the corrupting matrix table also can be analysed up to a certain limit into class 4 quadruple entries, leaving the remaining entries to be analysed into class 2 or class 1 quadruple entries. Looking now at the realistic zero-sum matrix table, these class 2 and class 1 corrupting quadruple entries will reveal their presence through the entries they produce in the E row and E column; but the class 4 corrupting quadruple entries produce no symptoms of this kind and we have no means of knowing to what extent they are present in the realistic matrix table.

ZSF

	1	2	3	4	5	E	Σ
FS				+ x		− x	0
FA: a			− z		+ z		0
b	+ y	− y					0
c			+ z		− z		0
E	− y	+ y		− x		+ x	0
Σ	0	0	0	0	0	0	0

Table 6.2

Suppose that our realistic matrix table has a complete set of non-zero entries in the identified matrix table and in the E row and the E column. As we know, the UK matrix table as published has had all the FA row/E column entries reduced to zero by the compilers (see Chapter 3 section 3); let us suppose that this has been done for all these entries except one, shown by +a in Table 6.3 (1). We can see how all these entries are reduced to zero by seeing how this last one is dealt with. Here we shall indicate the quadruple entries we shall use by four a entries, four b entries and four c entries, with the sign of each entry; all of them have the same magnitude.

The +a entry in an FA row and the E column, as in Table 6.3 (1), can be regarded conceptually as having emerged when corrupting quadruple entries were added to the correct matrix table; here, for our convenience we shall have our compilers believe that it was due to a single class 1 corrupting quadruple entry. The compilers expunge the +a entry by adding to the matrix table what they intend to be a correcting quadruple entry; this is the negative image of what they believe (implicitly or explicitly) to be the corrupting quadruple entry, and it is shown by the b entries in 6.3 (2). There we also show where the other a entries were in fact, and we can see that the compilers were mistaken about the location of the two left-hand entries; their two left-hand b entries have simply replaced the two corrupting a entries in the E column by two corrupting b entries in an institutional sector column, leaving us now with two corrupting entries, +b and – a (which have the same magnitude), in the identified matrix table in 6.3 (3) instead of one, – a, before. In practice the compilers would stop at this point. However, if they felt they had sufficient information, they could always decide to go further and remove the entries in the E row. They could aim to remove the whole class 2 corrupting quadruple entry in 6.3 (3) by adding to the matrix table a corresponding correcting quadruple entry c. We assume that they expunge the +a and – b entries in the E row with appropriate c entries, but that they are mistaken about the location of the – a and +b corrupting entries in the identified matrix table (Table 6.3 (4)), so that the other two c entries do not expunge them, but instead add two more corrupting entries into the identified matrix table, making a single class 4 corrupting quadruple entry (Table 6.3 (5)).

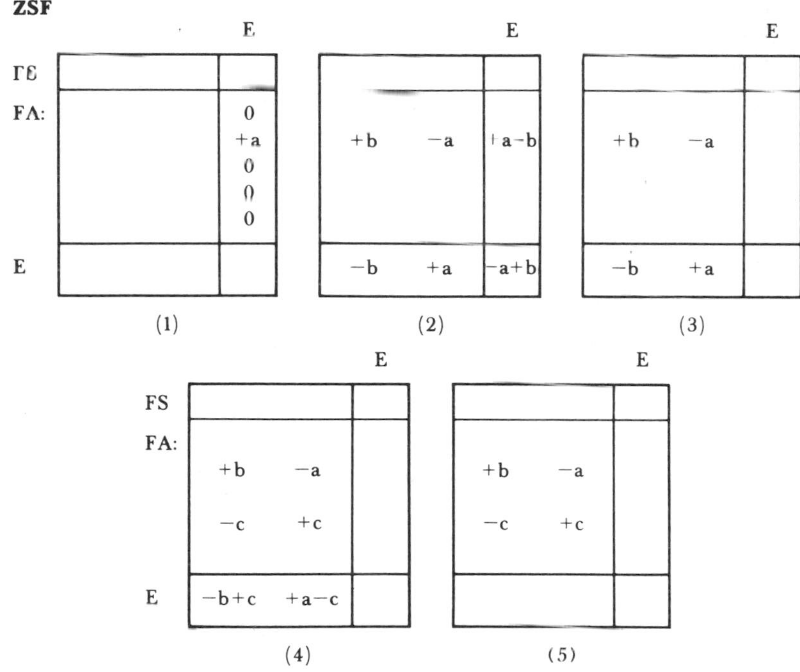

Table 6.3

The conclusion to be drawn from this example is clear. If the compilers, alerted by the presence of error entries, can acquire independent information which enables them to identify the true location of a corrupting quadruple entry and to remove it by adding to the matrix table a corresponding quadruple entry, then this will improve the quality of the entries in the identified matrix table. But if their information is incorrect, the main effect of the intended correcting quadruple entry is to move error entries (or components of error entries) from where they can be seen in the E row and E column as explicit symptoms of errors in the identified matrix table, into the identified matrix table itself where they cannot be seen at all.

The entries in the E row and the E column indicate net corrupting entries in the corresponding columns and rows of the identified matrix table. However, we have every reason to suppose that there will also be mutually offsetting corrupting entries in the identified matrix table, such as those arising from class 4 corrupting entries as illustrated in Table 6.3 (5), which will not reveal themselves in any E entries. The relationship between the gross total of absolute corrupting entries and the absolute net E entries can be clarified in two limiting cases and one intermediate case.

Beginning with the first limiting case, in the identified matrix table, in any transaction row or sector column, if all the corrupting entries $h_1, h_2 \ldots h_n$ have the same sign, then the absolute net error entry $|e|$ will be a correct measure of those corrupting entries:

$$\Sigma \; |h| \;=\; |e| \;>\; 0 \qquad \ldots(1)$$

In the second limiting case, the corrupting entries have different signs, but these entries all net out in the identified matrix table (as in the case of class 4 corrupting entries); the absolute net error entry will then be zero for any sum of the absolute corrupting entries:

$$\Sigma \; |h| \;>\; |e| \;=\; 0 \qquad \ldots(2)$$

In the intermediate case, the corrupting entries have different signs but do not net out in the identified matrix table; the absolute net error entry will then be greater than zero but less than the sum of the absolute corrupting entries:

$$\Sigma \; |h| \;>\; |e| \;>\; 0 \qquad \ldots(3)$$

It will be seen that in a zero-sum presentation of the UK matrix table, case (3) probably describes the situation in the sector columns and the FS row, while case (2) probably describes the situation in the financing account rows.

We have to accept that in transaction rows and sector columns the absolute sums, cell by cell of corrupting entries are, in all but a small number of financing account rows which record official bilateral transactions, virtually certain to exceed, to an unknown degree, the absolute net error entries. However, the net error entries in the E row and the E column are all that is available to us and we therefore have to work with these.

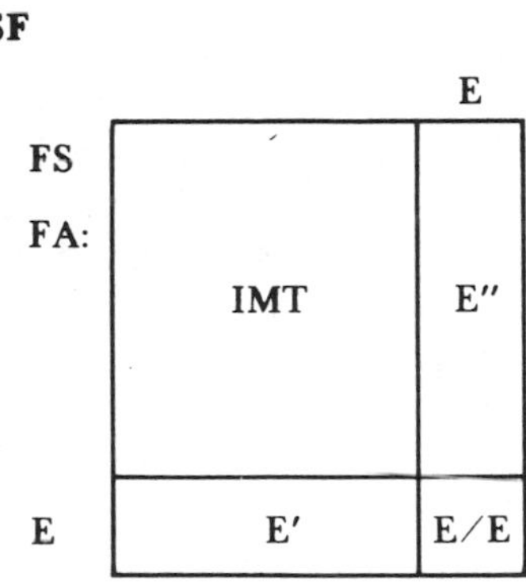

Table 6.4

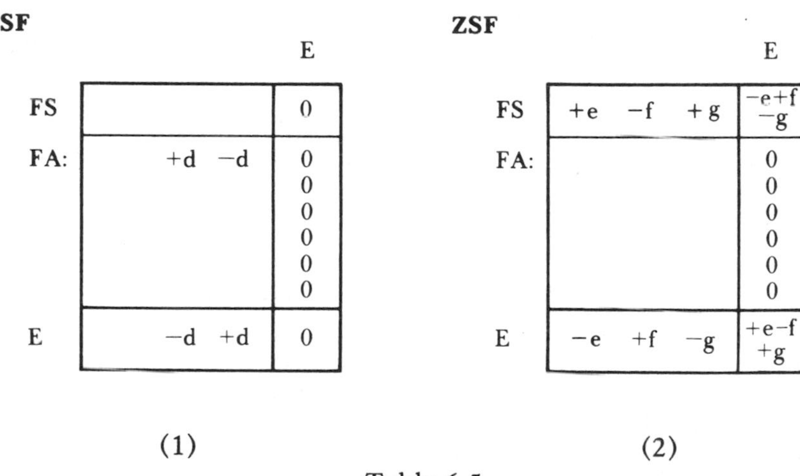

ZSF
E
FS
0
FA:
+d −d
0
0
0
0
0
0
E
−d +d
0
(1)
ZSF
E
FS
+e −f +g
−e+f −g
FA:
0
0
0
0
0
0
E
−e +f −g
+e−f +g
(2)

Table 6.5

We now turn to the question of how to establish some basis for a quantitative measure of the net corrupting entries in the identified matrix table. In Table 6.4 we have a zero-sum matrix table cross-partitioned into four fields. The first is the identified matrix table (IMT); the second is the cell in the E row and the E column (E/E); the third is the E row excluding E/E, which we label E′; the fourth is the E column excluding E/E, which we label E″.[2] Taking the UK matrix table in zero-sum format, the financing account rows are constrained to have zero entries in E″, and this is shown in Table 6.5 (1); there we model two corrupting entries in IMT by a single class 2 quadruple entry. In this case it is clear that the E′ entries taken individually provide an appropriate column by column measure of these net corrupting entries in IMT in terms of the net correcting entries needed to expunge them. Table 6.5 (2) models another case, using three class 1 corrupting quadruple entries of different magnitudes e, f and g, giving three different corrupting entries in IMT with a non-zero sum. Here again, the E′ entries taken individually appear to provide an appropriate measure; however, in 6.5 (1) the corrupting entries in IMT sum to zero, while in 6.5 (2) they do not. We have to take account of this, and we do so by including in our measure of the IMT net corrupting entries not only the E′ entries taken individually, but also the sum of the entries in E″, which in this case consists just of the FS/E cell entry. Using the E′ entries individually and the sum of the E″ entries gives us a measure of the IMT corrupting entries which is consistent for the cases illustrated in both 6.5 (1) and 6.5 (2). In the case of the UK matrix table, where the financing account rows are constrained to have zero entries in E″, more complex cases always reduce to combinations of class 2 and class 1 corrupting quadruple entries of the kind we have in 6.5 (1) and 6.5(2), so that our measure will always be consistent for them also. In the next section we shall make use of this measure of the net corrupting entries present in the IMT.

2 Magnitudes in the UK matrix table 1971–82

It is useful to have a general idea of the magnitudes and characteristic patterns of cell entries in the UK flow of funds matrix table. In Chapter 4 section 2 we were able to bring out the main features for the single year 1980 by taking account only of cell entries above a certain absolute magnitude. Here we shall make a different and more far-reaching simplication; we consider only the financial surplus (FS), identified financing (IF) and error (E) row entries, but for these we cover the twelve years 1971–82. Over this period there was a small amount of real growth in the British economy and a large amount of inflation, so that the figures for successive years are not comparable. Here we have corrected for this by multiplying all entries for each year by a factor which is the ratio of total final expenditure at current market prices (TFEcmp) in 1981 to TFEcmp in the year in question[3] thus roughly standardising all these annual entries on 1981 values. The resulting means of the corrected cell entries for these 12 years are shown in Table 6.6, each with its standard deviation (SD) in parentheses; this table follows the UK matrix table in using the CF presentation, so that in any sector column FS = IF + E. Throughout the rest of this section it will be this corrected data to which we are referring.

UK flow of funds matrix table

Means and SDs of annual data 1971-82, corrected to 1981 values, £bn.

CF

	Pub	Pers	ICC	O's	FC	E
FS	− 10.2	+ 12.8	− 1.5	+ 0.3	− 1.3	0
	(4.3)	(4.4)	(3.9)	(4.3)	(1.0)	(1.4)
IF	− 10.2	+ 14.0	− 2.7	− 0.3	− 0.9	0
	(4.6)	(3.7)	(3.4)	(4.4)	(1.1)	(0)
E	0	− 1.2	+ 1.1	+ 0.6	− 0.4	0
	(0.8)	(2.7)	(2.4)	(2.2)	(1.3)	(1.4)

(Standard deviations shown in parentheses)

Sources: see note 3.

Table 6.6

In Table 6.6 there is quite a clear pattern in the mean and standard deviation entries; to help in identifying this pattern we have the corresponding Table 6.7 which just indicates the matrix table cells and allocates them to three areas. Area 1 contains the FS and IF row entries for Pub and Pers, area 2 contains the FS and IF row entries for ICC and O's and area 3 contains the FS and IF row entries for FC and all the E row and E column entries except the IF/E entry which is excluded altogether because it is constrained to zero in all the underlying matrix tables. Looking at the mean cell entries in Table 6.6, in area 1 these all exceed 10 (£bn being understood throughout the rest of this section) in absolute magnitude while in areas 2 and 3 they are all less than 2.7 (and all but one under 1.5). Looking at the standard deviations, in areas 1 and 2 these all fall within the relatively narrow range of 3.4 to 4.6, while in area 3 they are all under 2.7. We thus have area 1 with high means and high standard deviations, area 2 with low means and high standard deviations and area 3 with low means and low standard deviations.

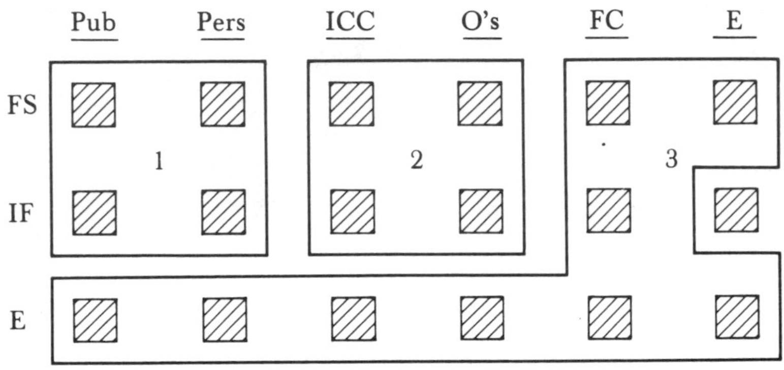

Table 6.7

We turn now to the error entries, which make explicit the mis-matching of the entries in the identified matrix table. Their means and standard deviations are shown in Table 6.6 and all fall in area 3 in Table 6.7. Here we are concerned with the importance of this mis-matching for the interpretation of the entries in the identified matrix table, and this raises a number of problems. Since we are concerned with mis-matching as such, we can deal with the absolute magnitudes of the error entries rather than their numerical values, but we require a yardstick by which to judge the importance of these absolute error entries. One possibility would be, in any sector column, to take the ratio of the absolute E row entry to the absolute FS or IF row entry; the problem here is that the FS and IF row entries can be positive, negative or zero, and as their absolute magnitudes approach zero, this ratio rises without limit and ceases to be helpful for our purposes. An alternative is to look at the matrix table as a whole and take an absolute measure of the E entries, $\Sigma\,|E|$, and express it as a ratio of the sum of the absolute FS row entries in the identified matrix table, $\Sigma\,|FS'|$, or as a ratio of the sum of the absolute IF row entries, $\Sigma\,|IF|$ (which is the same as the sum of the absolute IF row entries in the identified matrix table, since the IF/E entry is always zero).[4]

For our absolute measure of the error entries we go back to the previous section, where we proposed a measure consisting of the E′ entries taken individually plus the sum of the E″ entries. The sum of the E″ entries in the UK matrix table is the FS/E entry, which in absolute terms is equal to the E/E entry (as will be seen from Table 6.5 (2) above). We can therefore have an absolute measure of the error entries which consists of the sum of the absolute entries in E′ plus the absolute entry in E/E; this is the sum of the absolute entries in the whole E row, which we have already labelled $\Sigma\,|E|$.

Table 6.8 gives these variables (from annual matrix tables adjusted to 1981 values, using the sectorisation shown in Table 6.6) for 1971–82, together with the two error ratios derived from them.

The most striking figures in Table 6.8 are the means of the two error ratios (cols 4 and 5) – both in the region of .35 and indicating the very substantial scale of the discrepancies within the identified matrix table over this twelve year period.[5] The calculated standard deviations for both series are around .25, but these are to be regarded as descriptive only, since in fact the two error ratios cannot fall below zero. There is a distinct swing in the error ratios over time; this is due in part to cyclical swings in the dispersion of FS and IF row entries between sectors which is evident in cols 1 and 2, but also to the clear negative correlation between $\Sigma\,|E|$ and both $\Sigma\,|FS'|$ and $\Sigma\,|IF|$ (correlation coefficients of –.62 and –.67 respectively) for which there is no immediately obvious explanation.

3 Some implications of error entries

It is one of the uncomfortable virtues of the flow of funds matrix table that it has error entries which make explicit the internal inconsistencies in the entries in the identified matrix table (IMT). These inconsistencies would simply not be apparent if each of the constituent entries were to be presented in isolation. Here we shall use the example of the UK balance of payments on current account to illustrate some of the implications of such inconsistencies.

In Table 6.9 we set out a minimum zero-sum matrix table which has an IMT with only two rows (FS and IF) and two columns (UK and O′s). In the cells we note the corresponding national income and flow of

Error ratios

	adjusted to 1981 values				
	$\Sigma\lvert FS'\rvert$	$\Sigma\lvert IF\rvert$	$\Sigma\lvert E\rvert$	$\frac{\Sigma\lvert E\rvert}{\Sigma\lvert FS'\rvert}$	$\frac{\Sigma\lvert E\rvert}{\Sigma\lvert IF\rvert}$
	(1)	(2)	(3)	(4)	(5)
1971	14,483	19,776	13,006	.898	.658
1972	16,904	17,802	10,899	.645	.612
1973	25,508	33,260	9,526	.373	.286
1974	51,747	54,608	7,933	.153	.145
1975	43,591	41,370	5,396	.124	.130
1976	38,368	32,360	8,231	.215	.254
1977	24,792	29,450	10,548	.425	.358
1978	29,062	29,338	5,021	.173	.171
1979	32,467	35,342	8,541	.263	.242
1980	37,122	38,404	5,695	.153	.148
1981	35,355	30,708	10,712	.303	.349
1982	24,086	18,018	15,190	.631	.843
mean	31,122	31,703	9,225	.363	.350
SD	10,845	10,503	3,084	.245	.233

Sources: see note 3.

Table 6.8

funds terms; these national income terms have already been introduced in Chapter 2 section 2, see particularly Table 2.1, Treatment 2. In the E row and E column we use BI_{UK} for the balancing item in the UK balance of payments account, BI_0 for the corresponding item in the O's sector column and RE_{UK} for the residual error in the UK national income accounts. We have already seen that the IF/E entry is routinely

ZSF

	UK	O's	E	Σ
FS	$S_{UK} - I_{UK}$	$-(X_{UK} - M_{UK})$	RE_{UK}	0
IF	IF_{UK}	$-IF_{UK}$	0	0
E	BI_{UK}	BI_O	$-RE_{UK}$	0
Σ	0	0	0	0

Table 6.9

adjusted to zero by the compilers of the UK matrix table, so that IF_{UK} is a single term which appears twice (once with a positive sign and once with a negative sign) in the IMT. There are, therefore, three independently estimated entries in the IMT. If these were all correct they would each have the same magnitude and consistent signs, and the error entries would all be zero. But in practice the explicit non-zero error entries warn us that these three independent entries do not agree and that in this minimum IMT we have three different estimates each of which can be treated as an alternative estimate of each of the three independent cell entries. This is illustrated in Table 6.10, which corresponds to Table 6.9 but has example entries in each cell.

Starting with the FS/UK cell in Table 6.10, the direct estimate of that cell entry is + w and it is possible that this is the correct entry. Looking along the FS row shows that the FS/O's entry is - w - 10 and it is possible that *this* is the correct entry, in which case the correct FS/UK entry would be the negative image of this FS/O's entry:

$$FS/UK = - FS/O's = - (- w - 10) = + w + 10$$

Similarly, looking down the UK column, we find that the IF/UK cell has an entry of $- w + 5$ and it is possible that *this* is the correct entry, in which case the correct FS/UK entry would be the negative image of this IF/UK entry:

$$FS/UK = - IF/UK = - (- w + 5) = + w - 5$$

In this way we find ourselves with three alternative estimates of FS/UK:

$$+ w$$
$$+ w + 10$$
$$+ w - 5$$

In a similar way, these three terms with their signs reversed provide alternative estimates of FS/O's and IF/UK.

ZSF

	UK	O's	E	Σ
FS	+ w	− w − 10	+ 10	0
IF	− w + 5	+ w − 5	0	0
E	− 5	+ 15	− 10	0
Σ	0	0	0	0

Table 6.10

It is important to note that the simplicity and symmetry of these results arises first, because in looking at the UK balance of payments on current account we can restrict ourselves to the case of the minimum 2×2 IMT; and second, because we assume that each of these three estimates is equally likely to be correct, and these three are more likely to be correct than any others we might have chosen. It will be seen in the next section that the procedure followed above can be reproduced by manipulation of the matrix table by quadruple entries, and that the latter is the more general procedure.

So far we have made use of some cell entries in the UK sector column. However, in practice the UK flow of funds matrix table does not display a UK column; if we are to look at actual examples of these independent estimates of the UK balance of payments on current account, we have to derive them from the O′s and E column entries which do appear in the matrix table, and we have to ensure that they have signs which are correct for them as estimates of FS/UK. In Table 6.11 we show these three estimates in terms of UK national income and flow of funds definitions (column 1) and in terms of the available O′s and E column entries (column 2). It will be found helpful to relate the terms in rows (1), (2) and (3a) of Table 6.11 back to the corresponding entries in Tables 6.9 and 6.10, and to the three alternative estimates of FS/UK derived earlier. In practice the UK matrix table uses CF signs,

	estimate of FS/UK		matrix table cell entries	
ZSF and CF	$S_{UK} - I_{UK}$	=	$- FS/O's - FS/E$	... (1)
	$X_{UK} - M_{UK}$	=	$- FS/O's$	... (2)
ZSF	IF_{UK}	=	$+ IF/O's$	... (3a)
CF	$+ IF_{UK}$	=	$- IF/O's$	... (3b)

Table 6.11

and while this makes no difference to the terms in the FS row, and therefore in rows (1) and (2) in Table 6.11, it does mean that in order to use data from the UK matrix tables, we have to reverse the signs of row (3a) to produce row (3b).[6]

Using the three alternative estimates of the UK balance of payments in column 2 and rows (1), (2) and (3b) in Table 6.11, we can now produce figures for each of them from the UK CF matrix table. As an example this has been done for the 20 quarters from 1978/1 to 1982/4 and these time series are given in Table 6.12a and plotted in Table 6.12b.

Alternative estimates of the UK balance of payments on current account

CF signs, £ million

	− FS/O's	− IF/O's	− FS/O's − FS/E
1978/1	− 425	+ 350	− 37
2	+ 322	+ 730	+ 1182
3	+ 460	+ 661	+ 247
4	+ 661	+ 1426	+ 746
1979/1	− 917	+ 137	− 67
2	− 179	− 97	+ 1746
3	+ 378	− 11	− 237
4	− 135	− 566	− 325
1980/1	− 333	+ 1052	+ 1373
2	− 212	− 37	+ 2185
3	+ 1190	+ 418	+ 174
4	+ 2284	+ 1590	+ 1407
1981/1	+ 2536	+ 4039	+ 2987
2	+ 1495	+ 1749	+ 3714

3	+ 306	+ 451	+ 341
4	+ 1624	− 2	+ 1296
1982/1	+ 905	+ 304	+ 1867
2	+ 292	− 791	+ 2485
3	+ 707	+ 966	+ 167
4	+ 2044	− 1124	+ 430
mean	+ 650.2	+ 562.3	+ 1084
SD	953.7	1111	1142

X	Y	const	coeff on X	R^2	DW
− FS/O's	− IF/O's	+ 216.3 (.781)	+ .532 (2.18)	.209	1.47
− IF/O's	− FS/O's − FS/E	+ 830.9 (3.13)	+ .450 (2.07)	.192	2.14
− FS/O's	− FS/O's − FS/E	+ 788.4 (2.66)	+ .455 (1.74)	.144	1.90

t-values in parentheses.

Source: CSO, *Financial Statistics*, April 1983, Tables 1.1 and 1.11, not seasonally adjusted.

Table 6.12a

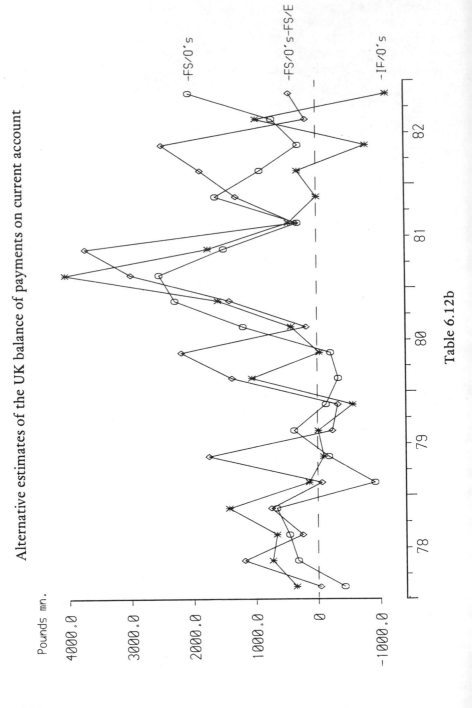

Alternative estimates of the UK balance of payments on current account

Table 6.12b

With three time series we have three possible pairs, and if in each pair we regress one series on the other, we have some indication of how closely the three series move together. These three regression results are shown with the three series in Table 6.12a; clearly the relationship between these three series is not very strong. Looking at the 20 quarters individually, 9 of them include both positive and negative estimates, and the range of the estimates (which shows an upward time trend) exceeds £1bn in 11 quarters and £3bn in 2 quarters. These series are used here to illustrate some of the problems that can arise in the particular case of the UK balance of payments on current account when we have inconsistencies in the IMT entries, reflected in the substantial error entries, and no attempt is made here to provide any interpretation of these results.

It can be claimed that recognising these alternative estimates of the UK balance of payments on current account gives a justifiably blurred picture for the user to act upon or suspend judgement upon. However, one practical limitation to their usefulness is that for those who need to follow the development of the UK economic situation very closely, the flow of funds accounts from which such estimates can be derived have the disadvantage of being available only quarterly with a lag of about four months. It is not surprising that such people are likely to pay more attention to the monthly figures for overseas trade and the balance of payments on current account (which appear with a lag of three to four weeks) because this provides them with much more recent single figure estimates. By the time the flow of funds matrix table has been published for one quarter, all three monthly figures for the UK balance of payments on current account for the following quarter will already have appeared.

4 Error entries: the attribution method

We saw in section 1 above that when error entries are expunged as a matter of course by the compilers of the flow of funds matrix table, there is the danger that instead of correcting the error entries, this may in effect lead to some error entries being concealed in the identified matrix table (IMT). It is quite a different matter if a user, concerned with a particular IMT cell entry and able to see its associated error entries (those in the same row and the same column), has information which gives him some reason to believe that these error entries are due (wholly or partly) to error in that cell entry, rather than to errors in other cell entries in the same row or the same column. Such a user can observe the effects on the particular IMT cell of expunging/attributing these error entries, and should have the chance of judging the results for himself. At least he will then know what is being done to the relevant entries, and this is the case for explicitly showing all error entries and the compilers' own preferred attributions, rather than the current practice of presenting the matrix table only after the (unpublished) error entries for the financing account rows have been attributed by the compilers.

If in a correct zero-sum matrix table we are concerned with a cell in the IMT which has the correct entry +u, then this cell and its associated empty error cells and the empty E/E cell (ignoring all other cells) can be shown as in Table 6.13 (1). If we add into these cells a corrupting quadruple entry of magnitude f with −f falling in the same cell as +u, we then have the situation shown in Table 6.13 (2) where the cell we are concerned with now has the entry +u−f and its two associated error entries are both +f. In this case these two error entries can be simultaneously expunged and attributed to the IMT cell we are concerned with by adding the correcting quadruple entry of magnitude f and with +f falling in the top left-hand cell, restoring the situation in Table 6.13 (1). However, in practice, associated error entries may be of different magnitudes and may have different signs.

Suppose now that we have a realistic zero-sum matrix table with a full complement of entries in the E column which have not yet been expunged/attributed by the compilers, as well as the usual entries in the E row, and that we are concerned with an IMT cell containing the entry +w (Table 6.13 (3)). If we believe that either one or the other of

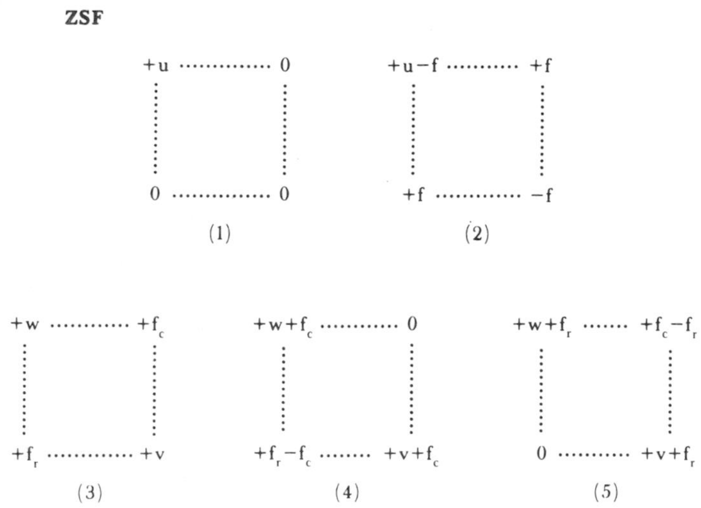

Table 6.13

the associated error entries f_r and f_c could be reflecting error in the +w entry, then we have reason to attribute first one error and then the other to the +w entry to see what effect this has. This is done by adding the appropriate quadruple entry of magnitude f_c to expunge the f_c entry in Table 6.13 (3) and attribute it to the cell with the +w entry, as shown in Table 6.13 (4), and adding a quadruple entry of magnitude f_r to expunge the f_r entry in Table 6.13 (3) and attribute it to the cell with the +w entry, as shown in Table 6.13 (5). This results in two additional estimates of the entry +w, making three in all:

$$+ w$$

$$+ w + f_c$$

$$+ w + f_r$$

Referring back to Table 6.10 and the comments upon it in the preceding section, it will now be seen that the examples there of alternative estimates of the three independent cell entries in the minimum 2 X 2 IMT can be expressed as attribution estimates of the FS/UK, FS/O's and IF/UK cell entries respectively (but see the comments on this below).

For any IMT cell entry, the attribution of one non-zero associated error entry will by definition reduce it to zero but will affect the other associated error entry, as can be seen from Table 6.13 (3), (4) and (5); these cross-effects need to be taken into account in assessing any particular attribution exercise. Here we examine them by means of a simple example: we set f_r at a positive value of 12 and sweep f_c through a series of negative and positive values, attributing first f_c and then f_r at each and looking at the cross-effects on f_r and f_c. The results for certain key values of f_c are shown in Table 6.14, where the left-hand column generalises the relationship between f_c and f_r, and the right-hand pair of columns show the qualitative change in the absolute size of the other error entry arising from the attribution. These results can easily be generalised further, and symmetries and phases can readily be seen; here we note particularly:

(1) if the signs of f_c and f_r are the same, the attribution of the absolutely smaller of the two will reduce the absolute value of the other and will not change its sign;

(2) if the signs of f_c and f_r are the same, there are two critical ratios where $f_c = f_r/2$ and $f_c = 2f_r$; between these ratios attribution of either error entry will cause the absolute value of the other to fall, but the attribution of the larger will cause the sign of the other to change.

ZSF

f_r is positive and:	before attribution f_c	f_r	attr. of	after attribution f_c	f_r	due to attribution f_c	f_r
$f_c < 0$	−12	+12	f_c	0	+24		rises
			f_r	−24	0	rises	
$f_c = 0$	0	+12	f_c	0	+12		const
			f_r	−12	0	rises	
$f_c = f_r/2$	+ 6	+12	f_c	0	+ 6		falls
			f_r	− 6	0	const	
$f_c = f_r$	+12	+12	f_c	0	0		falls
			f_r	0	0	falls	
$f_c = 2f_r$	+24	+12	f_c	0	−12		const
			f_r	+12	0	falls	
$f_c > 2f_r$	+36	+12	f_c	0	−24		rises
			f_r	+24	0	falls	

Table 6.14

So far we have considered only cases of 100 per cent attribution of f_c and f_r. In fact, if f_c and f_r have the same sign, the attribution of the smaller one will fall under (1) above, and it is always possible to attribute only part of the larger one such that the ratio between the smaller one and the attributed part of the larger one falls just within the critical ratios of 1/2 and 2. The partial attribution of the larger one will then fall under (2) above except for the fact that such partial attribution will cause the larger error to fall, but not to zero.

It will be seen that for the particular case of $f_c = 0$ (the case for all financing account rows in the UK flow of funds matrix table), attribution of f_r would always raise the absolute value of f_c; partial attribution of f_r provides no solution in this case. It will also be seen that where f_c and f_r have different signs, attribution always leads to a rise in the absolute value of the other associated error entry.

Conformity to (1) or (2) above provides two possible criteria for the acceptability of the cross-effects of attribution. However, (1) relates to single attributions and (2) relates to pairs of attributions; the two overlap to the extent that some of the single attributions under (1) form part of the pairs of attributions under (2). How rigorously such criteria should be applied is a matter to be judged by the user. In our alternative estimates for FS/UK in the preceding section, our example in Table 6.10 was a case in which f_c and f_r had different signs, and this was also the case in 4 out of 20 quarters for which actual estimates were reported in Table 6.12a, leaving 16 quarters in which single attributions could conform to (1) above, of which 7 conform to (2) above. One possible view is that in the minimum 2 X 2 IMT, the independent cell entries are all valid estimates of the correct entries which all have the same magnitude, and that in this limiting case the attributions which would produce the same estimates must therefore be acceptable, whether or not they conform to our two possible criteria. However, in a normal-sized IMT this highly constrained situation would not exist and our two possible criteria could then reasonably be applied.

The attribution method is a response to the internal inconsistencies in the IMT entries, which are made explicit in the error entries. Whether it is reasonable to apply the method to a particular cell entry in the IMT for a particular period, and the degree of credence to be attached to each of the resulting set of estimates, must depend upon the judgement of the user (including his judgement of the technical consequences of the attribution process).

1 With the E row at the bottom and the E column on the right (their conventional positions) and with the matrix table being adjusted using compact quadruple entries, as illustrated in Appendix 5, Table A5.1b, it will be seen that the compact quadruple entries adjusting the cells in the first r − 2 rows and the first c − 2 columns will have no entries in the E row/E column; these (r − 2)(c − 2) quadruple entries will therefore all be of class 4. The r − 2 rows will be completed by r − 2 quadruple entries and the c − 2 columns will be completed by c − 2 quadruple entries; each of these quadruple entries will have two entries in the E column and the E row respectively, giving (r − 2) + (c − 2) class 2 quadruple entries. There will then be one final quadruple entry to adjust the cell in the penultimate row and the penultimate column, and simultaneously the three corner cells in the E row/E column. This will be a class 1 quadruple entry, giving us altogether:

(a)	(r − 2)(c − 2)	class 4 quadruple entries
(b)	(r − 2) + (c − 2)	class 2 quadruple entries
(c)	1	class 1 quadruple entry.

Multiplying out (a) above and adding together (a), (b) and (c):

$$
\begin{array}{llrrr}
\text{(a)} & rc & -\ 2r & -\ 2c & +\ 4 \\
\text{(b)} & & r & & -\ 2 \\
 & & & c & -\ 2 \\
\text{(c)} & & & & +\ 1 \\
\hline
 & rc & -\ r & -\ c & +\ 1 \\
= & (r-1)(c-1) & & &
\end{array}
$$

which is the number of quadruple entries (compact or extended) required to adjust all the cell entries in an r × c matrix table.

2 Taking Tables 6.2 and 6.4 together, we can say something about the sums of cell entries in each of the four fields of the usual cross-partitioned flow of funds zero-sum matrix table, in which one field is the identified matrix table (IMT). From these two tables it will be seen that, in a zero-sum matrix table, adding a class 4 quadruple entry (such as the z entries) does not alter the sum of cell entries in the IMT field; that adding a class 2 quadruple entry (such as the y

entries) does not alter the sum of cell entries in the IMT field or in the E′ field; but that adding a class 1 quadruple entry (such as the x entries) will alter the sums of cell entries in the IMT and E/E fields each by + x and the sums of cell entries in the E′ and E″ fields each by − x. Since the entries in any zero-sum matrix table can be analysed into, or built up from, (r − 1)(c − 1) class 1 quadruple entries, it is not surprising that the relationship between the sums of entries in the four fields reflect the characteristic relationship between the entries in a class 1 quadruple entry: on one diagonal the sum of entries in the IMT field will equal the single entry in the E/E field, and on the other diagonal the sum of entries in the E′ field will equal the sum of entries in the E″ field; further, all four sums will have the same magnitude, with the signs of the sums on one diagonal being opposite to the signs of the sums on the other diagonal.

Our classification of quadruple entries can readily be generalised so that it can apply to any cross-partitioning of a zero-sum matrix table, with the conventional flow of funds cross-partitioning appearing as a special case:

A class 4 quadruple entry has all four entries in any one field and does not affect the sum of cell entries in that field.

A class 2 quadruple entry has two entries in each of any two adjacent fields, and does not affect the sum of cell entries in either of these fields.

A class 1 quadruple entry has one entry in each of the four fields and affects the sum of cell entries in each of them.

3 The annual TFEcmp series for 1971–81 was taken from CSO, *Economic Trends Annual Supplement 1983*, Table 7, and the figure for 1982 was taken from CSO, *National Income and Expenditure 1983*, Table 1.1. The resulting factors used to multiply the matrix table entries were:

1971	4.448	1977	1.659
1972	4.004	1978	1.466
1973	3.359	1979	1.247
1974	2.799	1980	1.089
1975	2.312	1981	1.000
1976	1.915	1982	0.910

Error ratios

	$\frac{\Sigma\lvert E\rvert}{\Sigma\lvert FS'\rvert}$	$\frac{\Sigma\lvert E\rvert}{\Sigma\lvert IF\rvert}$		$\frac{\Sigma\lvert E\rvert}{\Sigma\lvert FS'\rvert}$	$\frac{\Sigma\lvert E\rvert}{\Sigma\lvert IF\rvert}$
1952	.889	.682	1962	.883	.513
1953	.814	.808	1963	.597	.551
1954	.938	1.261	1964	.474	.350
1955	1.879	1.232	1965	.616	.434
1956	1.015	.801	1966	.531	.365
1957	1.011	.746	1967	.434	.400
1958	1.319	.998	1968	.664	.469
1959	1.152	.950	1969	.817	.469
1960	1.154	.867	1970	.319	.269
1961	.416	.342			

Source: calculated using data from Bank of England, *An introduction to flow of funds accounting: 1952–70.*

Table 6.8a

	const	coeff on time (t-value)	R^2	DW	no of obs
$\frac{\Sigma\lvert E\rvert}{\Sigma\lvert FS'\rvert}$	1.18	−.033 (5.86)**	.542	1.70	31
$\frac{\Sigma\lvert E\rvert}{\Sigma\lvert IF\rvert}$	.919	−.024 (5.15)**	.477	1.01″	31

Table 6.8b

The annual flow of funds matrix tables were taken from the following sources:

1971–76 Bank of England, *United Kingdom flow of funds accounts 1963–76.*

1977,78 *BEQB* June 1980.

1979,80 *BEQB* June 1981.

1981,82 *BEQB* June 1983.

4 Another way would be to express a sector's absolute E row entry as a ratio of the sum of that sector's gross absolute IMT entries (or just its FA entries) or to express $\Sigma|E|$ as a ratio of the sum of all sectors' gross absolute FA entries; these alternative measures have not been explored here.

5 Inspection of the more detailed revision data for 1970 and 1977 made it seem unlikely that there was sufficient regularity in the evolution of the error ratios arising from revisions to the matrix table entries to make it worthwhile standardising our data at a particular point in the revision cycle. However, revision is known to affect the error ratios, sometimes severely (see Appendix 9), so that the annual figures given in this section should be regarded as giving only a broad indication of magnitude.

Annual matrix tables are available back to 1952, and error ratios for the years 1952–70 are given in Table 6.8a. Combining the error ratio series in Tables 6.8 and 6.8a allows us to cover the 31 years 1952–82. A clear downward trend can be seen in both error ratios over this period, and taking an OLS linear regression on time (Table 6.8b) for each series shows that for both of them the t-value of the negative coefficient on time is significant at better than the 1 per cent level (indicated by **); however, the DW figure is poor (indicated by ″) for the second error ratio. No attempt has been made here to test for the stability of the coefficients over sub-periods.

6 For the CSO's reconciliation between the UK balance of payments and the O's sector column in the UK flow of funds matrix table see Appendix 8.

7 Successive revisions in the UK flow of funds accounts

1 The scale of the problem

After the initial publication of the flow of funds matrix table for a particular period, further information continues to accrue and this allows the compilers to revise entries in the matrix table. This process of revision goes on for years and leads to a number of problems for the users of the flow of funds accounts.

Flow of funds data is published each month in CSO, *Financial Statistics,* currently in section 1, Financial accounts. Table 7.1 gives a schematic view of the structure of this data. In the bottom row, the matrix table for quarter A makes its initial appearance in *Financial Statistics* for month 1 and is denoted here by A_1; after months 2 and 3 the matrix table for the next quarter, B, makes its initial appearance in month 4 and is denoted by B_4, followed in due course by C_7 and so on. However, each successive issue of *Financial Statistics* also contains successive further appearances of matrix table data for earlier periods. These we shall call successor matrix tables[1] and each of their entries (which may appear unchanged or revised to a new figure) we shall call successor entries. For any point in time at which a new monthly issue of *Financial Statistics* appears, the successor matrix tables (each with the time subscript for that issue) form a vertical column; this is most clearly seen in the case of the last such column in Table 7.1, which contains A_9, B_9, C_9; every fourth issue, this column of successor matrix tables will be accompanied by a new initial matrix table, as in the case of A_7, B_7, C_7. In due course the successor matrix tables for the earliest period will have appeared in their allotted number of issues; they then cease to appear and from then on this will mark the ceiling for the successive monthly columns of successor matrix tables. The structure of the annual data used here follows the same pattern, *mutatis mutandis.*

By definition revisions cannot appear in the initial matrix tables, but they can appear in all successor matrix tables. The number of potential revisions in the flow of funds data presented in any issue of *Financial Statistics* is therefore given by (1) the number of successor matrix tables that it presents and (2) the number of independently revisable cell entries in each of these successor matrix tables (which will consist of the IMT cells *less* null cells). In the mid-1960's each issue of *Financial Statistics* presented the data for 11 or 12 quarterly successor matrix tables, each with about 130 independently revisable cell entries, making about 18,000 revisable entries per year. By 1983 this had risen by a number of steps to about 20 quarterly successor matrix tables, each containing about 195 independently revisable cell entries and making about 47,000 revisable entries per year. Over the 19 year period 1965–83 this amounts to about 600,000 potentially revisable entries in *Financial Statistics*[2], of which an undetermined proportion were actual revisions.

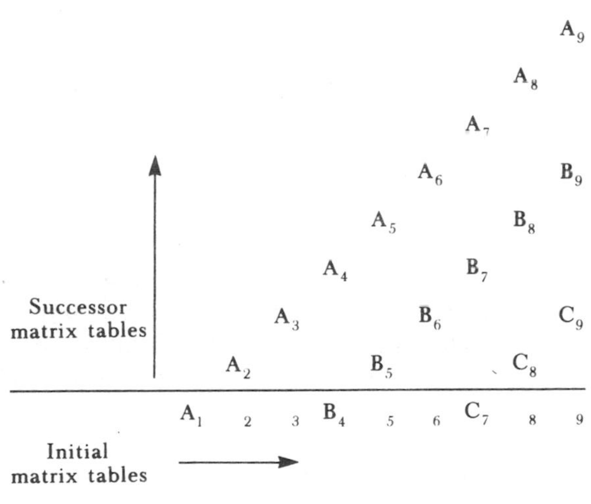

Table 7.1

Dealing with this amount of data would be a major undertaking, and here we shall restrict ourselves to some preliminary and exploratory investigations using only a very small part of it. We shall limit ourselves to the annual matrix tables for just two years: 1970 and 1977. These were chosen because the data for 1970 had just passed through its full cycle of appearances in *Financial Statistics* and *National Income and Expenditure,* and 1977 was then the latest available year which had passed through its full cycle of appearances in *Financial Statistics.* (The full cycle of appearances in the monthly *Financial Statistics* takes just under 5 years and consists of the initial matrix table and 57 or 58 successor matrix tables; in the annual *National Income and Expenditure* it takes 11 years and consists of the initial matrix table and 10 successor matrix tables.) Both these annual matrix tables are used here in the same highly aggregated form: they have IMTs consisting of only two rows (a financial surplus (FS) row and an identified financing (IF) row which is an aggregation of all the financing account rows) and five sector columns (Pub, Pers, ICC, FC and O′s), giving the same 10 IMT cell entries in each matrix table. We do not, of course, know how far 1970 and 1977 are in fact reasonably representative years. Finally, in looking at the revisions to these two annual matrix tables we are looking at the work of economic statisticians who compile the flow of funds figures. They have their own methods and guidelines for revising them and they are subject to the exigencies of time-tables for the production of these and other figures. Here we shall take no cognizance of these aspects; to us the revisions will simply be data which we shall describe and analyse.

We look first at the number of revisions when these two annual matrices were appearing in *Financial Statistics;* Table 7.2 shows the number of successor entries (SUs) for each cell, each of which is a potentially revisable entry, and the number of actual revisions, which we deal with in the form of 'non-zero revision first differences' (RFDs). Overall we have 32 per cent of potential revisions emerging as actual revisions; one noticeable feature is the rise in the percentage of RFDs in the IF row from 32 per cent in 1970 to 53 per cent in 1977 (although perhaps one-tenth of this 53 per cent could be due to the minimum RFD remaining at £1m while money GNP rose threefold between 1970 and 1977)., However, such a result from our two single, highly aggregated IF rows can tell us very little about the proportion of RFDs to SUs in the fully disaggregated financing account rows which are presented in the published matrix tables. Inspection indicates that RFDs are widespread throughout the financing account cells in the first few successor matrix tables, but that later they tend to occur in a much smaller proportion of rows/cells.

Table 7.3 shows the timing of these RFDs and the general tendency for the number to fall over successive 12 month periods in the cycle of successor matrix table presentations in *Financial Statistics;* it should be

Successor entries and revision entries

		Pub	Pers	ICC	FC	O's	Total	%
1970								
FS:	SUs	58	58	58	38	57	269	100
	RFDs	10	13	14	3	14	54	20
IF:	SUs	58	58	58	57	57	288	100
	RFDs	14	24	22	18	15	93	32
1977								
FS:	SUs	58	58	58	57	58	289	100
	RFDs	14	14	14	12	12	66	23
IF:	SUs	57	57	57	57	57	285	100
	RFDs	24	41	34	41	11	151	53
				Total:	SUs		1131	100
					RFDs		364	32

Table 7.2

noted that the last of these periods will contain only 9 or 10 months.

2 Revisions in the identified matrix table entries

We turn now to the revisions themselves. These are most easily appreciated when they are graphed and this is done in Table 7.4 for four (out of ten) cell entries for 1970 and for 1977. The main graphs all have the same horizontal scale, marked from 0 to 60; these indicate

		Month observation numbers					
		1–12	13–24	25–36	37–48	49–	Total
1970							
No of RFDs:	FS	17	12	12	9	4	54
	IF	40	18	15	9	11	93
1977							
No of RFDs	FS	20	17	15	9	5	66
	IF	44	37	27	26	17	151
Total		121	84	69	53	37	364

Table 7.3

the monthly points in time at which *Financial Statistics* appeared, carrying the entries shown. Month 0 is that in which the initial entry appeared (April 1971 for the 1970 data, April 1978 for the 1977 data) and months 1 to 60 are those in which the successor entries appeared; we shall call these the observation numbers of the entries. An RFD appears as a vertical step in the graph at the point where a revised successor entry is published; the RFD takes the observation number of this revised successor entry. The vertical axes may vary greatly in scale and this needs to be kept in mind in interpreting the graphs. For the 1970 cell entries, these graphs have an additional right-hand section showing (on a different horizontal scale, but the same vertical scale) the subsequent successor entries which appeared in the annual *National Income and Expenditure* published in the years shown, until the data for 1970 was dropped from publication after 1981.

A summary of the figures for all our 1970 and 1977 IMT cell entries as they appeared in *Financial Statistics* is given in Table 7.5. For each cell it gives the initial entry, the last successor entry, the change between the two, and the extreme levels reached outside the range set by the initial entry and the last successor entry; where appropriate the relevant observation number is shown in parentheses. The table also shows the mean, standard deviation (SD) and number (n) of the RFDs for each series. This indicates the evolution of our twenty original/successor entry series (which from now on we shall refer to simply as revision series) over their first five years or so; note that the entries are presented with the CF signs they have in *Financial Statistics*. The subsequent successor entries for the 1970 cells as these appeared with CF signs in *National Income and Expenditure* are given in full in Table 7.6.

One way of looking at revision series[3] is to regard them as a source of information about the structure of data revisions. Taking a typical IMT cell, for every period for which that cell has an original entry, it is likely also to have a revision series; from such a set of revision series it may be possible to model the structure of data revisions for that cell and so produce an optimal estimate for each entry in that cell while it is still in the process of revision. A paper by Harvey, McKenzie, Blake and Desai[4] refers to earlier work on the statistical methods which can be used to do this, and extends this work by showing how it can be done with data revisions which appear at irregular intervals (as is the case with the flow of funds accounts).

The key question here is whether the revision series for the flow of funds IMT cells will prove to have a well-determined structure of a kind which will allow this approach to produce useful results. With the limited group of revision series we are looking at here, it is possible to make one tentative step towards seeing if this is likely to be the case. If an individual revision series is to have a structure of this kind, then a necessary condition is that it shows convergence towards some particular level. We can test for this by regressing its absolute RFDs upon time (for which we use their observation numbers) and seeing if they reveal a statistically significant downward trend.

This was done for each of our 1970 and 1977 cells using OLS linear regression (some non-linear forms of estimation were also tried, but these did not appear to show any better performance overall). The results are reported in Table 7.7 (where there is no equation for IF/FC 1970, which has only 3 RFDs). Out of the 19 equations, 14 show the expected negative sign on the coefficient on time. R^2 was very low in all cases and the t-value of the coefficient on time shows that it was significant at the 5 per cent level or better in only two cases, IF/Pub 1977 and IF/ICC 1977, for both of which it was significant at the 1 per cent level (indicated by **). Although the Durbin–Watson figure was satisfactory for most equations, IF/Pub 1977 was one of the two for which it was unsatisfactory (indicated by "). It was also the only equation for which the regression line converged to zero (at observation number 46) within our data period. Out of these 19 equations, this leaves us with only one, that for IF/ICC 1977 (for which the DW figure

Revisions to cell entries

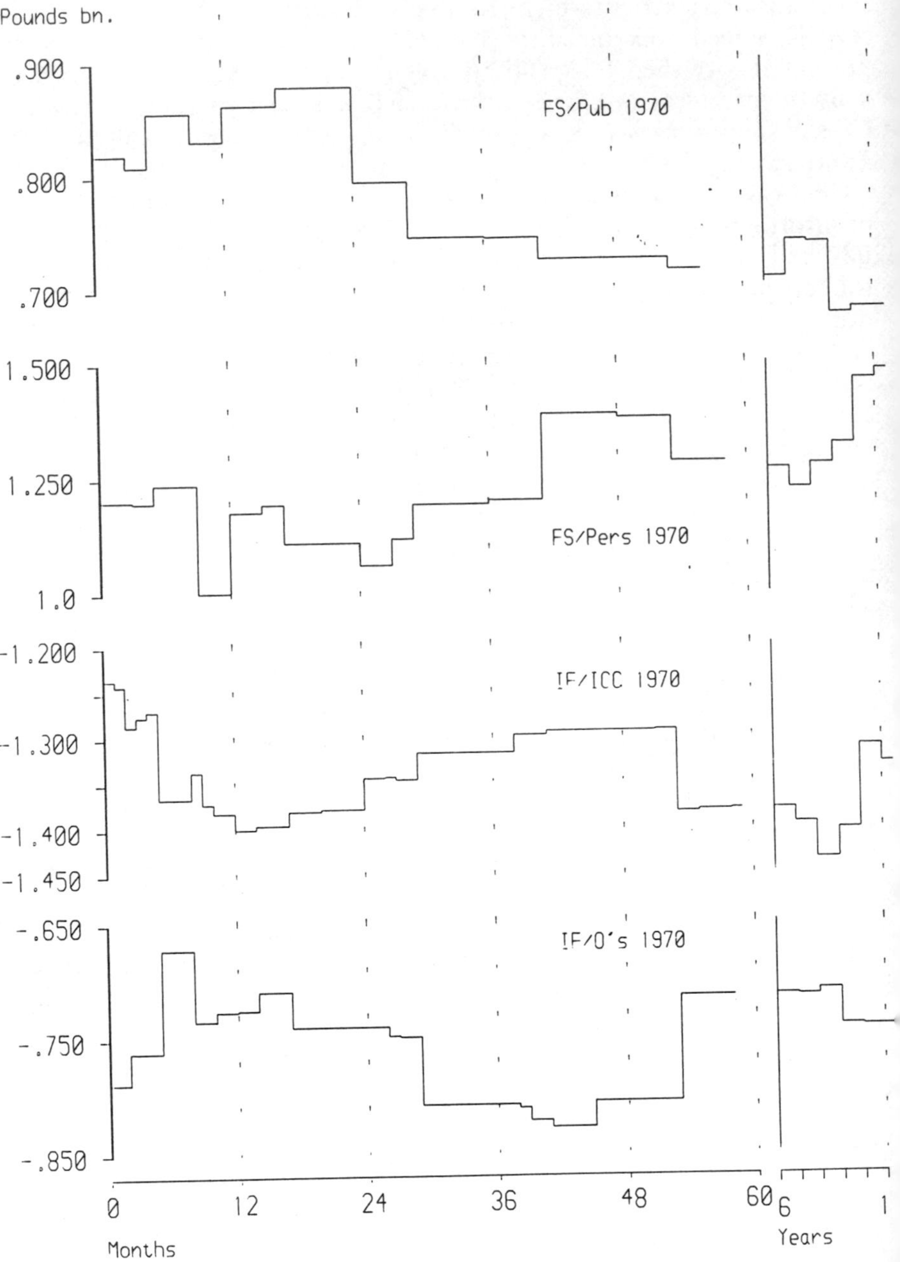

Table 7.4

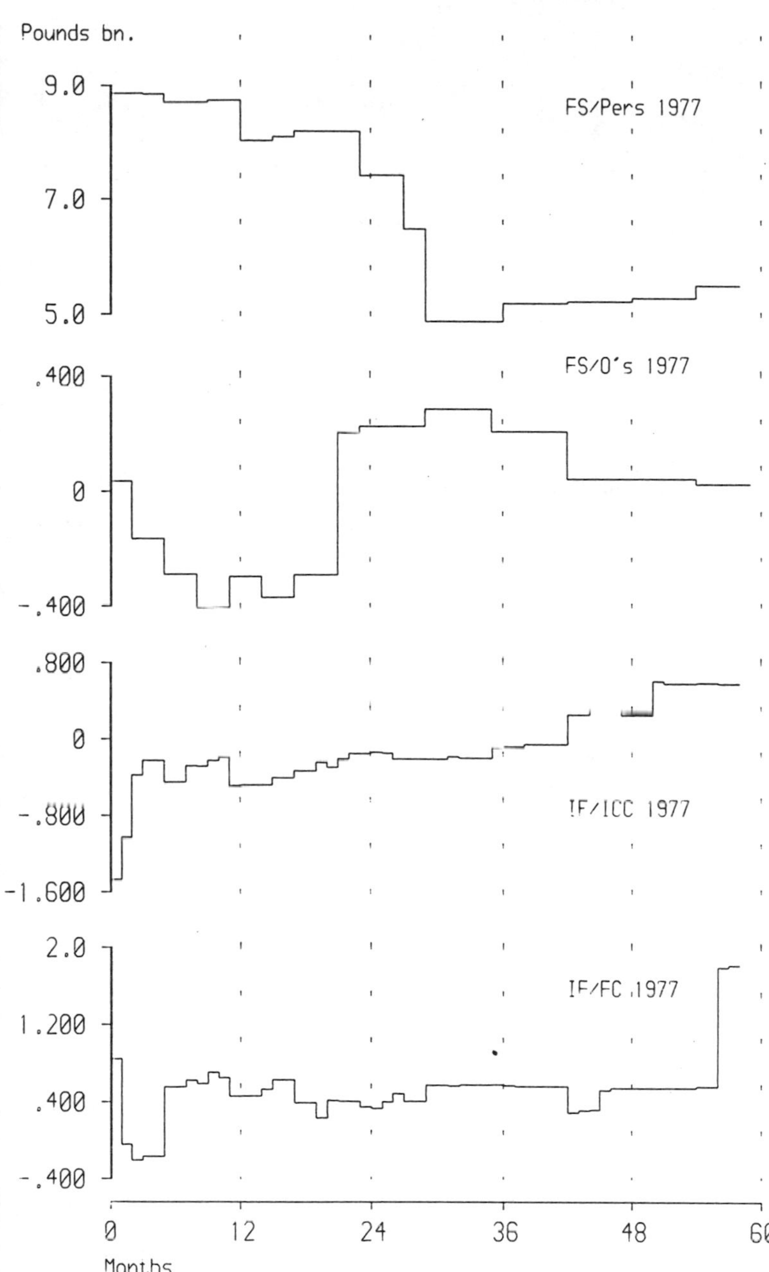

Table 7.4 (cont)

Revisions to cell entries

CF signs, £ million

1970	Initial entry	Last successor entry		Change, initial to last
FS/Pub	+ 819	+ 715	(58)	− 104
Pers	+ 1202	+ 1283	(58)	+ 81
ICC	− 977	− 899	(58)	+ 78
FC	− 245	− 265	(38)	− 20
O's	− 631	− 735	(57)	− 104
IF/Pub	+ 747	+ 727	(58)	− 20
Pers	+ 1677	+ 1736	(58)	+ 59
ICC	− 1236	− 1381	(58)	− 145
FC	− 400	− 362	(57)	+ 38
O's	− 788	− 715	(57)	+ 73
1977				
FS/Pub	− 5688	− 5948	(58)	− 260
Pers	+ 8859	+ 5498	(58)	− 3361
ICC	− 1758	+ 628	(58)	+ 2386
FC	− 1376	+ 430	(57)	+ 1806
O's	+ 35	+ 22	(58)	− 13
IF/Pub	− 5189	− 5695	(57)	− 506
Pers	+ 8376	+ 6492	(57)	− 1884
ICC	− 1471	+ 578	(57)	+ 2049
FC	+ 845	+ 1817	(57)	+ 972
O's	− 2561	− 3192	(57)	− 631

Source: *Financial Statistics*, Apr 1971 – Feb 1976 and Apr 1978 – Feb 1983

Table 7.5

Revisions to cell entries (cont.)

Extreme entries outside range between initial and last		RFDs: mean	SD	n
+ 878 (17)	–	− 10.4	38.0	10
+ 1002 (9)	+ 1387 (41)	+ 6.23	111	13
− 1175 (41)	–	+ 5.57	131	14
− 204 (17)	− 325 (5)	− 6.67	111	3
− 579 (5)	–	− 7.57	26.7	14
–	+ 619 (5)	− 1.43	31.0	14
–	+ 1838 (9)	+ 2.46	31.6	24
–	− 1400 (12)	− 6.6	33.5	22
–	–	+ 2.11	15.9	18
− 828 (41)	− 672 (5)	+ 5.00	43.3	15
− 5627 (12)	–	− 18.6	75.2	14
–	+ 4877 (29)	− 240	551	14
− 2501 (17)	–	+ 170	595	14
− 1454 (3)	–	+ 151	277	12
+ 284 (29)	− 406 (8)	− 1.08	185	12
–	− 5701 (22)	− 21.1	72.2	24
+ 8939 (2)	–	− 46.0	246	41
–	+ 606 (50)	+ 60.3	171	34
− 168 (2)	–	+ 23.7	283	41
–	–	− 57.4	165	11

Table 7.5 (cont)

Revisions to cell entries

CF signs, £ million

	CSO, Financial Statistics	*CSO, National Income and Expenditure* published in:					
	Last successor entry 1	**1976**	**1977**	**1978**	**1979**	**1980**	**1981**
1970							
FS/Pub	+ 715	+ 708	+ 740	+ 738	+ 676	+ 681	+ 681
Pers	+1283	+1267	+1224	+1276	+1320	+1461	+1481
ICC	− 899	− 759	− 515	− 537	− 621	− 541	− 541
FC	− 265	− 392	− 397	− 397	− 312	− 301	− 301
O's	− 735	− 733	− 695	− 731	− 776	− 781	− 823
IF/Pub	+ 727	+ 726	+ 740	+ 742	+ 693	+ 690	+ 684
Pers	+1736	+1756	+1732	+1771	+1786	+1802	+1791
ICC	−1381	−1381	−1397	−1436	−1404	−1313	−1332
FC	− 362	− 387	− 360	− 367	− 334	− 437	− 402
O's	− 715	− 714	− 715	− 710	− 741	− 742	− 742

1 These are entries for Jan 1976 (57) or Feb 1976 (58) except for FS/FC where it is the entry for June 1974 (38); for this latter cell we therefore have two earlier subsequent entries from NIE: Aug 1974, − 328 (40) and Aug 1975, − 339 (52).

Table 7.6

was in the range of uncertainty, indicated by '), which shows a significant downward trend in its RFDs and therefore the significant convergence towards some particular level which is a necessary condition for the successful application of the revision structure approach. Even in this case the estimated convergence is slow, and it is instructive to look back at the actual revision series for IF/ICC 1977 in Table 7.4.

So far we have used revision series covering just under 5 years, which are broadly comparable for 1970 and 1977; but for 1970 we can add to the RFDs used in Table 7.7 the further RFDs from *National Income and Expenditure* up to 1981. If we then re-run our regressions for 1970 we find the following main differences from those reported in Table 7.7: we now have an equation for FS/FC 1970 with a negative coefficient on time, while for FS/O's 1970 and IF/ICC 1970 their previously negative coefficients on time have become positive, but none of these three coefficients is significant at the 5 per cent level; for IF/FC 1970 the coefficient on time remains positive, but from being not significant at the 5 per cent level it has now become significant at the 1 per cent level, with a satisfactory DW figure. Overall, therefore, the ten year revision series for 1970 produces worse results in terms of convergence than did its five year revision series.

All of this represents a very limited and narrowly-based investigation. In particular, each of our IF revision series is an aggregation of all the individual financing account revision series for that sector. A number of these can be seen by casual inspection of the data to have only a few small and early revisions, if any. However, the other financing account revision series do not converge in this way and produce the results seen above for all but one of our aggregate IF revision series.[5]

3 Revisions in the error entries

We turn now from the IMT cells to the error (E) cells in our two annual matrix tables for 1970 and 1977. In the flow of funds matrix table the E entries are determined by the IMT entries, but the revision variability of the latter means that it is of some interest to look at the E cell revision series in their own right. The significant question with the E cell revision series is how far they show a tendency to converge on zero, indicating declining net discrepancies over time between the relevant IMT entries. Various statistical methods were considered for testing this but all presented problems and in the end a straightforward descriptive approach was found to be more effective.

The data on our E entries is summarised in Table 7.8 and covers their cycle of appearances in *Financial Statistics*. There we show all the E row cells for the institutional sector columns, but instead of an E/E cell we show FS/E (the residual error); with the CF signs used in Table 7.8 and with the IF/E entry always zero, the two cells will always have

OLS regression of absolute RFDs (£ million) on observation numbers

	Const	Coeff on time (t-value)	R^2	DW	Absolute RFDs Mean	Absolute RFDs SD[1]	n
1970							
FS/Pub	36.2	−.307 (.590)	.042	2.00	29.2	24.8	10
Pers	86.9	−.303 (.217)	.004	2.21	79.5	75.6	13
ICC	73.4	.938 (.634)	.032	2.45	97.4	84.0	14
FC	n.a.	n.a.	n.a.	n.a.	87.3	25.0	3
O's	24.2	−.234 (.639)	.033	2.34	18.3	20.4	14
IF/Pub	25.8	−.217 (.562)	.026	3.05″	21.6	21.5	14
Pers	25.2	−.278 (.980)	.042	1.90	19.0	25.1	24
ICC	24.3	−.148 (.469)	.011	2.37	20.9	26.7	22
FC	8.71	.146 (.654)	.026	1.15′	11.0	11.3	18
O's	30.9	−.074 (.136)	.001	1.48	29.1	31.5	15
1977							
FS/Pub	86.8	−1.26 (1.46)	.150	2.12	55.7	51.8	14
Pers	314	1.82 (.211)	.004	1.72	359	476	14
ICC	505	−2.95 (.374)	.012	2.29	429	433	14
FC	168	.797 (.172)	.003	2.46	188	251	12
O's	165	−1.70 (.683)	.045	2.56	128	127	12
IF/Pub	83.0	−1.82 (2.34)**	.200	1.19″	45.1	59.6	24
Pers	99.8	.985 (.490)	.006	2.24	12.6	215	41
ICC	185	−3.15 (2.08)**	.119	1.41′	104	148	34
FC	164	−1.23 (.507)	.007	1.91	130	251	41
O's	181	−2.91 (1.31)	.160	1.83	112	131	11

1 Since we are dealing with absolute RFDs, which cannot be negative, the SDs reported here are only descriptive.

Table 7.7

the same entries. The table gives for each revision series the initial entry, the last successor entry, the extreme entries outside the range of the last two, and the mean and SD of the entries, together with the number of observations and the number of RFDs. This gives an indication of the variability of these revision series; it should be noted that E/FC 1970 and FS/E 1970 have a lower number of entries.

The last columns in Table 7.8 summarise the extent to which the revision series for each cell has converged on zero over this cycle of appearances. For each cell we take the initial entry (which can be positive or negative) as 100 per cent and the zero level as 0 per cent. Then taking E/Pers 1970 as an example, this had an initial entry of -475 (£ million being understood here and in what follows) and a last successor entry of -453 (95 per cent of the initial entry), showing that over virtually five years it had only converged from 100 per cent to 95 per cent on its way (hopefully) to 0 per cent; this can be compared with E/Pub 1977 which showed a greater degree of convergence to 51 per cent over almost the same period. The initial entry for E/O's 1970 was +157 (100 per cent) and the last successor entry was -20 (-13 per cent), so that it had overshot zero but in absolute terms finished nearer to zero, so that it overshot/converged. On the other hand E/Pers 1977 had an initial entry of +483 (100 per cent) and a last one of -994 (-206 per cent), so that it overshot zero to a level which in absolute terms was further from zero than it was initially; it had overshot/diverged from zero. Our final example is E/ICC 1970 which had an initial entry of +259 (100 per cent) and a last one of +482 (186 per cent), showing that it had simply diverged from zero. If the initial entry is close to zero, this measure of convergence may be misleading; for this reason it is important to note the actual initial entry, and indeed the actual last successor entry. It will also be seen from Table 7.8 that the path from the initial entry to the last successor entry has been far from steady for most cells.

With these points in mind, we can go one step further by ignoring the signs on the percentages in the last column of the table and taking them in absolute terms as an index of the degree of convergence on zero. The results for the cells for 1977 are generally worse than those for 1970, and in most cases there is a marked dissimilarity between the results for corresponding cells in the two years. Taking the two years together, we have three cells showing the highest degree of convergence (to 10–20 per cent), three converging to around 50–60 per cent, two showing very slight convergence (to 90 per cent and 95 per cent) and four which diverge. Generally the picture is one of individual error entries changing but with little trend overall in either the 1970 or the 1977 entries.[6]

While these figures are comparable for our two years, for 1970 we have

Revisions to error entries

CF signs, £ millions

	Initial entry	Last successor entry	Extreme entries outside range between initial and last; ( ) = obs no		mean	SD	no of entries	no of RFDs	from start of 100%:	
1970										
E/Pub	+ 72	− 12	+ 237 (6)	–	+ 89.3	87.1	59	14	converged/overshot to	− 17%
Pers	− 475	− 453	− 836 (10)	− 390 (45)	− 570	127	59	27	converged to	95%
ICC	+ 259	+ 482	+ 120 (42)	+ 490 (16)	+ 307	111	59	26	diverged to	186%
FC	+ 155	+ 139	+ 176 (18)	+ 31 (13)	+ 119	51.8	39	18	converged to	90%
O's	+ 157	− 20	–	–	+ 91.8	43.1	58	15	converged/overshot to	− 13%
FS/E	− 168	+ 98	− 214 (16)	+ 234 (10)	− 8.02	114	45	11	converged/overshot to	− 58%
1977										
E/Pub	− 499	− 253	–	− 44 (25)	− 208	83.4	58	27	converged to	51%
Pers	+ 483	− 994	+ 688 (10)	− 3352 (30)	− 1510	1422	58	43	overshot/diverged to	− 206%
ICC	− 287	+ 50	− 2346 (23)	+ 236 (49)	− 897	801	58	37	converged/overshot to	− 17%
FC	− 2221	− 1387	–	− 129 (55)	− 934	605	58	42	converged to	62%
O's	+ 2596	+ 3214	+ 2416 (12)	+ 3225 (45)	+ 2975	287	57	14	diverged to	124%
FS/E	− 72	− 630	+ 1200 (9)	–	+ 550	597	59	21	diverged to	875%

Table 7.8

a later set of successor entries, those which appeared in *National Income and Expenditure (NIE)* 1981 when the figures for 1970 appeared there for the last time. These figures, shown in Table 7.9, can be compared with the corresponding ones in Table 7.8 both taking the same initial entry datum points to look at each cell's convergence upon zero. We then see that in the five years or so after the last successor entries in *Financial Statistics,* four of the cells show entries which have just moved further in the same direction as before, taking two nearer to zero (but only to 65 per cent after ten years) and two further away, while the remaining two cells have reversed their previous movements, taking one nearer to zero and one further away. Overall, however, the second five years showed a considerable worsening of the error entries for 1970.[7]

CF signs, £ million

	Fin. Stats. initial entry	*NIE* 1981 last successor entry	convergence from start of 100%:	
E/Pub	+ 72	− 3	overshot/converged to	− 4%
Pers	− 475	− 310	converged to	+ 65%
ICC	+ 259	+ 1035	diverged to	+ 400%
FC	+ 155	+ 101	converged to	+ 65%
O's	+ 157	− 81	overshot/converged to	− 52%
FS/E	− 168	− 742	diverged to	+ 442%

Table 7.9

4 The reliability of the UK flow of funds accounts

In looking at the various aspects of the reliability of the UK flow of funds accounts we have already noted the limitations of our data and procedures, and the consequent reservations about the results; these need to be kept in mind although we shall not repeat them here.

Even when full allowance is made for all the shortcomings, the picture that emerges is fairly clear. It would lead us to expect that the matrix table for a typical year would have discrepancies between the IMT entries which would show up in the form of sizeable error entries which are likely to produce error ratios (see Chapter 6 section 2) of around .3 or .4. Observing the FS and IF entries in the IMT as they are revised over time, we would expect most of them to show no significant convergence to any ultimate level over their first five years in publication. The revisions in the IMT cell entries lead to revisions in the error entries; but while some error cell entries would converge on zero, others would diverge and overall we would expect to see no clear pattern. As they are revised over their first five years in publication, therefore, we would expect to see FS, IF and E entries which drift and lurch about to a significant degree but in an apparently haphazard way. Looking at them over their second five years in publication, we would expect to see some further deterioration in terms of the error ratios.

It can readily be seen that sizeable error entries and instability due to revisions can cause real problems if we are using the matrix table figures for the direct description of events or for simple flow of funds studies. Their effects on macro-econometric models must also be adverse, but it would require specific investigation to see how significant this is. However, it is worth noting that, for the United States, Laurence Klein has pinpointed 'big data revisions' as one of the major technical reasons for the poor performance of econometric forecasts.[8]

Notes

1 In fact this successor matrix table data for each quarter appears in sector table form, but such data can readily be re-arranged into matrix tables and for convenience we shall refer to them as matrix tables.

2 This estimate does not include any annual successor matrix tables, whether or not they overlap the quarterly data, nor does it include the seasonally adjusted FS row data which may be subject to additional revisions arising from revision of the seasonal factors. Obviously it excludes the seasonally adjusted financing account data which appears regularly in *BEQB*, and the longer runs of annual successor matrix table data which appears in *NIE* annually.

3 It is important to note that although a revision series may look like an ordinary time series (as in Table 7.4, for example) it is in fact very different. This can be seen from Table 7.1; for ease of exposition, here we shall treat each term in that table as if it were a

single data observation rather than a matrix table of observations. A time series not subject to revision (as in the case of interest rates or exchange rates) would consist of the horizontal series A_1, B_4, C_7 ...; a time series subject to revision would normally consist of the latest successor entry for each observation, namely the vertical series A_9, B_9, C_9... . In these two cases each series is a run of simultaneously valid data observations. But a revision series (for example, the diagonal series A_1, A_2, A_3...) is not a series of simultaneously valid data observations because A_1 will have been superseded and replaced by A_2, which in turn will have been superseded and replaced by A_3, and so on.

4 'Irregular data revisions' by A.C. Harvey, C.R. McKenzie, D.P.C. Blake and M.J. Desai in A. Zellner (ed), *Applied Time Series Analysis of Economic Data,* Washington, Bureau of the Census (1983), pp. 329–50.

5 One would expect the CSO's reliability gradings for the (strictly, quarterly) IMT cell entries (see Chapter 3 section 3, particularly Table 3.6a) to be inversely related to the incidence of revisions. It is those rows whose entries all have the highest grading, shown in Table 3.6b above as those with our highest quantified reliability grading (which is 4), which casual inspection shows to have few and small revisions, if any; however, we have not gone any further in investigating this relationship.

6 The sum of absolute error entries for 1970 fell by about 6 per cent and that for 1977 rose by 6 per cent. See also Appendix 9.

7 See Appendix 9.

8 This is quoted from section 1 of the paper by Harvey et al; see note 4 above.

Appendices

Appendix 1
UK flow of funds matrix table: current presentations

Flow of funds: annual matrix 1982

£ millions

	Line	Central government	Local authorities	Public corporations	Public sector	Monetary sector	Other financial institutions	Industrial and commercial companies	Personal sector	Overseas sector	Residual error
Capital account											
Saving	1	– 3,256	+4,011	+5,683	+ 6,438		+3,970	+16,050	+22,004	– 3,948	
Taxes on capital and capital transfers	2	– 1,157	– 44	+ 572	– 629		– 403	+ 598	+ 434	—	
less:											
Gross fixed-capital formation at home	3	– 2,101	–1,823	–7,368	–11,292		–5,600	–15,554	– 9,211		
Increase in value of stocks and work in progress	4	– 214		–1,037	– 1,251		+ 31	– 443	– 193		
Financial surplus + /deficit –	5	**– 6,728**	**+2,144**	**–2,150**	**– 6,734**		**–2,002**	**+ 651**	**+13,034**	**– 3,948**	**– 1,001**
Changes in financial assets and liabilities											
Assets: increase + /decrease –											
Liabilities: increase – /decrease +											
Notes and coin	6	– 463		—	– 463	– 9	—	+ 278	+ 194	—	
Market Treasury bills	7	+ 359		– 13	+ 346	– 561	+ 2	+ 81		+ 132	
British government securities	8	– 6,457	+ 2	+ 21	– 6,434	– 147	+ 5,374	+ 201	+ 542	+ 464	
National savings	9	– 3,536	+ 1	– 56	– 3,591		+ 13	+ 220	+ 3,358		
Tax instruments	10	– 1,360		+ 347	– 1,013	– 31	– 23	+ 1,049	+ 18		
Net government indebtedness to Banking Department	11	– 156			– 156	+ 156					
Northern Ireland central government debt	12	– 19			– 19	+ 3	—	—	+ 16		
Government liabilities under exchange cover scheme	13	+ 68	– 1	– 67	—						
Other non-marketable government debt	14	+ 192		—	+ 192	– 192	—				
Issue Department's transactions in commercial bills	15	+ 4,714			+ 4,714			– 4,714			
Government foreign currency debt	16	+ 163			+ 163	—				– 163	
Other government overseas financing	17	+ 202			+ 202					– 202	
Official reserves	18	– 1,421			– 1,421					+ 1,421	

Local authority debt:											
Temporary	19.1	+ 19	+1,437	+ 91	+ 1,547	− 638	− 439	− 234	− 220	− 16	
Foreign currency	19.2		− 56		− 56	—	—			+ 56	
Other listed securities	19.3	—	+ 167	+ 2	− 169	− 173	+ 158		− 161	+ 7	
Other long-term	19.4	+ 1,388	− 1,231	− 4	− 153	− 618	+ 420	− 34	+ 80	− 1	
Public corporation debt:											
Foreign currency	20.1			+ 16[illegible]	+ 169	− 52	—			− 117	
Other	20.2	+ 2,352	− 20	−2,25[illegible]	+ 77	− 3	− 4	—	—	− 70	
Deposits with banks:											
Sterling sight	21.1	− 101	+ 74	+ 3[illegible]	+ 8	− 4,187	+ 857	+ 509	+ 2,127	+ 686	
Sterling time	21.2	+ 21	+ 446	+ 3[illegible]	+ 498	− [illegible],874	+ 1,958	+ 92	+ 1,516	+ 3,81[illegible]	
Foreign currency	21.3	+ 35	+ 6	− 3	+ 38	−20,403	− 224	+ 1,033	+ 193	+19,36[illegible]	
Deposits with building societies	22						−10,154	+ 88	+10,059	+ [illegible]	
Bank lending (excluding public sector):											
Foreign currency	24.1					+17,785	− 894	− 611	− 213	−16,067	
Sterling	24.2					+11,747	− 913	− 1,940	− 4,860	− 4,034	
Credit extended by retailers	25			− 3	− 3			+ 112	− 109		
Identified trade credit:											
Public corporations (domestic)	26.1			+ 7[illegible]8	+ 738			− 710	− 28		
Import and export	26.2	− 462		+ [illegible]0	− 372		—	+ 228		+ 144	
Loans for house purchase:											
Building societies	27.1						+ 7,855		− 7,855		
Other	27.2	—	− 541	+ 3[illegible]5	− 866	+ 5,041	+ 161		− 6,068		
Other public sector lending	28	+ 538	—	+ [illegible]78	+ 616		—	− 374	− 27	− 2[illegible]5	
Other lending by financial institutions	29			—	—		+ 427	− 267	− 160		
Unit trust units	30						− 177		+ 177		
UK company securities	31	− 380		+ 76	− 304	− 791	+ 2,892	− 307	− 1,963	+ 473	
Overseas securities	32	—		—	—	+ 2,173	+ 4,008	+ 1,104	− [illegible]35	− 7,150	
Life assurance and pension funds	33	− 132			− 132		−13,090		+13,222		
Miscellaneous domestic instruments	34	—		—	—	—	+ 6	− 5	− 1	—	
Direct and other investment abroad	35					− 3	+ 73	+ 2,794		− 2,864	
Overseas direct and other investment in United Kingdom	36					− 129	− 129	− 2,586		+ 2,844	
Miscellaneous overseas instruments	37	− 465		+ 32	− 43[illegible]		− 27	− 1,166		+ 1,626	
Accruals adjustment	38	− 1,075	+ 90	+ 131	− 85[illegible]	− 14	+ 72	+ 732	+ 64		
Financial transactions	39	**− 5,976**	**+1,456**	**− 235**	**− 4,7[illegible]5**	**+ 1,080**	**− 1,798**	**− 4,427**	**+ 9,766**	**+ 134**	
Unidentified	40	− 752	+ 688	−[illegible],915	− 1,9[illegible]9	−1,284		+ 5,078	+ 3,268	− 4,082	−1,001

— nil or less than £½ million.

Source: *Bank of England Quarterly Bulletin* June 1983 p. 252 (this is the presentation termed here OP (BE), see Chapter 2 section 2).

Table A1.1

13.2 Financial transactions[1] Analysis by sector and type of asset, 1982

£ million

	Private sector					Public sector			
			Financial institutions						
	Personal sector	Industrial and commercial companies	Monetary	Life assurance and superannuation funds	Other	Public corporations	Central government	Local authorities	Overseas sector
CAPITAL ACCOUNT									
Saving	20 174	17 653	2 758	-	3 623	5 891	-3 412	3 608	-5 428
Capital transfers (net receipts)	521	584	-100	-	-339	527	-1 055	-138	-
less Gross domestic fixed capital formation	9 963	14 723	544	1 709	3 552	7 221	2 134	2 326	-
less Increase in value of stocks and work in progress	445	1 257	-55	-	-	918	180	-	-
Financial surplus or deficit[3]	10 287	2 257	2 169	-1 709	-268	-1 721	-6 781	1 144	-5 428
FINANCIAL TRANSACTIONS ACCOUNT									
Notes and coin	625	-160	-9	-	-	-	-463	-	7
Market treasury bills	-	82	-561	-	1	-13	359	-	132
British government securities	820	238	-147	3 122	1 938	21	-6 457	2	463
National savings	3 445	114	-	7	7	-3	-3 571	1	-
Tax instruments	18	1 049	-31	-	-23	347	-1 360	-	-
Net government indebtedness to Banking Department	-	-	156	-	-	-	-156	-	-
Northern Ireland central government debt	20	-	3	-	-4	-	-19	-	-
Government liabilities under exchange cover scheme	-	-	-	-	-	-67	68	-1	-
Other non-marketable debt	-	-	-192	-	-	24	168	-	-
Issue Department's transactions in commercial bills	-	-4 714	-	-	-	-	4 714	-	-
Government foreign currency debt	-	-	-	-	-	-	278	-	-278
Other government overseas financing	-	-	-	-	-	-	87	-	-87
Official reserves	-	-	-	-	-	-	-1 421	-	1 421
Local authority debt:									
Temporary	-454	-234	-638	66	-513	91	251	1 437	-16
Foreign currency	-	-	-	-	-	-	-	-58	58
Sterling securities	-	-	-173	-11	142	2	-242	167	-
Other sterling debt	264	-34	-618	46	346	-4	1 352	-1 229	-8

Public corporations debt									
Foreign currency	-	-	-52	-	-	169	-	-	-117
Sterling	-1	-	-3	-4	-5	-2 241	2 391	-66	-71
Deposits with monetary sector									
Sterling sight	2 302	359	-4 362			35	-101	74	686
Sterling time	1 343	89	-7 685	640	2 120	38	21	446	3 791
Foreign currency	204	1 073	-21 001			-2	36	6	19 888
Deposits with building societies	10 059	88	-	121	-10 275	-	-	-	7
Deposits with other financial institutions	-	-	-	-	-	-	-	-	-
Bank lending (excluding public sector)									
Foreign currency	-214	-633	18 428			-	-	-	-16 673
Sterling	-4 843	-959	11 750	-348	-2 474	-	-	-	-4 034
Credit extended by retailers	-109	112	-	-	-	-3	-	-	-
Identified trade credit									
Domestic	-28	-579	-	-	-28	614	21	-	-
Import and export	-	205	-	-	-	75	-478	-	198
Loans for house purchase									
Building societies	-7 841	-14	-	-	7 855	-	-	-	-
Other	-6 074	-	5 041	118	43	324	-	548	-
Other public sector lending	7	-123	-	-	-	78	269	-	-231
Other lending by financial institutions	-180	-209	-	101	288	-	-	-	-
Unit trust units	177	-	-	302	-479	-	-	-	-
United Kingdom company securities	-2 422	409	-791	3 309	-391	76	-380	-	190
Overseas securities	175	770	2 205	3 047	1 045	-	-	-	-7 242
Life assurance and pension funds	12 938	-	-	-12 803	-	-	-135	-	-
Miscellaneous domestic instruments	23	-244	-	387	-166	-	-	-	-
Direct and other investment abroad	-	3 470	-3	-	68	-	-	-	-3 535
Overseas direct and other investment in the United Kingdom	-	-2 639	-129	-	-181	-	-	-	2 949
Miscellaneous overseas instruments	-	-1 601	-	9	1 067	27	-437	-	935
Accruals adjustment	159	1 402	-1	349	-211	95	-1 774	-19	-
Total financial transactions	10 413	-2 683	1 187	-1 542	170	-317	-6 969	1 308	-1 567
BALANCING ITEM[4]	-126	4 940	982	-167	-438	-1 404	188	-164	-3 861[5]

1 Acquisition of assets or reduction in liabilities is shown positive; sale of assets or increase in liabilities negative.
2 Before providing for depreciation, stock appreciation and additions to tax reserves.
3 The sum of the entries in this row equals, apart from the change in sign, the Residual error shown in table 1.2.
4 A sector analysis of balancing items in other years is given on page 93.
5 The Balancing item in the balance of payments accounts.

Source: CSO, *National Income and Expenditure* 1983 p. 31 (this is the presentation termed here OP (NIE), see Chapter 2 section 2).

Table A1.2

Appendix 2

UK flow of funds matrix table: row headings of earlier presentations

	Line
Capital account	
Saving	1
Taxes on capital and capital transfers	2
less:	
Gross fixed-capital formation at home	3
Increase in value of stocks and work in progress	4
Financial surplus + /deficit – (b)	5
Changes in financial assets and liabilities	
Assets: increase + /decrease –	
Liabilities: increase – /decrease +	
Government debt to Banking Department	6
Life assurance and pension funds	7
Loans by the UK Government	8
Central government external transactions:	
Direct official financing	9.1
Other	9.2
Other public sector direct official financing	9.3
Banks' net external transactions (excluding securities):	
Borrowing for official financing	10.1
Other	10.2
Miscellaneous investment overseas (net)	11
Notes and coin	12
Bank deposits of domestic sectors	13
Deposits with other financial institutions	14
National savings	15.1
Tax instruments	15.2
Bank lending to domestic sectors	16
Instalment lending by retailers	17
Loans for house purchase	18
Other loans and accruals	19
Marketable government debt held by domestic sectors:	
Treasury bills	20
Stocks	21
Other local authority debt	22
UK company and overseas securities:	
Capital issues	23
Other transactions	24
Unit trust units	25
Identified financial transactions	26
Unidentified(b)	27
Total = financial surplus + /deficit – (b)	28

Source: *Bank of England Quarterly Bulletin* June 1980 p. 186 (these are the row headings from the presentation termed here BEP, see Chapter 2 section 2).

Table A2.1

Capital account

Savings[2]
Capital transfers (net receipts)
less Gross domestic fixed capital formation
less Increase in value of stocks and work in progress

Net acquisition of financial assets[3]

Financial transactions account

Notes and coin
Market Treasury bills
British government and government guaranteed securities
National savings:
  Deposits
  Certificates and bonds
Tax instruments
Net government indebtedness to Bank of England, Banking Department
Northern Ireland central government debt
Local authority debt:
  Temporary borrowing
  Listed securities and negotiable bonds
  Other long-term borrowing
Deposits with banking sector
Deposits with savings banks
Deposits with building societies
Deposits with finance houses
Deposits with other financial institutions
Banking lending (except general government):
  Advances and loans
  Commercial bills
  Market loans
Credit extended by retailers
Identified trade credit (net)
Loans for house purchase
Transactions in commercial bills by Issue Department, Bank of England
Other loans by public sector to private sector
Loans by superannuation funds to parent organisation
Other loans and mortgages by financial institutions (excluding banks)
Unit trust units
Company and overseas securities:
  United Kingdom capital issues
  Capital issues overseas
  Other
Funds of life assurance and superannuation schemes
Other identified home assets
Allocation of Special Drawing Rights
Official reserves
Inter-government loans (net)
Transactions with IMF, etc.
Refinanced export and shipbuilding credits
Intra-company investment by UK companies overseas
Intra-company investment by overseas companies in the UK
Other identified overseas assets
Accruals adjustment

Total identified financial assets

Unidentified items[3]

Net acquisition of financial assets[1 3]

Source: CSO, *National Income and Expenditure* 1980 p. 91 (these are the row headings from the presentation termed here CSOP (NIE), see Chapter 2 section 2).

Table A2.2

Appendix 3

The United States flow of funds matrix table. (Chapter 2 section 1)

The United States was the first country to publish flow of funds accounts, and a very clear and useful introduction to these, together with a bibliography, is given in Board of Governors of the Federal Reserve System, *Introduction to Flow of Funds* (June 1980). In Appendix Table S.1 this gives an annual matrix table for the US, shown here in Table A3.1, and it is instructive to make a brief comparison between this and the corresponding presentation for the UK given in Appendix 1 and looked at in some detail in Chapters 2 and 3.

The most striking difference between the UK and US presentations is that in the UK accounts each sector has a single column of net cell entries, while in the US accounts each sector has its entries in two sub-columns headed U (Uses of funds, or payments) and S (Sources of funds, or receipts) respectively, so that in place of single net cells, the US matrix table has pairs of sub-cells. An easy way of looking at these sub-columns in the financing account rows is to regard them as being derived from balance sheet assets (A) and liabilities (L) columns respectively (US balance sheets being set out in the opposite order from the L/A presentation used in the UK). Changes in assets are then defined as being uses of funds and changes in liabilities as being sources of funds:

$$U \equiv \Delta A \qquad \text{... (1)}$$

$$S \equiv \Delta L \qquad \text{... (2)}$$

There are certain conventions (some of which are noted below) about placing particular types of entry in the U or S sub-columns, and both sub-columns can contain negative as well as positive entries.

Just as liabilities can be regarded as negative assets, so sources of funds can be regarded as negative uses of funds. For any sector the U and S sub-columns can be collapsed into a single column of net entries, as in the UK accounts, by reversing the signs of the entries in one sub-column and adding them, row by row, to the entries in the other sub-column. Conversely, if the figures were available, there would be no difficulty in presenting the UK matrix table in a Sources/Uses format (the order of the sub-columns in this case reflecting the UK balance sheet convention).

Turning to the row and column structure, the US matrix table presentation has more sub-total rows and columns than the UK presentations, and this combined with the Uses/Sources format tends to make the US matrix table appear rather complicated. This arrangement may well give easier access to certain particular figures, but it would seem to produce a matrix table which is not particularly easy to use directly in conjectural variation and forecasting exercises.

The institutional structure of rows and columns for the US has a general family resemblance to that for the UK, the differences largely reflecting the institutional differences between the two economies. The more general considerations (the need to compromise between detail and compactness in the matrix table, to separate out the main transactors and transaction entries and to have these in reasonably homogeneous groups, subject to the availability of data) are common to both.

However, there is more to say about the general row structure in the US matrix table. Perhaps the easiest way for a new user of the US matrix table to understand this row structure is to use the entries in the Households sector column in Table A3.1 for numerical examples and to start from rows 14 to 43 which make up the financing account (remembering that three of these are sub-total rows). It will be seen that this block of rows contains entries in both the Uses and Sources sub-columns; each of these sub-columns is summed over these rows, giving (in billions of dollars throughout what follows) a total of Financial Sources of 166.4 in row 13 and a total of Financial Uses of 248.3 in row 12. These two entries in turn are by convention netted out as explained above, by reversing the sign of the total Financial Sources entry in row 13 and adding it to the total Financial Uses entry in row 12, the resulting figure of 81.9 being entered as Net Financial Investment (NFI) in the Uses sub-column of row 11.

Moving now from the financing account to the capital account, we have in row 1 Gross Saving (S) of 338.3 entered by convention in the Sources sub-column. In row 5 we have Private Capital Expenditure (PCE) of 298.2 entered by convention in the Uses sub-column (this is what we would normally term Investment (I) in national income accounting). We now add NFI of 81.9 in row 11 to PCE of 198.2 in row 5 to get Gross (financial and real) Investment (I′) of 380.1 in row 4, all of these entries being in the Uses sub-column. In principle, Gross Saving and Gross Investment on these definitions should be equal. In practice this is virtually never the case and a reconciling entry will normally be required in the Sector Discrepancies row (row 44) where by convention it is always placed in the Uses sub-column; in the present case this reconciling entry is −41.8.

Looking now at this row structure more analytically, we use the abbreviations introduced above, together with E for the discrepancy entries and subscripts $_u$ and $_s$ for the sub-columns in which the entries appear (naturally we exclude any double-counting arising from sub-total rows and columns). Under the identities we again give as examples the corresponding entries taken from the Households sector column of the

Summary of flow of funds accounts for the year 1978

Billions of dollars

Transaction category / Sector	Private domestic nonfinancial sectors								Rest of the world		U.S. government	
	Households		Business		State and local governments		Total					
	U	S	U	S	U	S	U	S	U	S	U	S
1 **Gross saving**	....	338.3	....	195.6	....	7.6	....	541.5	....	23.5	....	−34.9
2 Capital consumption	....	181.0	....	172.7	....	....	....	353.7	....	....	....	....
3. Net saving (1−2)	....	157.3	....	22.9	....	7.6	....	187.7	....	23.5	....	−34.9
4 **Gross investment (5+11)**	380.1	....	174.1	....	.5	....	554.8	....	12.7	....	−36.6	....
5 Private capital expenditures	298.2	....	249.9	....	....	....	548.1	....	....	....	−2.0	....
6 Consumer durables	200.3	....	....	....	....	....	200.3	....	....	....	....	....
7 Residential construction	92.0	....	16.3	....	....	....	108.3	....	....	....	....	....
8 Plant and equipment	5.9	....	209.3	....	....	....	215.2	....	....	....	....	....
9 Inventory change	....	....	22.3	....	....	....	22.3	....	....	....	....	....
10 Mineral rights	....	....	2 0	....	....	....	2.0	....	....	....	−2.0	....
11 **Net financial investment (12−13)**	81.9	....	−75.7	....	.5	....	6.7	....	12.7	....	−34.7	....
12 **Financial uses**	248.3	....	84.6	....	25.1	....	358.0	....	55.7	....	28.9	....
13 **Financial sources**	....	166.4	....	160.4	....	24.6	....	351.4	....	43.0	....	63.5
14 Gold and official foreign exchange	....	....	....	....	....	....	....	....	1.2	.2	−2.6	....
15 Treasury currency	....	....	....	....	....	....	....	....	....	....	....	.5
16 Demand deposits and currency	18.2	....	5.4	....	−1.1	....	22.5	....	−.2	....	4.0	....
17 Private domestic	18.2	....	5.4	....	−1.1	....	22.5	....	....	....	....	....
18 Foreign	....	....	....	....	....	....	....	....	−.2	....	....	....
19 U.S. government	....	....	....	....	....	....	....	....	....	....	4.0	....
20 Time and savings accounts	105.2	....	2.0	....	8.1	....	115.2	....	1.1	....	.1	....
21 At commercial banks	44.1	....	2.0	....	8.1	....	54.1	....	1.1	....	.1	....
22 At savings institutions	61.1	....	....	....	....	....	61.1	....	....	....	....	....
23 Fed funds and security RPs	....	....	5.5	....	2.0	....	7.5	....	....	....	....	....
24 Money market fund shares	6.9	....	....	....	....	....	6.9	....	....	....	....	....
25 Life insurance reserves	12.0	....	....	....	....	....	12.0	....	....	....	....	.3
26 Pension fund reserves	65.8	....	....	....	....	....	65.8	....	....	....	....	6.9
27 Net interbank claims	....	....	....	....	....	....	....	....	5.4	....	....	....
28 Corporate equities	−6.2	....	....	2.6	....	....	−6.2	2.6	2.4	−.5	....	....
29 Credit market instruments	58.0	162.6	−1.2	125.6	14.6	23.6	71.4	311.8	37.7	32.8	20.4	53.7
30 U.S. Treasury securities	17.3	....	−7.1	....	9.8	....	20.0	....	28.2	....	....	55.1
31 Federal agency securities	9.7	....	.7	....	2.8	....	13.3	....	....	....	7.7	−1.3
32 State and local govt. securities	3.3	....	.2	3.2	1.0	25.1	4.5	28.3	....	....	....	....
33 Corporate and foreign bonds	−1.4	....	....	20.1	....	....	−1.4	20.1	1.6	4.0	....	....
34 Mortgages	14.5	104.8	....	43.3	1.0	....	15.5	148.2	....	....	−.4	−.1
35 Consumer credit	....	50.6	3.2	....	....	....	3.2	50.6	....	....	....	....
36 Bank loans n.e.c.	....	3.4	....	33.9	....	....	....	37.3	....	18.3	....	....
37 Open-market paper	14.6	....	1.7	5.2	....	....	16.3	5.2	7.9	6.6	....	....
38 Other loans	....	3.8	....	19.9	....	−1.6	....	22.2	....	3.9	13.0	....
39 Security credit	1.4	1.4	....	....	....	....	1.4	1.4	0	0	....	....
40 Trade credit	....	1.4	54.9	45.5	....	1.0	54.9	47.9	3.4	−.3	2.7	2.4
41 Taxes payable	....	....	....	3.4	1.6	....	1.6	3.4	....	....	3.5	....
42 Equity in noncorporate business	−20.8	....	....	−20.8	....	....	−20.8	−20.8	....	....	....	....
43 Miscellaneous	7.6	1.1	18.1	4.0	....	....	25.7	5.0	4.7	10.8	.7	−.3
44 **Sector discrepancies (1−4)**	−41.8	....	21.4	....	7.0	....	−13.3	....	10.8	....	1.7	....

Source: Board of Governors of the Federal System, *Introduction to Flow of Funds* (June 1980), Appendix Table S.1.

Table A3.1

Financial sectors										All sectors		Discrepancy	National saving and investment
Total		Sponsored agency and mtg. pools		Monetary authority		Commercial banking		Private nonbank finance					
L	S	U	S	U	S	U	S	U	S	U	S	U	
....	**18.4**	....	**1.0**	....	**.7**	....	**3.4**	....	**13.3**	....	**548.5**	....	**524.9**
....	6.0	....	....	....	....	....	2.7	....	3.3	....	359.7	....	359.7
....	12.4	....	1.0	....	.7	....	.7	....	10.0	....	188.7	....	165.2
20.7	....	**.5**	....	**.7**	....	**9.6**	....	**9.8**	....	**551.6**	....	**−3.1**	**539.0**
5.6	....	....	....	....	....	4.2	....	1.4	....	551.8	....	−3.3	551.8
....	....	....	....	....	....	....	....	....	....	200.3	....	....	200.3
−.3	....	....	....	....	....	....	....	−.3	....	108.0	....	....	108.0
5.9	....	....	....	....	....	4.2	....	1.7	....	221.1	....	....	221.1
....	....	....	....	....	....	....	....	....	....	22.3	....	....	22.3
....	....	....	....	....	....	....	....	....	....	....	....	....	....
15.0	....	**.5**	....	**.7**	....	**5.4**	....	**8.4**	....	**−.2**	....	**.2**	**−12.7**
400.8	....	**46.7**	....	**13.3**	....	**141.2**	....	**199.6**	....	**843.4**	....	**.2**	**43.0**
....	**385.7**	....	**46.2**	....	**12.6**	....	**135.8**	....	**191.2**	....	**843.6**	....	**55.7**
1.6	....	....	....	1.6	....	....	....	....	....	.2	.2	....	....
.6	....	....	....	.6	....	....	....	....	....	.6	.5	*	....
2.6	28.2	*	....	....	6.3	.3	22.0	2.3	....	28.9	28.2	−.7	....
2.6	24.8	*	....	....	9.3	.3	15.5	2.3	....	25.1	24.8	−.3	....
....	−.2	....	....	....	.1	....	.3	....	....	−.2	−.2	....	....
....	3.7	....	....	....	−3.1	....	6.8	....	....	4.0	3.7	−.3	....
7.8	124.2	....	....	....	....	....	65.0	7.8	59.2	124.2	124.2	....	....
9.7	65.0	....	....	....	....	....	65.0	9.7	....	65.0	65.0	....	....
−2.0	59.2	....	....	....	....	....	....	−2.0	59.2	59.2	59.2	....	....
4.0	20.9	1.4	....	....	....	....	18.8	2.6	2.1	11.5	20.9	9.4	....
....	6.9	....	....	....	....	....	....	....	6.9	6.9	6.9	....	....
....	11.7	....	....	....	....	....	....	....	11.7	12.0	12.0	....	....
....	58.9	....	....	....	....	....	....	....	58.9	65.8	65.8	*	....
9.5	15.6	....	....	3.6	5.9	5.9	9.7	....	....	14.9	16.6	.7	....
7.6	1.7	....	....	....	....	*	1.1	7.5	.5	3.7	3.7	....	....
348.4	79.8	44.6	41.4	7.0	....	128.7	6.9	168.1	31.5	478.0	478.0	....	....
6.9	....	.5	....	7.7	....	6.5	....	5.2	....	55.1	55.1	....	....
19.1	41.4	.1	41.4	−.4	....	7.0	....	12.3	....	40.1	40.1	....	....
23.8	....	....	....	....	....	9.6	....	14.2	....	28.3	28.3	....	....
31.3	7.5	....	....	....	....	−.3	[illegible]	21.6	7.3	31.6	31.6	....	....
133.9	.9	30.6	....	....	....	35.0	....	68.3	.9	149.0	149.0	....	....
17.3	....	....	....	....	....	26.9	....	20.4	....	50.6	50.6	....	....
58.4	2.8	....	....	0	....	58.4	....	....	2.8	58.4	58.4	....	....
2.2	14.6	−1.2	....	−.4	....	−1.3	6.7	5.1	7.9	26.4	26.4	....	....
25.5	12.5	14.6	0	....	....	....	....	10.9	12.5	38.6	38.6	....	....
−1.1	−1.0	....	....	....	....	−2.9	....	1.8	−1.0	.4	.4	....	....
1.3	....	....	....	....	....	....	....	1.3	....	62.3	50.0	−12.3	....
....	1.7	....	....	....	....	....	.3	....	1.4	5.2	5.2	*	....
....	....	....	....	....	....	....	....	....	....	−20.8	−20.8	....	....
18.5	37.1	.6	4.8	.5	.5	9.1	11.9	8.2	19.9	49.6	52.6	3.0	....
−2.3	....	.5	....	0	....	−6.3	....	3.5	....	−3.1	....	−3.1	−14.1

Table A3.1 (cont)

US flow of funds matrix in Table A3.1. The row structure can then be set out as follows:

	S_s	=	I'_u	+	E_u	... (3)
Households:	338.3	=	380.1	−	41.8	
	(row 1)		(row 4)		(row 44)	

We have already seen that Gross Investment I'_u is the sum of PCE_u and NFI_u and that PCE_u is what would normally be termed investment, I_u. Substituting these terms into (3) above we have:

	S_s	=	I_u	+	NFI_u	+	E_u	... (4)
Households:	338.3	=	298.2	+	81.9	−	41.8	
	(row 1)		(row 5)		(row 11)		(row 44)	

We can change the matrix table from a Sources/Uses format to a net entries format by reversing the signs of all the Uses sub-column entries and adding them, row by row, to the Sources sub-column entries, so that all entries then become Sources entries. This procedure is the equivalent of moving what were the Uses terms in (4) above to the other side of the identity and giving them Sources subscripts:

	S_s	−	I_s	−	NFI_s	−	E_s	= 0 ... (5)
Households:	338.3	−	298.2	−	81.9	+	41.8	= 0

The Sources subscripts then become redundant, since all entries are sources, either positive or negative as shown by the signs. Identity (5) above shows, therefore, that the US matrix table can be rearranged on to a net (sources) entry basis with zero-sum columns.

By comparison with the row structure, the column structure of both the UK and US matrix tables is simple – merely an exhaustive sectorisation of the world of transactors. This exhaustive sectorisation in principle produces zero-sum rows in the financing account (rows 14–43) and in the E row (row 44), (although in practice this generally requires E column entries); but this is not the case with the S and I (= PCE) rows. As it stands, therefore, even on a net entries basis the US matrix table cannot be displayed as a zero-sum matrix table. To do this we would have to add to the matrix table a financial surplus (FS) row which for each sector would contain an entry for S − I. We could then treat the S and I rows as headnote or memorandum rows, and the matrix table consisting of the FS row, the financing account rows and the E

row would be a zero-sum matrix table. Following on from (5) above, this matrix table could be set out with a row structure given by the following identity:

	FS	-	NFI	-	E	=	0	... (6)
Households:	40.1	-	81.9	+	41.8	=	0	

Finally we can compare this zero-sum format (ZSF) with its rearrangement which produces the conventional format (CF) row structure used in the UK matrix table presentations:

	FS	=	NFI	+	E	... (7)
Households:	40.1	=	81.9	-	41.8	

From what has been said here and in Chapter 3, it is clear that both the US and UK matrix tables can be rearranged into net (sources) entry zero-sum matrix table format (accompanied by the appropriate subtotal etc rows and columns). Conversely, starting from such a zero-sum matrix table we can follow out the various modifications required to arrive at the US and UK matrix tables respectively, and in this way see how their formats are related.

Relating the two matrix tables in this way raises again some issues which have been discussed in the past. The Uses/Sources format allows the display of some grossness in the matrix table entries, but it is striking that in the US matrix table rows 14 to 42 (that is, the financing account rows excluding the Miscellaneous row 43) there are 129 cells in the institutional sector columns which have entries in either the Uses or Sources sub-cell, but only 30 of these have entries in both sub-cells. (We exclude the Miscellaneous row 43, which has entries in both sub-cells in all institutional sector columns except State and local government, where it has no entries, because this is probably due to the non-homogeneity of the entries.) This seems rather a small amount of grossness to buy at the cost of almost doubling the number of columns of figures to be looked at and establishing a set of conventional rules about placing particular entries in particular sub-columns. Grossness clearly has some information value, but quite apart from the old question of the optimum of grossness, is the matrix table the right place to display it? The difference in this respect between the US and the UK matrix tables seems to reflect interestingly different judgements (as well, perhaps, as some relative deficiencies in the UK data).

The quadruple entry nature of the US matrix table is made clear when it is reduced to a zero-sum matrix table. However, in the normal US presentation this characteristic is not clear, nor is it easy to make use of, although it is implicitly recognised in the comments in the last paragraph of Section 2, sub-section 9 which appears on p. 26 of *Introduction to Flow of Funds.*

Although the financing account and sector discrepancy (or error) rows are zero-sum rows, this is not made clear in either the US or the UK matrix tables. One interesting difference is that in the US matrix table some of the financing account rows require discrepancy column (Uses) entries to bring about this zero sum while, as explained in Chapter 3 section 3, the UK financing account entries are estimated in ways which remove the need for such discrepancy (or error) column entries.

Appendix 4

The relationship between e′ in Treatment 1 and e in Treatment 2. (Chapter 2, section 4)

Starting with the identity:

$$S - I \equiv X - M \qquad \dots (3)$$

we further define the domestic economy (UK) and the overseas sector (O′s) with subscripts UK (now for S, −I as well as for X,M) and o respectively. We also define identity (3) above as being in normal form and when re-arranged into $S - I - X + M \equiv 0$ as being in zero-sum form. Now looking at Table A4.1 we begin by using our identities in the classification form, so that all E column/E row entries are zero. Then along the UK row we have the terms of identity (3) for the domestic economy in zero-sum form, and along the O′s row we have the terms of identity (3) for the overseas sector in zero-sum form. Summing these two identities, we get identity (3) for the closed world economy in zero-sum form. In this identity the X,M terms cover all X and M (in negative image form, since the identity is in zero-sum form), and for the closed world economy these must sum to zero, as shown in the X,M column. Similarly, for a closed world economy all S,I terms must sum to zero, as shown in the S,I column. All these S,I and X,M entries in the table we shall call primary entries.

	S,I	X,M	E	Σ
UK	$+ S_{UK} - I_{UK}$	$- X_{UK} + M_{UK}$	$+ e$	0
O′s	$+ S_o - I_o$	$- X_o + M_o$	$+ e''$	0
E	$+ e'$	$+ e'''$	$- e^*$	0
Σ	0	0	0	0

Table A4.1

We now move over to the estimation form of the identities set out in Table A4.1 so that the error entries in the table need not be zero.

Then it can be seen that e' in our Treatment 1 is the same as e' in the S,I column, and e in our Treatment 2 is the same as e in the UK row. The X,M column and the O's row are given the error entries e''' and e'' respectively, and we enter $-\ e^*$ in the E column/E row. Since the primary entries in the table must have the same sum down the S,I *plus* X,M columns and along the UK *plus* O's rows, it follows that:

$$e + e'' \equiv e' + e''' \equiv e^*$$

and that the E column and E row will both sum to zero. The relationship between e' in Treatment 1 and e in Treatment 2 is:

$$e \equiv e^* - e''$$

$$e' \equiv e^* - e'''$$

and

$$e \equiv e' - e'' + e'''.$$

Appendix 5

Construction of a specified zero-sum matrix table using compact quadruple entries. (Chapter 5 section 1)

Here we again construct the specified set of entries in the zero-sum matrix table shown in Chapter 5 section 1, Table 5.1a (= Table A5.1a here), in a previously empty matrix table, Table A5.1b. As before, we use sequential cell selection, but this time we use compact quadruple entries. During the construction process the 1, 2 or 4 individual entries falling in a cell in Table A5.1b are shown in light type and in the locations shown below, and the cell total is shown in heavy type (T).

Cells receiving one entry:	1 — **T**
Cells receiving two entries:	1 2 **T**
Cells receiving four entries:	1 2 3 4 **T**

We now begin the process of adding the entries from Table A5.1a to the previously empty Table A5.1b.

1 we select cell r_1 c_1 in Table A5.1b, which initially has a zero entry; we choose compact quadruple entry r_1 c_1/r_2 c_2 so as to achieve the desired entry (−5) in r_1 c_1 and add it to the matrix table.

2 we select cell r_1 c_2 in Table A5.1b which now has an entry of + 5 from the preceding quadruple entry; choose quadruple entry r_1 c_2/r_2 c_3 with − 2 falling in r_1 c_2 so as to achieve the desired total of + 3 in that cell.

3 we select cell r_1 c_3 and proceed as above. This completes all the entries in row 1 in Table A5.1b which now has the same entries as row 1 in Table A5.1a.

4 we select cell r_2 c_1 and proceed as above, and so on through Table A5.1b.

	1	2	3	4
1	−5	+3	−1	+3
2	+4	+2	−7	+1
3	−1	−1	+12	−10
4	+2	−4	−4	+6

Table A5.1a

	1	2	3	4
1	−5	+5	+2	+3
		−2	−3	
	−5	**+3**	**−1**	**+3**
2	+5	−5+2	−2+3	−3
	−1	+1+4	−4−4	+4
	+4	**+2**	**−7**	**+1**
3	+1	−1−4	+4+4	−4
	−2	+2+2	−2+6	−6
	−1	**−1**	**+12**	**−10**
4	+2	−2	+2	+6
		−2	−6	
	+2	**−4**	**−4**	**+6**

Table A5.1b

At stage 3 the third quadruple entry completed the third and fourth cell entries for row 1. The reason for this is the same as in the earlier case: the first three quadruple entries produce the desired entries in the first three cells and maintain the zero sum of the row; the third quadruple entry must, therefore, produce the desired dependent entry in that row. This is shown in Table A5.2. Again as in the earlier case, the quadruple entries completing the penultimate row will also complete the final row.

		col 1		col 2		col 3	col 4	Σ
row 1	entry pair sums:	= 0		= 0		= 0		
	entry pairs:	− 5	+ 5	− 2	+ 2	− 3	+ 3	0
	required cell totals:	− 5	= + 3		= − 1		+ 3	0

Table A5.2

Appendix 6

Some exploration of obstruction matrices. (Chapter 5 section 1)

This Appendix gives a brief and self-contained account of obstruction matrices, and records the results of some exploration of this type of matrix; this exploration has, of course, no mathematical pretensions whatever.

Consider an empty zero-sum matrix table (one with all zero entries) into which we wish to enter a specified set of zero-sum entries by the addition of (zero-sum) quadruple entries. We define an indicator matrix which corresponds cell by cell with this zero-sum matrix table; the indicator matrix contains only a + or a - sign in each cell, the + sign indicating that the corresponding cell in the zero-sum matrix table is unadjusted and does not yet contain its specified entry, and the - sign showing that it is adjusted and does contain its specified entry.

The process of adjusting the cell entries in the underlying zero-sum matrix table (the construction process) is reflected in the progressive change from + cell entries to - cell entries in the indicator matrix. It has already been noted above that, because of the zero-sum characteristic, a zero-sum matrix table cannot have only a single unadjusted cell entry and any row or column; it follows that in the indicator matrix there can never be only a single + sign in any row or column. From now on we shall deal only with the indicator matrix and for simplicity we shall confine ourselves to square matrices.

Since the construction process is done by means of quadruple entries, if we select unadjusted cells at random in order to adjust them, it is possible for a pattern of + and - entries to emerge such that no further + entry can be adjusted to - without disturbing at least one existing - entry and changing it to +. A matrix of order n with such a pattern of + and - cell entries will be termed an obstruction matrix of order n, O_n. When such a matrix cannot contain any more + entries and remain an O matrix, it can be termed a saturated O matrix; in what follows we shall deal only with such saturated matrices.

The smallest possible O matrix is of order 3, and it is quite easy to construct this and other low order O matrices by inspection. For O_3 this produces a pattern of cell entries which is immediately reminiscent of that appearing in an Hadamard matrix of order 4. At this point, therefore, we turn to look briefly at Hadamard matrices. A survey of the subject will be found in A. Hedayat and W.D. Wallis, 'Hadamard matrices and their applications', *The Annals of Statistics,* 1978 No 6, pp. 1184 – 1238, referred to below as H & W.

An Hadamard matrix of order n, which we denote by H_n, can be defined as a matrix with entries which are either + 1 or - 1 (abbreviated to + or -) and in which any pair of rows (or any pair of columns), when placed next to each other, will have half the adjacent pairs of cell entries matching (+, + or -, -) and half non-matching (+, - or -, +), and the sum of the products of the adjacent cells (the inner product of the rows or columns) is equal to zero. Examples of H_n for n = 2, 4 and 8 (taken from H & W p. 1222, Table 2) are shown in Table A6.1.

n = 2	n = 4	n = 8
+ +	+ + + +	+ + + + + + + +
+ -	+ + - -	+ + + - + - - -
	+ - + -	+ - + + - + - -
	+ - - +	+ - - + + - + -
		+ - - - + + - +
		+ + - - - + + -
		+ - + - - - + +
		+ + - + - - - +

Table A6.1

H matrices of order 4 and above are confined to orders which are multiples of 4.

From the definition of an H matrix given above, it will be seen that the ordering of the rows and columns is immaterial. However, the H matrices displayed in Table A6.1 are all shown in normalised form, that is, with the first row and first column containing only + entries. (In passing, we shall define a reduced H_n matrix as one with the first row and first column of + entries removed; we shall denote it by H^*_{n-1}.)

Perhaps the easiest type of H matrix to construct is the tensor product type. The tensor product of two matrices H_m and H_n consists of H_m with every cell with a + entry replaced by the whole H_n matrix, and every cell with a - entry replaced by the negative image of the H_n matrix (H_n with all its signs reversed) which we denote by $-H_n$. As an example, it can readily be seen that, in Table A6.1, H_4 with its two central rows reversed in order is the tensor product of two H_2 matrices. Another type of H matrix we shall term the diagonal type; in this type the rows and columns (excluding row 1 and column 1, which contain all + entries) are, or can be, arranged to form a pattern of all + sign diagonals or all - sign diagonals. It will be seen from Table A6.1 that both H_4 and H_8 are of this type. H_4 in that table is therefore both a tensor product and a diagonal type of H matrix.

Returning now to O matrices, these can be constructed by successively selecting each cell with a - entry and changing it to a + entry if this can be done while maintaining the obstruction condition. Such a procedure can be applied to matrices containing all - entries or to ones with prior + entries (providing these are compatible with the resulting matrix being an O matrix). Different obstruction patterns of cell entries are likely to emerge with different cell selection procedures and with different patterns of prior + entries (or, indeed, specified unalterable - entries).

Here we shall consider one such procedure which we shall apply to a matrix containing only - entries. The procedure starts with the leading diagonal and searches down it from top left to bottom right, testing each cell and replacing the - entry with a + entry if this can be done while maintaining the obstruction condition. It then moves to the next diagonal below the leading diagonal and carries out the same procedure as before; if no + entries were made, it would move to the next diagonal on the same side and so on; if one or more + entries are made in a diagonal, it switches to the next untested diagonal on the other side of the leading diagonal and so on.[1] Table A6.2 shows O_3, O_7 and O_{11} constructed by this procedure. We shall call this the diagonal (1) family of O matrices. Since

n = 3

+	-	+
+	+	-
-	+	+

n = 7

+	-	+	-	-	-	+
+	+	-	+	-	-	-
	+	+	-	+	-	-
-	-	+	+	-	+	-
-	-	-	+	+	-	+
+	-	-	-	+	+	-
-	+	-	-	-	+	+

n = 11

+	-	+	-	-	-	-	-	+	-	
+	+	-	+	-	-	-	-	-	+	-
-	+	+	-	+	-	-	-	-	-	+
-	-	+	+	-	+	-	-	-	-	-
-	-	-	+	+	-	+	-	-	-	-
+	-	-	-	+	+	-	+	-	-	-
-	+	-	-	-	+	+	-	+	-	-
-	-	+	-	-	-	+	+	-	+	-
-	-	-	+	-	-	-	+	+	-	+
-	-	-	-	+	-	-	-	+	+	-
-	-	-	-	-	+	-	-	-	+	+

Table A6.2

obstruction matrices, like Hadamard matrices, are independent of the ordering of their rows and columns, it can now be seen that the

n	m:	$r_m c_1$					$r_1 c_m$		
3					2	1	3			
4					2	1	3			
5					2	1	3			
6				6	2	1	3			
7				6	2	1	3	7*		
8				6	2	1	3			
9				6	2	1	3	9		
10				6	2	1	3	9		
11				6	2	1	3	9		
12			12	6	2	1	3	9		
13			12	6	2	1	3	9	13*	
14			(12)	6	2	1	3	9		
15				6	2	1	3	9		
16			16	6	2	1	3	9		
17			16	6	2	1	3	9		
18			16	6	2	1	3	9		
19			16	6	2	1	3	9	19	
20			16	6	2	1	3	9	19	
21			16	6	2	1	3	9	19	
22		22	16	6	2	1	3	9	19	
23		22	16	6	2	1	3	9	19	23*
24		(22)	16	6	2	1	3	9	(19)	
25			16	6	2	1	3	9	(19)	25*
26			16	6	2	1	3	9	(19)	(21)
27		27*	16	6	2	1	3	9	(19)	(21)
28		28	16	6	2	1	3	9		21
29		28	16	6	2	1	3	9		21
30		28	16	6	2	1	3	9		21

31					28	16	6	2	1	3	9	21	31				
32					28	16	6	2	1	3	9	21	31				
33					28	16	6	2	1	3	9	21	31				
34				34	28	16	6	2	1	3	9	21	31				
35				34	28	16	6	2	1	3	9	21	31	35*			
36				(34)	(28)	16	6	2	1	3	9	21	(31)				
37				(35)	(28)	16	6	2	1	3	9	21	(31)	37*			
38			38*	(35)	(28)	16	6	2	1	3	9	21	(31)				
39				(35)	(28)	16	6	2	1	3	9	21	(31)				
40				(32)	(28)	16	6	2	1	3	9	21	37				
41				(32)	(28)	16	6	2	1	3	9	21	37				
42				(32)		16	6	2	1	3	9	21	37				
43				32		16	6	2	1	3	9	21	37				
44			44	32		16	6	2	1	3	9	21	37				
45			44	32		16	6	2	1	3	9	21	37				
46			44	32		16	6	2	1	3	9	21	37				
47			44	32		16	6	2	1	3	9	21	37	47			
48			44	32		16	6	2	1	3	9	21	37	47			
49			44	32		16	6	2	1	3	9	21	37	47			
50		50	44	32		16	6	2	1	3	9	21	37	47			
51		50	44	32		16	6	2	1	3	9	21	37	47	51*		
52		(50)	(44)	32		16	6	2	1	3	9	21	(37)	(47)			
53			(44)	32		16	6	2	1	3	9	21	(37)	(47)	53*		
54		54	(44)	32		16	6	2	1	3	9	21	(37)	(47)	(50)		
55		54	(44)	32		16	6	2	1	3	9	21	(37)	(47)	(49)	55*	
56		54	(44)	32		16	6	2	1	3	9	21	(37)		(49)		
57			(43)	32		16	6	2	1	3	9	21	(37)		(49)	(53)	(55)
58	(54)	(44)	(43)	32		16	6	2	1	3	9	21	(37)		(49)	(53)	(55)
59		54	(43)	32		16	6	2	1	3	9	21	(37)	(45)	(50)	57	
60		54	(43)	32		16	6	2	1	3	9	21	(37)	(45)	(50)	57	

Table A6.3

O_3 matrix in Table A6.2 is equivalent to the negative image of H_3^*, the reduced H_4 matrix from Table A6.1, and that O_7 in Table A6.2 is equivalent to H_7^*, the reduced H_8 matrix from Table A6.1. (This is most easily seen by taking the bottom row of H_7^* and placing it above the top row.)

The question at this point is whether these links between O and H matrices (which were the reason for choosing the method used above in constructing the diagonal (1) family of O matrices) continue to hold for higher order matrices. Unfortunately, when we try to relate H_{12} and O_{11}, we find that H_{11}^* is not an obstruction matrix. Further, it will be recalled that the cell entries in H matrices shown above as +/- are in fact + 1/- 1. Interpreting the entries in the diagonal (1) O matrices in the same way, it will be seen that since the inner products of H_4 and H_8 are zero by definition, the inner products of H_3^*, $-H_3^*$, O_3 and H_7^*, O_7 will all be -1. However, O_{11} has non-constant inner products. At this point, therefore, we abandon this particular line of enquiry and turn to consider the diagonal (1) family of O matrices in its own right to see if anything of interest can be said about it.

Table A6.3 summarises the cell pattern in O_3 through O_{60} in the diagonal (1) family of matrices. In this table diagonals containing + entries are identified by their top left hand cells. The left hand side of the table shows these diagonals which are below the leading diagonal, each identified by its value of m in r_m c_1, while the right hand side of the table shows these diagonals which are above the leading diagonal, each identified by its value of m in r_1 c_m. The central column in the table shows the leading diagonal for which m = 1 in either of the above formulae. A single + corner entry which does not develop into a diagonal as n rises is marked *; diagonals which are not completely filled with + entries are in parentheses. (It is helpful here to relate the O matrices in Table A6.2 to their entries in Table A6.3.)

This table shows that as n rises, a central body of + diagonals becomes established and does not change thereafter, but that there are also transient extreme diagonals (which may consist of only a single + entry and which may appear as normally growing + diagonals only to lose their + entries progressively and disappear again, or behave in other ways). These two groups of transient diagonals interact with each other via the central body of stable diagonals, but the existence of these groups seems to be due to scale effects as n rises, which can be seen in the relationship between the first and last rows and the first and last columns as n rises. This can most easily be seen by visualising each O matrix in the form of a torus, so that the first and last rows/columns appear adjacent to each other along what we shall term the seams of such a toroidal display. We then find that, in our range of O_3 to O_{60}, in most cases some of the + diagonals are discontinuous across the

n	constant row/column weight (w)	inner products (p)
O_3	2	− 1
O_7	3	− 1
O_{13}	4	+ 1
O_{23}	5	+ 7
O_{35}	6	+ 15
O_{51}	7	+ 27

Table A6.4a

seams, but that in six cases all the + diagonals are continuous across the seams; each of these six cases has a pattern of + and − diagonals such that each individual diagonal makes a single helical turn round the minor circumference of the torus as it makes a single circuit round the major circumference. These six cases are shown in Table A6.4a where each will be seen to have its own characteristic and constant row and column weight (measured by the number of + entries) and its own characteristic and constant inner products (found, as before, by interpreting +/− as + 1/− 1). It is to be noted that this series contains O_3 and O_7. The second differences of both n and p in this series are alternately 2 and 4; extrapolating on this basis leads to the prediction that the next two cases in this series will be :

n	w	p
69	8	41
91	9	59

Table A6.4b

In matrices of the diagonal (1) family, as n rises, total weight rises, but the first differences of the total weights tend to be erratic. At least for lower orders, some weights can be formulated in terms of n for triplets of values of n (Table A6.5); these are interspersed with two triplets (n = 6,7,8 and 12,13,14) whose weights cannot be formulated with the same degree of simplicity.

	total weight
n = 3, 4, 5	3 (n − 1)
n = 9, 10, 11	4 (n − 2)
n = 15, 16, 17	6 (n − 5) + 1
n = 18, 19, 20	7 (n − 9) − 1

Table A6.5

Since we have devoted most of our attention to the diagonal (1) family, it is worth while looking at examples of other sub-families of O matrices. In Table A6.6 are three further examples of O_{11} matrices (which may be compared with the diagonal (1) O_{11} matrix in Table A6.2):

(a) shows O_{11} in what we could call the diagonal (2) family. This is constructed by cell selection down the diagonals, as with diagonal (1), but the diagonals are taken in a different order; the leading diagonal is taken first, then those above it are taken in order from left to right and then those below it in order from top to bottom.

(b) is constructed by 'square spiral' cell selection, starting with cell r_6 c_6 and going on to cells r_6 c_7, r_7 c_7, r_7 c_6, r_7 c_5, r_6 c_5 and so on.

(c) is constructed by sequential cell selection along the top row from left to right, then the second row from left to right and so on, but it has a specified unalterable − entry in cell r_1 c_1.

(At this point it is worth giving the warning that, while there are many other procedures which will generate valid O matrices, there are some which produce matrices which look like O matrices but which are invalid because they have at least one row or column in which there is only one + entry.)

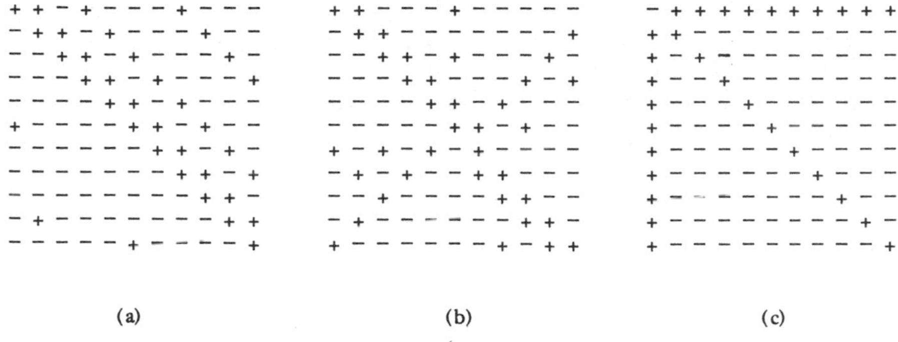

$$\begin{array}{ccccccccccc}
+ & + & - & + & - & - & - & + & - & - & - \\
- & + & + & - & + & - & - & - & + & - & - \\
- & - & + & + & - & + & - & - & - & + & - \\
- & - & - & + & + & - & + & - & - & - & + \\
- & - & - & - & + & + & - & + & - & - & - \\
+ & - & - & - & - & + & + & - & + & - & - \\
- & - & - & - & - & - & + & + & - & + & - \\
- & - & - & - & - & - & - & + & + & - & + \\
- & - & - & - & - & - & - & - & + & + & - \\
- & + & - & - & - & - & - & - & - & + & + \\
- & - & - & - & - & + & - & - & - & - & +
\end{array}$$

(a)

$$\begin{array}{ccccccccccc}
+ & + & - & - & - & + & - & - & - & - & - \\
- & + & + & - & - & - & - & - & - & - & + \\
- & - & + & + & - & + & - & - & - & + & - \\
- & - & - & + & + & - & - & - & + & - & + \\
- & - & - & - & + & + & - & + & - & - & - \\
- & - & - & - & - & + & + & - & + & - & - \\
+ & - & + & - & + & - & + & - & - & - & - \\
- & + & - & + & - & - & + & + & - & - & - \\
- & - & + & - & - & - & - & + & + & - & - \\
- & + & - & - & - & - & - & - & + & + & - \\
+ & - & - & - & - & - & - & + & - & + & +
\end{array}$$

(b)

$$\begin{array}{ccccccccccc}
- & + & + & + & + & + & + & + & + & + & + \\
+ & + & - & - & - & - & - & - & - & - & - \\
+ & - & + & - & - & - & - & - & - & - & - \\
+ & - & - & + & - & - & - & - & - & - & - \\
+ & - & - & - & + & - & - & - & - & - & - \\
+ & - & - & - & - & + & - & - & - & - & - \\
+ & - & - & - & - & - & + & - & - & - & - \\
+ & - & - & - & - & - & - & + & - & - & - \\
+ & - & - & - & - & - & - & - & + & - & - \\
+ & - & - & - & - & - & - & - & - & + & - \\
+ & - & - & - & - & - & - & - & - & - & +
\end{array}$$

(c)

Table A6.6

If we take the diagonal (1) O_{11} matrix from Table A6.2 together with the above three O_{11} matrices, we find that all four are saturated but that all have different weights (39, 36, 38 and 32 respectively). This is the easiest way of proving that these are four different O_{11} matrices and that none of them can be converted into one of the others by the permutation of their rows or columns. It can readily be seen that the weight of a type (c) matrix of order n is 3 (n − 1), which is the same as that of the diagonal (1) O_3, O_4, O_5 matrices in Table A6.5. It seems intuitively clear that 3 (n − 1) is the minimum possible weight for a saturated O matrix of order n, but there is no correspondingly intuitive indication of maximum weight.

It is also clear that a type (c) matrix of any order will contain as sub-matrices all lower order members of its own family. The situation is more complicated in the case of diagonal (1) matrices. As can be seen from Table A6.3, O_7 contains as sub-matrices all lower members of the diagonal (1) family; O_8 to O_{13} each contains all lower order members except O_7; O_{15} to O_{23} each contains all lower order matrices except O_7 and O_{12}, O_{13}, O_{14} and so on with growing blocks of exceptions. Without going further into the question of the extent to which a matrix O_n contains as sub-matrices lower order members of its own and other families, it is worth noting that all the four methods of construction (or families) of O matrices we are looking at generate the same O_3 matrix and (what is not the same thing) this O_3 matrix appears as a sub-matrix in all our four examples of O_{11} matrices; indeed, it appears 9, 8, 2 and 1 times respectively in the diagonal (1), (a), (b) and (c) O_{11} matrices.

Note

1 The higher order obstruction matrices referred to here were constructed using a program written by Mark Alford and run on the Prime computer system at the University of Surrey.

Appendix 7

Two types of quadruple entry system. (Chapter 2 section 4)

In Chapter 1 section 3 it is shown that in a zero-sum matrix table (ZSMT) a transaction is recorded by a quadruple entry (QE), and the cell entries in a ZSMT can be regarded as the cell-by-cell sum of such QEs over a particular period. (Further, it is shown in Chapter 5 that any pattern of entries in a ZSMT can be built up from, or analysed into, a much smaller number of formally identical QEs which we term composite QEs.) This type of QE we shall term QE1.

Inspection of Treatment 1 and Treatment 2 in Table 2.1 shows that the capital account (CA) can in a similar way be looked at as a QE system in which the QEs are of a different kind which we shall term QE2.

A QE2 is specified as follows: it consists of four identical entries in two rows and two columns, forming a quadrilateral of cell entries. These entries may be positive or negative and if, for example, each of these four entries is + x then the magnitude of that QE2 is + x. To look at the CA as a QE2 system, we have to define a permissible set of QE2s and such a set has to conform to two constraints:

1 the location constraint: each QE2 must have one entry in the Σ row/Σ column cell (Note that in the CA, the Σ row is the FS row.)
2 the zero-sum constraint: the magnitudes of the set of QE2s must sum to zero.

Table A7.1 shows a schematic picture of the CA divided into four fields:

Field A covers the non-FS rows/non-Σ columns.
Field B covers the FS row/non-Σ columns.
Field C covers the non-FS rows/Σ column.
Field D covers the FS row/Σ column (= Σ row/Σ column).

The location constraint means that every QE2 will have one cell entry in field D, and therefore one each in fields A, B and C. The specification of a QE2 means that each QE2 will contribute the same entry to each of these fields. The zero-sum constraint means that the sum of entries in each of these fields will be zero: in field A these entries appear individually; in B we have column sums of these entries, in C we have the row sums of these entries and in the single-cell D field we have the

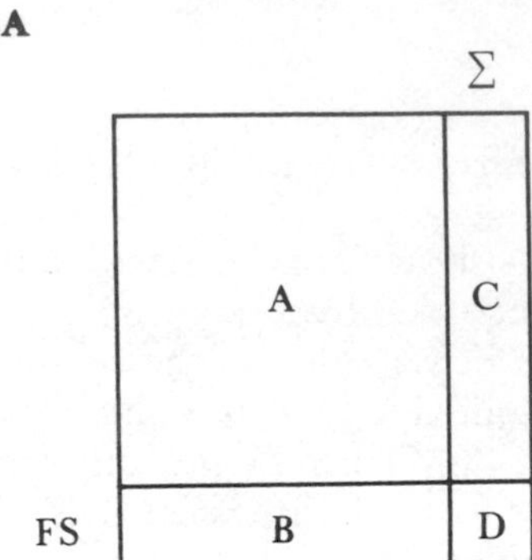

Table A7.1

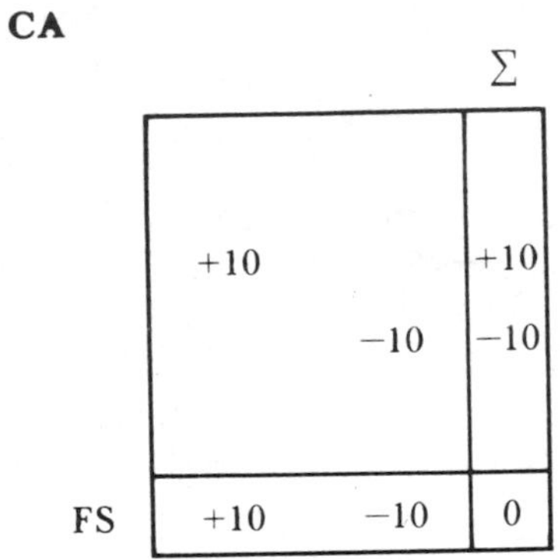

Table A7.2

overall sum of these entries, which is zero by constraint. The zero-sum constraint means that the unit of entry, or unit of variation, in the CA is a pair of QE2s with magnitudes which sum to zero. Such a pair is illustrated in Table A7.2.

Now looking at Treatment 1 and Treatment 2 in Table 2.1 in the light of this QE2 system, it is easy to trace out the QE2s of magnitude S_1 etc, $-I_1$ etc, e' etc and $-X_{UK} + M_{UK}$, and to see their zero-sum made explicit in the FS row/Σ column cell, which is field D above.

Two examples of inconsistencies in the CA were noted in Chapter 2 section 4 above, and both of these can now be seen as arising from an incomplete QE2. The first case occurs in CSOP(NIE), where the QE2 of magnitude $-X_{UK} + M_{UK}$ has its entry explicitly present in field B (and implicitly present in field D, which is not displayed) but explicitly absent from field A (and implicitly absent from field C, which is not displayed). The second case occurs in OP(BE), and also in BEP quarterly version, where there is an explicit E column; there the QE2 with the magnitude of the residual error (RE) has its entry explicitly present in B and implicitly present in D, but explicitly absent from A and implicitly absent from C. Both of these cases result in inconsistencies between the entries in fields B and D on the one hand and those in fields A and C on the other, so that the CA is internally inconsistent.

ZSMT

		Σ
FS	B	D
	E	G
Σ	F	H

Table A7.3

Two additional points can be made about the QE2 system. First, like the QE1 system, it can be regarded as consisting either of transaction QE2s or of composite QE2s; in this Appendix we are implicitly using composite QE2s. Second, the entries in the TCCT row, which was only omitted from Treatments 1 and 2 for simplicity, will always sum to zero; it follows that the sub-set of QE2s producing the TCCT row entries must have magnitudes which sum to zero, which is an additional sub-constraint within the zero-sum constraint already mentioned.

Fields B and D in the CA also form part of the ZSMT, which also contains four further fields E, F, G and H (Table A7.3). Looking at the ZSMT as a QE1 system, the QE1s are confined to fields B + E, with fields F, H, G and D containing only zero entries. However, it is evident that any QE1 of magnitude x can be expressed as the cell-by-cell sum of four QE2s, specified as above and subject to the location and zero-sum constraints. Such a quartet will be made up of two pairs, each pair containing QE2s of magnitude +x and -x (so that the QE2 unit of entry in the ZSMT is equivalent to two QE2 units of entry in the CA). In such a quartet of QE2s, conformity to the location constraint means that each QE2 must have one entry in the Σ row/Σ column cell, which in this case is field H. Conformity to the zero-sum constraint is ensured by the zero-sum character of the QE1 which we are aiming to express in terms of a quartet of QE2s. Any such quartet will require an additional general constraint to ensure that it will sum cell-by-cell to a QE1 or a specific constraint to make it sum to a specific QE1. The former would be the requirement that all the quartet entries fall in any two rows and any two columns, the latter that all the entries fall in two specified rows and two specified columns.

While it is possible in this way to express the ZSMT entries in terms of QE2s, it is less convenient than using QE1s and does not link up directly with the recording of individual transactions, as do QE1s. However, seeing both the CA and the ZSMT as expressible in terms of (differently constrained) sets of QE2s does help to reveal the common elements and the differences between the two. It will be seen that while the QE1 system in the ZSMT can be expressed in terms of appropriately constrained QE2s, the QE2 system in the CA cannot be expressed in terms of QE1s.

Appendix 8

Reconciliation between the financial accounts for the Overseas sector and the balance of payments account for the UK. (Chapter 2 section 1 and Chapter 3 section 3 and particularly note 4)

Supplementary table S22 in *Financial Statistics,* Oct 1983, pp. 144–5 (see also the note on p. 150), is one of an annual series which for the latest year (in this case 1982) gives a matrix table reconciliation between the entries in the sector column of the Overseas sector (SC_0) and those in the balance of payments account of the UK (BP_{UK}). In principle this reconciliation is quite straightforward, and it is set out schematically in Table A8.1:

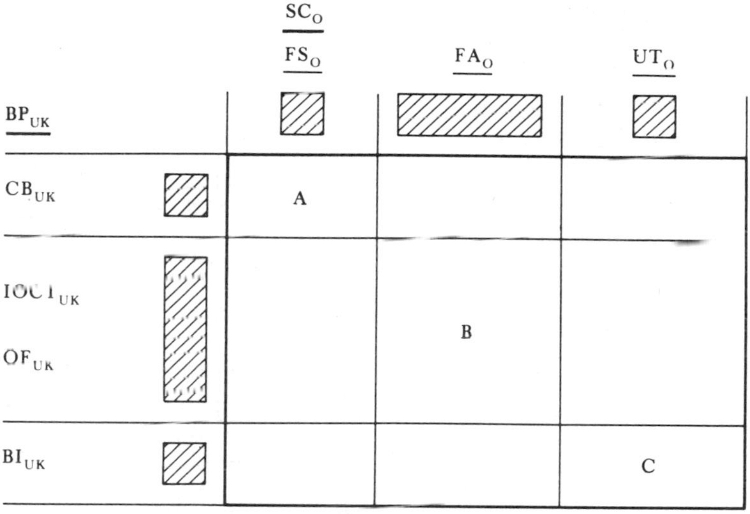

		SC_O		
		FS_O	FA_O	UT_O
BP_{UK}				
CB_{UK}		A		
$IOCT_{UK}$ OF_{UK}			B	
BI_{UK}				C

Table A8.1

The components of SC_0 shown in the top row are FS_0 (the financial surplus or deficit of O's), FA_0 (the financing account entries of O's) and UT_0 (the unidentified transactions entry of O's). The corresponding components of BP_{UK} shown in the left-hand column are CB_{UK} (the current balance, or financial surplus, of the UK); $IOCT_{UK}$ (investment and other capital transactions) and OF_{UK} (official financing) which make up the financing account entries of the UK; and finally BI_{UK} (the balancing item of the UK). The entries under the components of SC_0 are represented by the row of shaded rectangles, and those under the components of BP_{UK} by the column of shaded rectangles. (Here we ignore the rounding, timing and coverage differences (RTCD); this is a row of entries which can be regarded as summing to zero in field B.)

The body of Table A8.1 contains three labelled fields, the others being irrelevant. Fields A and C will each contain just a single reconciling entry; that in field A will reconcile FS_0 and CB_{UK}, and that in field C will reconcile UT_0 and BI_{UK}. Field B, on the other hand, will contain many cells (23 x 20 = 460 in the CSO matrix table we are considering), with a number of reconciling entries (45 in this case, plus a further 6 RTCD entries); the column sums of these entries produce the individual entries under FA_0, and the row sums produce the individual entries under $IOCT_{UK}$ and OF_{UK}.

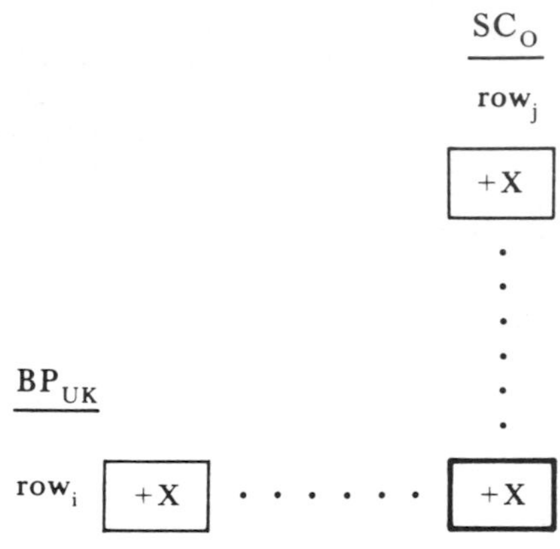

Table A8.2

Table A8.2 illustrates this reconciliation in the basic case, where there is only one reconciling entry (shown with its cell heavily outlined) in a particular row and a particular column. This is the case in fields A and C, and would be the simplest case in field B. It is obvious that for reconciliation to be possible, the entries to be reconciled must have the same sign. However, SC_0 records transactions from the point of view of the O's sector, while BP_{UK} records them from the point of view of the UK[1]; using the same sign rules for each, therefore, would lead to the SC_0 and BP_{UK} entries having opposite signs (as illustrated in the

UK and O's sector column entries in Table 1.2, Chapter 1 section 2 above) so that in Table A8.2 these entries would be +x and −x, and there would be no possible reconciling entry. The solution is to present SC_0 and BP_{UK} on opposite sign rules, which will offset their opposite viewpoints and allow them to be reconciled.

		CA		FA	E		presentation	
SC_O	(1)	FS_O	≡	FA_O	$+UT_O$		CF	normal presentations
BP_{UK}	(2)	CB_{UK}		$-(IOCT_{UK}+OF_{UK})$	$-BI_{UK}$	≡ 0	ZSF	
	(3)	CB_{UK}	≡	$(IOCT_{UK}+OF_{UK})$	$+BI_{UK}$		CF	
	(4)	$-CB_{UK}$	≡	$-(IOCT_{UK}+OF_{UK})$	$-BI_{UK}$		−CF	

Table A8.3

This brings us to Table A8.3, where rows (1) and (2) show the normal presentations, SC_0 using CF and BP_{UK} using ZSF (for the introduction to these sign rules see Chapter 3 section 2 above). The opposite sign rules necessary for reconciliation to be possible will appear here as opposite signs on the SC_0 and BP_{UK} terms in the CA column, in the FA column and in the E column. Because one is on CF and the other is on ZSF, we find that they have the opposite signs necessary for reconciliation in the FA column and in the E column, but not in the CA column. The CSO solves the problem by simply reversing the sign of CB_{UK}, which produces the presentation in row (4). Comparing this with the CF presentation of BP_{UK} in row (3) shows that the effect of reversing the sign of CB_{UK} is to switch BP_{UK} from ZSF presentation in row (2) to negative CF presentation (− CF) in row (4). We then have SC_0 on CF presentation and BP_{UK} on − CF presentation, and it is these opposite presentations which make the two reconcilable in the CSO's matrix table. However, it leaves us with a presentation of BP_{UK} which is significantly different from its normal presentation and for which no explanation has been given.

Note

1 In the title and elsewhere in table S22 it is not made clear that UK and O's are the two sectors involved, while in *Financial Statistics Explanatory Handbook* 1983, p. 122, the note to table S22 refers to the financial accounts (evidently meaning SC_0) as analysing transactions *with* O's (implying that this is from the point of view of UK) when in fact SC_0 analyses transactions *by* O's, from the point of view of O's.

Appendix 9

Revisions and error ratios. (Chapter 7 section 3, n.6 and n.7)

Revisions can significantly affect the error ratios defined in Chapter 6 section 2. This is shown in Table A9.1 where we calculate the error ratios for 1970 and 1977 using (a) the initial entries, (b) the last successor entries (all taken from *Financial Statistics* and shown in Tables 7.5 and 7.9 above) and (c), for 1970 only, the last successor entries taken from *National Income and Expenditure* 1981 (shown in Tables 7.6 and 7.9 above). For 1970 both error ratios fall from (a) to (b) and then nearly double to (c), while for 1977 both rise from (a) to (b), one by 10 per cent and the other by 50 per cent.

	$\frac{\Sigma\lvert E\rvert}{\Sigma\lvert FS'\rvert}$		$\frac{\Sigma\lvert E\rvert}{\Sigma\lvert IF\rvert}$	
1970: from *Fin. Stats.*				
(a) using initial entries	.332	(100)	.277	(100)
(b) using last successor entries	.309	(93)	.245	(88)
from *NIE* 1981				
(c) using last successor entries	.594	(180)	.459	(166)
1977: from *Fin. Stats.*				
(a) using initial entries	.348	(100)	.334	(100)
(b) using last successor entries	.521	(150)	.367	(110)

Table A9.1

It so happens that the error ratios reported in Chapter 6 for 1970 (.319 and .269; see n.5, Table 6.8(c)) and 1977 (.425 and .358; see Chapter 6 section 2, Table 6.8) fall roughly mid-way between the respective (a) and (b) estimates in Table A9.1.

Glossary of abbreviations

AV	assets view	Ch 3 sect 2
B/S	balance sheet	Ch 4 sect 1
BA	balancing account	Ch 3 sect 4
BEP	Bank of England presentation of the matrix table, pre-1981	Ch 2 sect 2
BEQB	*Bank of England Quarterly Bulletin*	Ch 2 sect 2
BI	balancing item	Ch 3 sect 4
Bkg	banking sector	Ch 2 sect 2
Bks	banking sector	Ch 2 sect 2
BOBOTM	'bad old Board of Trade method'	Ch 4 n. 8
BP	balance of payments	Appendix 8
C	consumption expenditure	Ch 2 sect 4
c	1. number of columns in a matrix table	Ch 5 sect 1
	2. (with subscript n): column n in the matrix table	Ch 5 sect 1
CA	capital account	Ch 1 sect 5
CB	current account balance	Appendix 8
CD	certificate of deposit	Ch 3 sect 2
CF	conventional format	Ch 3 sect 2
CFAL	changes in financial assets and liabilities	Ch 3 sect 4
CG	central government	Ch 2 sect 2
CSO	Central Statistical Office	Ch 2 sect 5
CSOP	CSO presentation of the matrix table, pre-1981	Ch 2 sect 2

CSOP(FinS)	CSO presentation of the matrix table in *Financial Statistics,* pre-1981	Ch 2 sect 2
CSOP(NIE)	CSO presentation of the matrix table in *National Income and Expenditure,* pre-1981	Ch 2 sect 2
D	discrepancy	Ch 3 sect 3
E,e	error (column, row or entry)	Ch 2 sect 2
FA	financing account	Ch 1 sect 5
FAT	financing account total	Ch 3 sect 4
FinS	CSO, *Financial Statistics,* monthly	Ch 2 sect 2
FIOB	financial institutions other than banks	Ch 2 sect 2
FOF	flow of funds (matrix table)	Ch 4 sect 1
FS	financial surplus	Ch 1 sect 5
FS/D	financial surplus/deficit	Ch 3 sect 4
FT	financial transactions	Ch 4 sect 4
FTA	financial transactions account (later revised to financial account)	Ch 3 sect 4
g	stock appreciation	Ch 2 sect 3
HN	headnote	Ch 1 sect 5
I	investment	Ch 2 sect 3
ICC	industrial and commercial companies sector	Ch 2 sect 2
IF	identified financing	Ch 3 sect 3
IFT	identified financial transactions	Ch 3 sect 4
IMT	identified matrix table	Ch 6 sect 1
IOCT	investment & other capital transactions	Appendix 8
LA	local authorities	Ch 2 sect 2
LASF	life assurance and superannuation funds	Ch 2 sect 2
M	imports	Ch 2 sect 4
M′	money	Ch 5 sect 4
Mon	monetary sector	Ch 2 sect 2
MTP	matrix table proper	Ch 1 sect 5
NAFA	net acquisition of financial assets	Ch 2 sect 4
NFW	net financial wealth	Ch 4 sect 1
NIE	CSO, *National Income and Expenditure,* annual Blue Book	Ch 2 sect 2
O	overseas sector (subscript)	Ch 2 sect 4
OF	official financing	Appendix 8
OFI	other financial institutions	Ch 2 sect 2
OFI′	other financial institutions (alternative definition)	Ch 2 sect 2
OP	official presentation of the matrix table, post-1981	Ch 2 sect 2

OP(BE)	Bank of England version of the official presentation, post-1981	Ch 2 sect 2
OP(FinS)	CSO version of the official presentation used in *Financial Statistics*, post-1981	Ch 2 sect 2
OP(NIE)	CSO version of the official presentation used in *National Income and Expenditure*, post-1981	Ch 2 sect 2
O's	overseas sector	Ch 2 sect 2
PC	public corporations	Ch 2 sect 2
Pers	personal sector	Ch 2 sect 2
PPV	purchasing power view	Ch 1 sect 4
Pri	private sector	Ch 5 sect 4
PSBR	Public Sector Borrowing Requirement	Ch 3 sect 1
Pub	public sector	Ch 2 sect 2
r	1. number of rows in a matrix table	Ch 5 sect 1
	2. (with subscript n): row n in the matrix table	Ch 5 sect 1
RE	residual error	Ch 2 sect 2
RFD	revision first difference	Ch 7 sect 1
RTCD	rounding, timing and coverage differences	Appendix 8
S	saving	Ch 2 sect 3
SC	sector column	Appendix 8
SD	standard deviation	Ch 7 sect 2
SU	successor entry	Ch 7 sect 1
T	target cell	Ch 5 sect 2
TCCT	taxes on capital and capital transfers	Ch 2 sect 3
TFT	total financial transactions	Ch 3 sect 4
TIFA	total identified financial assets	Ch 3 sect 4
U	unidentified	Ch 3 sect 4
UI	unidentified items	Ch 3 sect 4
UK	United Kingdom (also subscript)	Ch 2 sect 4
UKFOFA	Bank of England, *United Kingdom flow of funds accounts 1963-1976*	Ch 3 sect 5
Un	unallocated	Ch 2 sect 2
UT	unidentified transactions	Ch 3 sect 4
W	world (subscript)	Ch 2 sect 4
X	exports	Ch 2 sect 4
Y	income	Ch 2 sect 4
ZSF	zero-sum format	Ch 3 sect 2
ZSMT	zero-sum matrix table	Ch 1 sect 5